Hither Shore

Interdisciplinary Journal
on Modern Fantasy Literature

Jahrbuch der
Deutschen Tolkien Gesellschaft e. V.

Nature and Landscape in Tolkien

Natur und Landschaft in Tolkiens Werk

Interdisziplinäres Seminar der DTG
9. bis 11. Mai 2014, Jena

Herausgegeben von:
Thomas Fornet-Ponse (Gesamtleitung),
Marcel Aubron-Bülles, Julian Eilmann,
Thomas Honegger, Rainer Nagel,
Alexandra Velten, Frank Weinreich

SCRIPTORIUM OXONIAE

Bibliografische Information
der Deutschen Bibliothek

Die Deutsche Bibliothek verzeichnet diese
Publikation in der Deutschen Nationalbibliografie;
detaillierte bibliografische Daten sind im
Internet über http://dnb.ddb.de abrufbar.

ISBN 978-3-9810612-9-1

Hither Shore, DTG-Jahrbuch 2014
veröffentlicht im Verlag »Scriptorium Oxoniae«

Deutsche Tolkien Gesellschaft e. V. (DTG)
E-Mail: info@tolkiengesellschaft.de

Scriptorium Oxoniae im atelier für TEXTaufgaben e. K.
Brehmstraße 50 · 40239 Düsseldorf · Germany
E-Mail: rayermann@scriptorium-oxoniae.de

Hither Shore, Gesamtleitung: Thomas Fornet-Ponse
E-Mail: hither-shore@tolkiengesellschaft.de

Vorschläge für Beiträge in deutscher oder englischer Sprache (inklusive
Exposé von ca. 100 Wörtern) werden erbeten an o.g. E-Mail-Adresse.

Alle Rechte verbleiben beim Autor des jeweiligen Einzelbeitrags.
Es gilt als vereinbart, dass ein Autor seinen Beitrag innerhalb der nächsten
18 Monate nach Erscheinen dieser *Hither-Shore*-Ausgabe nicht anderweitig
veröffentlichen darf.

Abwicklung: Susanne A. Rayermann, Düsseldorf
Layout/Design: Kathrin Bondzio, Solingen
Umschlagillustration: Anke Eißmann, Herborn
Druck und Vertrieb: Books on Demand, Norderstedt

Alle Rechte vorbehalten.

Inhalt

Preface / Vorwort 6

Tolkien Seminar 2014

Tolkien's Living Landscapes 8
Alan Turner (Jena)

Old Forest and Barrow-downs: A Natural Prelude to LotR 18
Jonathan Nauman (Usk Valley Vaughan Association)

Melian's Girdle:
Boundaries and Hidden Thresholds in Arda 32
Guglielmo Spirito (Assisi)

Sympathetic Backgrounds in Tolkien's Prose 52
Annie Birks (Angers)

Romantische Landschaften in Tolkiens Werk 64
Julian Tim Morton Eilmann (Aachen)

Landscapes as Metaphor in LotR 80
Thomas Kullmann (Osnabrück)

What Tolkien's Landscapes Owe to Medieval Storytelling 92
Tatjana Silec (Paris)

The Role of Nature in LotR and *La Saga de los Confides* 104
Natalia González de la Llana (Aachen)

The Dead Marshes and *oikoumene*:
the Limits of a Landscape in Middle-earth 116
Michaël Devaux (Livarot)

Approach and Sojourn: Structures of
Arriving and Staying in *The Lord of the Rings* 130
Martin Sternberg (Bonn)

Die dunkle Seite des Waldes? Konkrete und gefühlte
Bedrohungen durch natürliche Räume 142
Patrick Peters (Mönchengladbach)

Zusammenfassungen der englischen Beiträge 156
Summaries of the German Essays 163

Reviews / Rezensionen

John S. Ryan: Tolkien—Cult or Culture 166
Helen Conrad-O'Briain & Gerard Hynes (Eds.):
J.R.R.Tolkien: the Forest and the City 168
Stefan Ekman: Here Be Dragons. Exploring Fantasy Maps
and Settings 173
Peter Hunt (Ed.): J.R.R. Tolkien. New Casebooks Series 176
John S. Ryan: In the Nameless Wood 178
Roberto Arduini & Claudio A. Testi (Eds.): Tolkien and Philosophy 180
Thomas Honegger & Dirk Vanderbeke (Eds.):
From Peterborough to Faëry 183
Raymond Edwards: Tolkien 184
Fastitocalon. Vol. 4-1&2. Crime and the Fantastic 185
Deborah A. Higgens: Anglo-Saxon Community in J.R.R. Tolkien's
The Lord of the Rings 187
Stuart D. Lee (Ed.): A Companion to J.R.R. Tolkien 189
Friedhelm Schneidewind & Heidi Steimel (Hg.): Musik in Mittelerde 191

Our Authors / Unsere Autorinnen & Autoren 194

Siglen-Liste 200

Index 202

Preface

The deep significance of nature and landscape in Tolkien's works, perceived by many readers and critics, prompted the 11th Seminar of the German Tolkien Society, 9-11 May 2014 in Jena, to take a look at this topic. Be it the antipathy against industrialisation and the linked destruction of nature expressed frequently by J.R.R. Tolkien, the reception by the green movement, the often uttered perception of long-winded descriptions of landscape, or the also often mentioned detailed geography of the secondary world: especially *The Lord of the Rings* offers ample opportunity to look at conception, meaning and relevance of nature and landscape from various disciplinary angles.

It thus does not come as a surprise that most articles focus on this particular work in their deliberations—for example with a view to the "sympathetic background", i.e. the reaction of landscape to deeds or emotions of characters or their imitation, especially in the Dead Marshes, the Old Forest and the Barrow-downs, or the risk potential of woods in general, to the metaphoric character of landscape portrayal, in that it amongst other things illustrates character traits, or to the various types of locations as either detached from normal space and time, embedded in time and space or as a sanctuary. A lot of these analyses show in which traditions—for example the medieval story telling or realistic literature—specific aspects are rooted. But other texts, especially the *Silmarillion* corpus, are not neglected either, as seen in the contributions to Romantic landscape or the Girdle of Melian as a paradigm for a (hidden) border.

Even though this volume collects fewer articles on the conference topic as many of its predecessors, the ones in hand clearly show how rewarding the further analysis of nature and landscape in Tolkien's work can be, and offers ample opportunity and impetus for it. The seminar contributions are complemented, as per usual, by in-depths reviews of topical secondary literature on Tolkien.

In closing, I would like to thank Prof. Dr. Thomas Honegger and his team at the Friedrich-Schiller-University in Jena as well as Walking Tree Publishers for their generous support. Further thanks go to all contributors, the co-editors from the board, Marie-Noëlle Biemer for her translation of the preface, our publisher Susanne A. Rayermann and Kathrin Bondzio for the layout. Without all these people, the 11th volume of *Hither Shore* could not have been realised.

Thomas Fornet-Ponse

Vorwort

Die von vielen Rezipienten wahrgenommene hohe Bedeutung von Natur und Landschaft in Tolkiens Werk gab Anlass für das 11. Tolkien Seminar der Deutschen Tolkien Gesellschaft vom 9. bis 11. Mai 2014 in Jena, sich genau dieses Themas anzunehmen. Sei es die von J.R.R. Tolkien ausgedrückte Antipathie gegenüber der Industrialisierung und der damit verbundenen Zerstörung der Natur, die Aufnahme durch die ökologische Bewegung, die oft geäußerte Empfindung sehr langatmiger Landschaftsschilderungen oder die ebenfalls oft angeführte Detailfülle der ausgearbeiteten Geographie der Sekundärwelt: Insbesondere *The Lord of the Rings* bietet ausreichend Gelegen-heit, Gestaltung, Bedeutung und Relevanz von Natur und Landschaft aus unterschiedlichen fachlichen Disziplinen in den Blick zu nehmen.

Insofern verwundert es nicht, wenn die meisten Beiträge hier ebendieses Werk in den Vordergrund stellen – beispielsweise mit Blick auf den „mitfühlenden Hintergrund", d.h. die Reaktion der Landschaft auf Taten oder Emotionen der Charaktere oder deren Nachahmung, auf den besonderen Charakter der Totensümpfe, des Alten Waldes und der Hügelgräberhöhen oder auf das Gefahrenpotential von Wäldern, auf den metaphorischen Charakter der Landschaftsschilderungen, insofern sie u.a. Charaktereigenschaften illustrieren, oder auf die unterschiedliche Art der Orte als von Normalraum und -zeit abgetrennt, als in Zeit und Raum eingebettet oder als Rückzugsort. Bei vielen dieser Untersuchungen wird ferner deutlich, in welchen Traditionen – etwa der mittelalterlichen Erzählweise oder der realistischen Literatur – bestimmte Aspekte stehen. Aber auch andere Texte, insbesondere aus dem *Silmarillion*-Komplex, werden nicht vernachlässigt, wie die Beiträge zur romantischen Landschaft oder zu Melians Gürtel als Paradigma einer (verborgenen) Grenze belegen.

Wenngleich dieser Band weniger Beiträge zur Seminarthematik versammelt als viele seiner Vorgänger, zeigen die vorhandenen doch deutlich, wie lohnend die weitere Auseinandersetzung mit Natur und Landschaft in Tolkiens Werk sein kann, und bieten ausreichend Gelegenheit und Anstöße dafür. Wie üblich, werden die Seminarbeiträge durch ausführliche Rezensionen zu aktueller Tolkien-Sekundärliteratur ergänzt.

Abschließend sei für den Erfolg des Seminars herzlich Prof. Dr. Thomas Honegger und seinem Team von der Friedrich-Schiller-Universität Jena sowie dem Verlag *Walking Tree Publishers* für die großzügige Unterstützung gedankt. Ebenfalls danke ich sehr allen Beitragenden, den Mitgliedern im Board of Editors, Marie-Noëlle Biemer für die Übersetzungen und schließlich der Verlegerin Susanne A. Rayermann sowie Kathrin Bondzio für die Vorlagenerstellung – ohne sie alle hätte dieser elfte Band von Hither Shore nicht erscheinen können.

Thomas Fornet-Ponse

Tolkien's Living Landscapes
Allan Turner (Jena)

The significance of landscapes in Tolkien's fiction has been clear for a long time. It is a commonplace of Tolkien criticism to assert that Middle-earth can be seen almost as a character in its own right. Brian Rosebury, for example, has given an often-cited detailed commentary of the description of the approach to Bree (Rosebury 15-19).

Undoubtedly the landscapes of Middle-earth have given great pleasure to readers. However, more recently, Nils Ivar Agøy has questioned how detailed Tolkien's descriptions really are. He disputes the claims of Elle van Wijk that they are "boring, unspecific and repetitive", arguing that, unlike in a realistic visual representation, Tolkien's depictions deliberately concentrate on elements which give a sense of atmosphere, leaving others only suggested, so that readers are invited to complete the details as they visualise them from their own experience.

In support of this view, Agøy cites Tolkien's own comments in *On Fairy-stories* on the collaboration between writer and reader:

> If a story says "he climbed a hill and saw a river in the valley below," the illustrator may catch, or nearly catch, his own vision of such a scene; but every hearer of the words will have his own picture, and it will be made out of all the hills and rivers and dales he has ever seen, but specially out of The Hill, The River, The Valley which were for him the first embodiment of the word.   (TL 70)

So it is in large part the open-endedness of the description which gives the reader the pleasure of collaborating in its realisation, just as Parish helps to fill in the gaps of Niggle's landscape.

I don't wish to disagree with Agøy's conclusion, but rather to supplement it. A part of what attracts readers is the fact that the landscapes are not inert surfaces which are merely seen, but rather Tolkien partly creates living, sensual landscapes with beating hearts to which the reader can relate almost physically. It is my contention that this is achieved partly through the unobtrusive use of cognitive metaphors which present landscapes in terms of living beings.

First I need to say what I mean by *metaphor*. For this purpose we are not dealing with normal literary rhetorical figures, which are conceived as being striking, creative and original, such as the personification of time in Ralph Hodgson's poem:

> Time, you old gipsy man,
> Will you not stay,

Put up your caravan
Just for one day?

Another example of a literary metaphor may be the conceit in Shakespeare's Sonnet 18, "Shall I compare thee to a summer's day?", which is an extended comparison of the transience of summer and nature with the permanence of art. In both these cases the unexpected and even arresting association of two normally quite distinct ideas is intended to offer a new, deeper insight into the topic.

In this article I am more interested in the concept of metaphor (and metonymy) as understood by cognitive linguistics. In brief, we perceive the world in terms of similarities and differences, allowing us to assign things to categories, which are then encoded in our language. In particular we perceive external objects in relation to our own bodies and designate them in similar terms.

For example, a table stands on legs and a chair has arms. At a deeper level of abstraction, the stairs have a foot, as in "at the foot of the stairs", which in this case is not a part of the woodwork resembling a human foot but is rather a metonymy designating a position at the bottom of the stairs corresponding to the position of the feet at the bottom of the human body. Directions may be viewed in a similar way, with movement up (towards the head) seen as positive and movement down (towards the feet) seen as negative. For example, we turn the music up to make it louder and down to make it softer.

All these expressions use metaphors, although they may not be accepted as such by literary scholars, who would be tempted to regard an expression like "the long arm of the law" as a cliché, that is to say a metaphor which has become so conventional and unoriginal that it is no longer recognised as one. For linguists, however, "clichés", that is predictable combinations or collocations, are a basic principle of how language works.

In many cases the extended uses have become lexicalised; that is to say, the originally metaphorical meaning is now given as a separate definition in dictionaries. For example, after listing the literal bodily meanings of *leg* as section I, the *Oxford English Dictionary* then gives as a new heading for further definitions: "II. Something more or less resembling a leg, or performing its function as a support for a 'body'." The inverted commas around *body* imply that this, too, is being used as a corresponding metaphor. The meaning of *leg* as part of a table comes in definition 12: "One of the comparatively long and slender supports of a piece of furniture or the like."

The type of cognitive metaphor that I am concerned with here can best be illustrated by a single sentence from *The Lord of the Rings*, where the hobbits set off across the edge of the Barrow-downs:

> Their way wound along the floor of the hollow, and round the green <u>feet</u> of a steep hill into another deeper and broader valley, and then over the <u>shoulders</u> of further hills, and down their long <u>limbs</u>, and up their smooth <u>sides</u> again, up on to new hill-tops and down into new valleys. (136; I, 8)

This is in itself an unremarkable description; as Agøy suggests, it contains no topographical detail which could enable the reader to form a particularised image, although anyone who has seen downland will be able to supply their own realisation of this scene. What is important are the underlined nouns; underlining will be used in quotations throughout this article to mark words which suggest, however remotely, characteristics of human, or at least animate, beings. There is some variation in the extent to which the different meanings have been lexicalised.

Many people would not recognise *side* as being necessarily related to the human body. Indeed, it could be applied to both persons and objects already in the Old English period,[1] suggesting that the metaphorical link may date back to a much earlier period of language development.[2] *Foot* has already been commented on, though its application here is more concrete than in the previous example, where it simply denoted a position. *Limb* is perhaps the least lexicalised of the four nouns; the OED offers:

> **4.** Transferred senses.
> **b.** In various uses, chiefly of material things and more or less technical: A projecting section of a building, e.g. the outworks of a castle; one of the four branches composing a cross; a member or clause of a sentence, or the like; a spur of a mountain range; one of the pieces which compose the lock of a gun; the part of a compound core of a transformer, electromagnet, etc., on which a coil is wound.

The number of quite distinct referents under a single heading suggests that this word is still to some extent experienced as a metaphor which can be applied in many different situations, rather than as a lexical item which can be given a fixed definition. It is precisely this interplay between more and less lexicalised

---

1 All lexicological information in this article is taken from the online version of the *Oxford English Dictionary*.
2 Anyone who questions the relevance to Tolkien of cognitive linguistics, with its insistence on the centrality of metaphor, should look at *Poetic Diction* by his fellow-Inkling Owen Barfield, which he claimed had a great influence on him. Barfield contends that in sacral terms such as *spirit*, the concrete sense ("breathing") and the abstract sense ("essence of life") were both present in the bundle of meanings which accompanied the word from its very beginnings. In other words, the metaphor is an integral part of the language and not something imposed upon it by art.

items that produces a liminal effect, in which the depiction of the landscape is neither altogether concrete nor altogether impressionistic.

Mountains

Before pursuing any further theoretical discussion, it will be useful to examine some additional examples of Tolkien's use of cognitive metaphors. A landscape feature which plays a prominent role in *The Lord of the Rings* and is similar yet significantly different to the downs already considered because of the vaster scale is mountains.

The verb which most commonly collocates with mountains in Tolkien is *march*: mountains are perceived as lines of marching soldiers. One example among many is the view from the Anduin of "a dark line, where marched the southernmost ranks of the Misty Mountains" (381; II, 9). However, descriptions of mountains also use the metaphors of heads, shoulders, arms, knees, laps and faces, as in Pippin's first view of Minas Tirith: "to his right great mountains reared their heads" (750; VI, 1). Shortly afterwards he glimpses Mindolluin, "its tall face whitening in the rising day. And upon its out-thrust knee was the Guarded City" (751; VI, 2). From the Ford of Bruinen, "the tall mountains climbed, shoulder above shoulder, and peak beyond peak, into the fading sky" (212; I, 12). Nen Hithoel above Rauros is "fenced by steep grey hills whose sides were clad with trees, but their heads were bare" (393; I, 9). The Hornburg stands on "a heel of rock thrust outward by the northern cliff" (528; III, 7), while the Firienfeld at Dunharrow is "laid upon the lap of the great mountains beyond" (794; VI, 3).

Another organic feature of mountains in Tolkien is that they have roots. This is surely an intertextual echo of the title of William Morris's romance *The Roots of the Mountains*. Sometimes he uses it in Morris's more obviously metaphorical sense of 'foothill'[3] as in the case of Treebeard's hill, which is "the abrupt end of some long root thrust out by the distant mountains" (462; III, 4). But more typically, Tolkien uses it to mean the internal spaces deep below the peaks, as in Gollum's riddle:

> What has roots as nobody sees,
> Is taller than trees,
> Up, up it goes,
> And yet never grows? (*H*, 97)

Of course, the word play here is all about the mingling of the living and the non-living, vegetable and mineral, botany and geology. This conceit is played

---

3　*Foothill* is of course in origin another metaphor which has become more thoroughly lexicalised.

upon further in *The Lord of the Rings*, where Gollum, at least as interpreted by Gandalf, is particularly interested in "roots and beginnings" (53; I, 2), so that on first seeing the Misty Mountains he thinks: "The roots of those mountains must be roots indeed" (54; I, 2).

Some intermediate Remarks

At this stage I would like to bring up two points in order to clarify further what I see as the main thrust of this article. First, it is important to differentiate clearly between the essentially linguistic approach to metaphor as understood here and the explanations of literary devices as given in the standard dictionaries of literary terms. For example, the remains of Amon Sûl on Weathertop are described as "a tumbled ring, like a rough crown on the old hill's head" (185; I, 11). Here we certainly have the cognitive metaphor of the head as the topmost part of the hill, and the ruins are associated metonymically with the crown worn on the head of a king. However, this sentence contains two specifically *literary* devices. One of these is personification, which, although it is ultimately derived from metaphor, is normally seen as a separate phenomenon, and the other is simile. Both of these are essentially rhetorical figures which are intended to draw attention to themselves; the reader is meant to notice and admire them, or even be moved by them. If s/he fails to appreciate the writer's skill, or perceives the devices as unoriginal or flawed, then they have lost their whole point and the writer may justly be criticised.[4]

The question of literariness is irrelevant in this context, and may even be a distraction, since I am concerned rather with the action of metaphor at a deeper, less conscious level of language. We have seen that because of the varying degree of lexicalisation, some of the metaphorical meanings are more overt than others, and it is these overt examples which are perhaps the most dangerous. To look at it from a personal point of view, in researching this topic I had to draw up a list of everything that I considered to be a cognitive metaphors in *The Lord of the Rings*. Looking through this list inevitably draws my attention to individual words and tempts me to evaluate them as literary figures, at which point I am dismayed by how trite and conventional they appear. On the other hand, I know that I gain great satisfaction from reading the landscape descriptions, so it must be the case that in their context the words in question are not prominent enough to stand out as effects which require evaluation; they are an integral part of the texture. The important point is not that Tolkien uses such

---

4 As it happens, in this case the description is made by a character, Aragorn, rather than by the narrative voice. Therefore, if anyone cares to call the phrase in question a cliché, then it is Aragorn's cliché and he is (presumably) characterised as someone with poor literary taste.

expressions, since they are an essential part of the language and must surely be used unconsciously to some extent by all other authors. In any case, it would be simplistic to attempt to reduce the effect of a text to any single feature. What is significant above all is their distribution, concentrated around certain passages of topographical description and combined with other factors to create an impression of animate landscapes.

This leads directly into the second main point; in *The Lord of the Rings* we are dealing with a secondary world which is suffused with mythology. I would contend that the tale is not itself a myth, but nevertheless there is an underlying Secondary World mythology which keeps breaking through to the surface. If we look at the description of Caradhras, we can add sides and flanks to the list of cognitive metaphors as we learn that "the grim flanks of Caradhras towered up invisible in the gloom" (288; II, 3), while shortly before "[i]ts sides were now black and sullen, and its head was in grey cloud" (287; II, 3). On the surface these descriptions look just like the ones that have already been considered, but in addition we are presented here with a mountain that is, or at least appears to some of the characters to be, an agent in itself, as Gimli observes: "Caradhras has not yet forgiven us... He has more snow yet to fling at us, if we go on" (291; II, 3).

Furthermore, we need to be aware that the cosmogonic myths of the *Silmarillion* are also tacitly present as Tolkien assimilated his 'New Hobbit' more and more to the materials of the First Age which had already been elaborated in considerable detail. Light and darkness are often treated in terms which can make them appear like tangible substances, as Tolkien conceived them already in *The Book of Lost Tales*, so that just before leaving Bag End, Frodo sees "shadows creep out of the corners" (69; I, 3). There are also references to the myth of Eärendil, the intercessor who became a star to keep watch over Middle-earth, as when from Mordor Sam sees a star "peeping among the cloud-wrack" (922; VI, 2). Similarly, the observation in Rivendell that "[t]he Hunter's Moon waxed round in the night sky, and put to flight all the lesser stars" (274; II, 3) relies on a knowledge of the early mythology in which the moon is a hunter who chases the stars. Even the use of the pronouns *he* and *she* to refer to the moon and the sun respectively has its origin in the interface between myth and language which is typical of the *Silmarillion*.[5]

It remains only to look at three other areas of landscape description in which metaphors play an important part, and in some cases may be associated with an underlying myth. This can be done quite briefly, since the principles are now clear and will not need detailed further explanation.

---

5   Of course German readers are used to *der Mond* and *die Sonne*, but poetic imagery in English, being dominated by Latin and the Romance languages, almost always presents the sun (*sol*) as masculine and the moon (*luna*) as feminine.

Water

There is rather less to say about the metaphors used to characterise water in *The Lord of the Rings*. Its sound is often compared to human speech, such as "the rush and chatter of water upon stone" at the Fords of Isen, or the "stony voice" of the Morgulduin (697; IV, 7). Pastoral poems and popular songs are notorious for their babbling brooks and murmuring streams, so some readers might possibly groan at the seeming conventionality when they read that Galadriel takes Frodo to a hollow "though which ran murmuring the silver stream" (361; II, 7). However, it can be pointed out in mitigation that this landscape feature has its own myth too; only a few pages before, as the company enters Lothlórien, the sound of another stream has been associated with the voice of its eponymous nymph Nimrodel. Perhaps this murmuring is specially associated with Lothlórien, since the metaphor does not appear elsewhere.

Another river, flowing down from the mountains, is described with cognitive metaphors which emphasise its fast movement over stones, with a hint of personification: "Down the hillside the young Entwash, leaping from its springs high above, ran noisily from step to step to meet them" (469; III, 4). Again there are different degrees of lexicalisation involved here: *run* for the flowing of water dates back to the Old English period, while *young* to dignify a watercourse close to its source is attested from 1550. *Leap* looks as if it should be an invention of the Romantic poets, such as Tennyson's "And the wild cataract leaps in glory",[6] although in fact it was already used of the movement of waves in Layamon's *Brut*.

Trees

As might be expected in Tolkien, there are a number of unobtrusive cognitive metaphors associated with trees and forests. The sound of the wind in the leaves and branches is similar to that of water, as we are made to hear "fir-trees sighing in the wind" (334; II, 6), or are told that "leaves were whispering" (77; I, 3). In their appearance, the unbroken lines of trees in a forest are presented, like mountains, as armies on the move. When the company are leaving Lothlórien, they see that "the woodlands still marched on southwards" (371; II, 8), and "bare woods stalked along either bank" (379; II,8). The tops of deciduous trees may appear like human heads; above Rauros there are "steep slopes upon which trees climbed, mounting one head above another" (396; II, 10), while from Fangorn Aragorn sees "the heads of the trees descending in ranks towards the plain" (492; III, 5). But the trees have not only heads as human attributes, but also hands and fingers. Sometimes the fingers are the

---

6 From "The Princess" and available, for example, at: http://www.poetryfoundation.org/poem/174652

bare twigs bearing the new season's buds: the trees at Edoras in the south are already "blushing red at their fingertips" (507; III, 6). Elsewhere the leaves themselves may be shaped like fingers; Aragorn, Gimli and Legolas camp under a tree like a chestnut which has "broad brown leaves of a former year, like dry hands with long splayed fingers" (441; III, 2).

This last example is particularly interesting because again it is a simile, that is an overt literary figure which is meant to draw attention to itself. It involves a stronger personification than any that has been mentioned before, since it is even suggested that the tree seems glad of the camp fire, like a sentient being warning itself. However, it is significant that this episode takes place on the edge of Fangorn and acts as an anticipation of the appearance of Treebeard and the Ents.

The Ents have too much individuality and corporeality to be considered as either metaphors or myths, but nevertheless they represent a point where cognitive metaphor breaks through into real, independent life, since they incorporate all the treeishness of trees but are nevertheless animate personalities with the free will to defend themselves against their enemies who want to cut down the forests. The reader who is familiar with them is now in a position to appreciate more consciously the metaphors which suffuse Tolkien's language at an almost subliminal level; trees will no longer be seen purely as trees.

An intermediate stage is represented by the Huorns, the trees that can move but have no individual personalities; their emotions seem not to rise above a generalised desire for revenge on Saruman and his orcs. The non-human air of threat about them is characterised by overt similes which repeat some of the metaphors seen above: "The ends of their long sweeping boughs hung down like searching fingers, their roots stood up from the ground like the limbs of strange monsters, and dark caverns opened beneath them" (546; III, 8). The Riders of Rohan hear "the creaking and groaning of boughs, and far cries, and a rumour of wordless voices, murmuring angrily" (ibid.). Even more than the Old Forest, this is an animate wood.

Metaphors of Mordor

All the landscapes mentioned above are in some way perceived as pleasant by the protagonists, or at least neutral, such as the trees which appear like marching armies without posing any definite threat. It is noticeable, for example, that there is a concentration of cognitive metaphors around the episode on the house of Tom Bombadil, such as the first example in this article. This is perhaps not surprising since it represents a safe refuge where the inhabitants are particularly close to the land and the rhythms of nature. But what about the presentation of the hostile landscapes, in particular those around Mordor where evil is incarnate? In brief, here the metaphors appear less frequently and usually have negative connotations; for example, as we have seen, the Morgulduin has a voice, but it is "stony". The pass of Cirith Ungol is "deep-cloven between two black shoulders; and on either shoulder was a horn of stone" (710; IV, 8). Certainly the human-sounding shoulders are present, but they are now associated with horns, which belong to animals and are used aggressively. The landscape features in Mordor tend to be the product of human (or humanoid) activity, acting against nature rather than in harmony with it, such as the Towers of the Teeth: "Stony-faced they were, with dark window-holes staring north and east and west, and each window was full of sleepless eyes... None could pass the Teeth of Mordor and not feel their bite" (636; IV, 3). The emphasis here as elsewhere is on teeth and eyes, to suggest that intruders are likely to be seen and attacked; Sauron is indeed the Eye that sees everything. The metaphors of evil are overt and have a clearly symbolic function. To this extent they are quite different from the examples considered above, which do not draw attention to themselves but are rather an essential part of the texture of the language.

Conclusion

I have attempted to show that Tolkien's landscape descriptions do not depend for their effect on the complete visualisation which would depend on a wealth of purely external description. Rather they offer a matrix into which they tempt the reader to enter, not only because individual readers can fill in the details from their own memories as Agøy suggests, but also because these landscapes have a life of their own which the reader can experience almost physically because of the large number of cognitive metaphors more or less hidden in the text, which by their nature draw upon a subconscious level of human perception.

To conclude, I would like to bring the wheel full circle. At the end of the tale, after the destruction of the Ring, the Elves, who have always had a close identification with nature, particularly trees, appear to melt back into the landscape themselves: "none saw them pass, save the wild creatures; or here and there some wanderer in the dark who saw a swift shimmer under the trees, or a light and shadow flowing through the grass as the Moon went westward" (1029; VI, 9). Or again: "If any wanderer had chanced to pass, little would he have seen or heard, and it would have seemed to him only that he saw grey figures, carved in stone, memorials of forgotten things now lost in unpeopled lands" (985; VI, 6). The synthesis is now complete; the landscape has become living and the living have become landscape.

Bibliography

Agøy, Nils Ivar. "Vague or Vivid? Descriptions in *The Lord of the Rings*". Tolkien Studies 10 (2013): 49-67

Hodgson, Ralph. "Time, You Old Gipsy Man". http://www.bartleby.com/103/109.html

Rosebury, Brian. *Tolkien: A Cultural Phenomenon*. Basingstoke: Palgrave Macmillan, 2003

Tolkien, J.R.R. *The Hobbit*. London: HarperCollins, 1998

---. *The Lord of the Rings* (50th Anniversary Edition). London: HarperCollins, 2005

Old Forest and Barrow-downs: A Natural Prelude to *The Lord of the Rings*

Jonathan Nauman (Usk Valley Vaughan Association)

> 'If there are no worse things ahead than the Old Forest, I shall be lucky,' said Frodo. 'Tell Gandalf to hurry along the East Road: we shall soon be back on it and going as fast as we can.'   (LotR I 156)

This inaccurate farewell to Fredegar Bolger in *The Fellowship of the Ring* is Frodo's last statement before leaving the Shire. Although the remark correctly forebodes that the Ring-bearer and his companions will encounter dangers on their journey far greater than any of those generally associated with the Old Forest in hobbit folklore, Fredegar's worry that his friends "will need rescuing before the day is out" (LotR I 156) proves to be well-founded. The East Road is not so easily attained, and J.R.R. Tolkien's readers must pass through three chapters of unforeseen adventures before the narrative reaches it—extraneous chapters, many have thought, both in the mid-twentieth century[1] and more recently.[2]

I will here attempt to demonstrate, on the contrary, that the Old Forest and Barrow-downs episodes perform an important, even an integral function in *The Lord of the Rings*, introducing the reader to a memorable and distinctive aspect of Tolkien's heroic romance at large. It is rightly observed that Old Man Willow, Tom Bombadil, and Goldberry are outside of the tale's central narrative, not motivated by or particularly concerned with the Quest of the Ring of Power; however, this is not a narrative flaw, but an ample and indeed elegant instance of contextualization establishing the complexity, dignity, and real agency of the natural world in Tolkien's Middle-earth. As Tolkien himself repeatedly said, the peculiar, marginal figure of Tom Bombadil, presiding genius of these episodes, was retained intentionally in order to show that "the power of the Ring ... is not the whole picture" (L 192). Within the fiction it is clear that the outcome of the Ring Quest will be as crucially important for Tom Bombadil as for any elf, man, dwarf, or hobbit, since no power in Middle-earth would be invulnerable if Sauron were to regain the One Ring (LotR I 348). But the entities that Tom Bombadil and Goldberry rejoice in and represent—the flora, fauna, topography, winds and weather of Middle-earth—function as dynamic agents quite apart from the intentions of other "Free Peoples of the World" (LotR I 361); and as the romance proceeds, their actions, though disengaged

---

1 Tolkien wrote shortly after *The Lord of the Rings* was published that many of his readers found Tom Bombadil (and, by implication, the narratives associated with him) "an odd or indeed discordant ingredient in the plot" (L 192).
2 Peter Jackson's 2001 movie skips them altogether; see Tom Shippey's comments on this in Road 417 and 435, n. 6.

from pursuit of the Ring, often act as unforeseen wild cards (so to speak) in the overarching providence of the divine Creator, Eru Ilúvatar. All of Tolkien's natural beings are conceived not as organic machines or necessary elements in self-propagating ecosystems,[3] but—rational or not—as willed beings with their own aesthetics, memories, and esprits de corps.

Such tribal presence in Middle-earth's forest communities makes entering them very much analogous with encountering alien and potentially hostile human tribes; and this aspect of the situation is highlighted at the start of the Old Forest episode.[4] Meriadoc Brandybuck, as a Buckland hobbit who has lived near the Old Forest most of his life,[5] acts as master of ceremonies at this juncture, recounting a history of conflict between Buckland and the Old Forest—the trees' attempt to destroy the High Hay, and the hobbits' felling of the aggressive dryads and burning of them in a fire of such proportions that the soil of the Bonfire Glade remains too ashen to support tree life. With hostilities of this sort in the background, Frodo's decision to enter the Old Forest is clearly a choice to evade evil spiritual peril—the Black Riders—under risk of expected natural animosities, a risk that he and his company seem quickly to lose, despite Meriadoc's frontiersmanly experience and poise; for Old Man Willow's spell has its way, and the hobbits are inexorably driven into the Old Forest's Withywindle valley, the "centre," as Merry had warned, "from which all of the wood's queerness comes" (LotR I 160). The malicious natural magic is orchestrated by an ancient and perverse dryad whose will has come to dominate the other trees of the Old Forest almost completely. Once the hobbits are successfully herded into his valley, and then into his immediate vicinity, the tree proceeds to seduce them, one after the other, into sleeping in vulnerable positions—Pippin first, with Merry and Frodo quickly following. Interestingly, Sam's sturdy tribal practicality shows strongest resistance to the dryad's spells, as he rescues Frodo from drowning and attempts to follow up on the hobbits' former victories over the trees by threatening the Willow with fire; but this action merely provokes a forest-wide commotion and unanswerable threats of retaliation, voiced through Pippin and Merry as the Willow's hostages. The

---

3   One notes the insistent mechanical metaphors that inform these current and regnant descriptions of the biological universe. Modern ecological discourse, however benevolent, tends to be much-implicated in the post-Enlightenment impulse to portray the world as a machine.
4   It is also in evidence when Bilbo senses a "watching and waiting feeling" at the threshold of Mirkwood, and implicit in Merry and Pippin's response to the "dim, and frightfully tree-ish" peripheries of Fangorn; see H 137 and LotR II 81.
5   Tolkien's portrayal of Buckland as an outlying colony of the Shire seems intentionally reminiscent of England's border on Wales, with the proximity of Tom Bombadil's realm reflecting the long English association of the "Celtic fringe" with natural magic. The Brandybucks have Welsh-style names; see Tolkien's passing comments on this in LotR III 516-517. Also, Crickhollow, the outlying village to which Frodo moves before leaving the Shire, further anglicises the Breconshire town name Crickhowell; and there is a manor house called Buckland Hall just a few miles from Crickhowell up the River Usk.

hobbits' situation seems irremediable. Frodo, however, moved by an unreasoned but accurate impulse, runs for help; and his calls find an answer in the fortuitous appearance of Tom Bombadil, a nature sprite[6] and "one-member category" or *lusus naturae*, as Tom Shippey calls him (Shippey 120), singing rhymes in unreflective joy that exult in sounding the name of his spouse:

> Hey! Come merry dol! derry dol! and merry-o,
> Goldberry, Goldberry, merry yellow berry-o!   (LotR I 168)

Bombadil has already noticed Old Man Willow's amplified rage in response to Sam's fire, but dismisses it with an offhand line—"*Poor old Willow-man, you tuck your roots away*" (LotR I 168). For Bombadil, the hobbits' presence and distress are no surprise. As he later reveals, their entry into the Forest, their predictable redirection to the Withywindle valley, their eventual need for rescue, and even the matter of Frodo's quest—all of this has already come to his attention (LotR I 175-176, 184). But for Bombadil, all such concerns are subordinated to routine duties, as expressed in his last words to the hobbits upon their departure from the Downs three days later: "*Tom has his house to mind, and Goldberry is waiting!*" (LotR I 203).

In his good-humored but incontestable authority, his uncalculated benevolence, Bombadil figures as a sort of demigod for Tolkien's prelapsarian classical and Christian take on nature—a world patterned and functional, unaccountable and beautiful, securely prior to actual corruptions caused by postlapsarian evils. The captured hobbits are freed through an exhortation sending their captor tree back toward primal health. "You let them out again, Old Man Willow!" Bombadil says.

> What be you a-thinking of? You should not be waking. Eat earth!
> Dig deep! Drink water! Go to sleep! Bombadil is talking!
>   (LotR I 169)

---

6   When I describe Tom Bombadil and Goldberry as "nature sprite" and "naiad," I take for the moment a standpoint exterior to Tolkien's fiction, positioning the characters in terms of their classical and folk literary antecedents without meaning to reduce them to instances of such traditions. Within the purview of Tolkien's legendarium, Bombadil and his spouse seem likely to be Maiar, the order of Valar "of less degree" (S 30) to which Sauron and Gandalf also belong. My account here thus largely agrees with Gene Hargrove's article on "Tom Bombadil" and Katherine Hesser's article on "Goldberry", though I do not feel that the personalities of Tom Bombadil and Goldberry are similar enough to those of the Valar Aulë and Yavanna to support Hargrove's and Hesser's suggestions that the two pairs might be identified.

The Willow's vindictive and monstrous aggression is suddenly reduced to functional health, with Merry and Pippin restored to a hobbit's natural freedom of movement.

The climax of Tolkien's chapter "The Old Forest" does not however coincide with the hobbits' rescue, but rather with their arrival at their unplanned destination: their welcome by Tom Bombadil at his house and their first meeting with the naiad Goldberry:

> Then another clear voice, as young and as ancient as Spring, like the song of a glad water flowing down into the night from a bright morning in the hills, came falling like silver to meet them:
>
> *Now let the song begin! Let us sing together*
> *Of sun, stars, moon and mist, rain and cloudy weather,*
> *Light on the budding leaf, dew on the feather,*
> *Wind on the open hill, bells on the heather,*
> *Reeds by the shady pool, lilies on the water:*
> *Old Tom Bombadil, and the River-daughter!*
>
> And with that song the hobbits stood upon the threshold, and a golden light was all about them.   (LotR I 171)

These words inaugurate a strange interim of preternatural country hospitality—good food, enchanted storytelling, and at night for Frodo, clairvoyant dreams that reach backward and forward to encompass much of the narrative of his quest. Tom and Goldberry preside over the natural world of the Old Forest and Barrow-downs together; and, as the imagery makes clear, they are also living emblems of the dynamic beauties of nature.[7] One sees this especially

---

[7] This aspect of Tom Bombadil and his spouse has garnered considerable notice in criticism; see, for instance, Anne Petty's references to Bombadil as "the nature deity par excellence" and "Tolkien's perfect personification of the powers of nature" (Petty 38, 97). One must note, however, that Tolkien probably would not have wished Bombadil to be characterised as an emanation of the earth, a reading that many of Tolkien's anthropologically-oriented myth critics have tended to suggest, and which Petty seems to endorse in citing the "perennial philosophy" of Alan Watts and stating that Bombadil "is nature in Watts' terms" (97). Assessments of Bombadil at the Council of Elrond (LotR I 348) seem rather to imply an individual of transcendent origin whose powers, invested in natural phenomena, are therefore analogous to and limited by that phenomena. Bombadil epitomises nature by choice rather than necessity: as a creature of Ilúvatar who gives himself completely to understanding and interacting with the distinctive motives and dynamics of the elements, plants, and animals of the Old Forest and Barrow-downs, he has effectively taken a "vow of poverty" toward the politics in the world at large (L 179), and this choice circumscribes his actions while maximizing his personal independence.

in Goldberry's panoply of splendid dress, which changes to match her environment or the weather in the world about: she is first seen seated amidst water lilies in earthenware vessels, wearing a gown "green as young reeds" (LotR I 172); then, on the rainy day following, the hobbits encounter her "clothed all in silver with a white girdle, and her shoes were like fishes' mail" (LotR I 183). Even Tom Bombadil's trademark costume, comically rearranging the colors of sky and sun—hat with blue feather, blue coat, yellow boots (LotR I 168)—can be adjusted at dinnertime with a crown of autumn leaves (LotR I 174) or a complete set of blue clothing and green stockings (LotR I 183). Tom and Goldberry also display, as epitomes of the natural world at large, a comic yet ideal masculine and feminine complementarity that the hobbits especially notice during meal preparation.

> Then Tom and Goldberry set the table; and the hobbits sat half in wonder and half in laughter: so fair was the grace of Goldberry and so merry and so odd the caperings of Tom. Yet in some fashion they seemed to weave a single dance, neither hindering the other, in and out of the room, and round about the table; and with great speed food and vessels and lights were set in order.
> (LotR I 183)

In healing reparation for the horrors of the Willow, the hobbits receive multiple assurances and benisons attesting to the wholesomeness and safety of their new refuge: Goldberry's first action, upon the hobbits' arrival, is to greet them demonstratively and run past them to close the door.

> "For you are still afraid, perhaps, of mist and tree-shadows and deep water, and untame things. Fear nothing! For tonight you are under the roof of Tom Bombadil!" (LotR I 172)

Likewise, upon leaving them for the evening, Goldberry wishes them a peaceful night, enjoining them to "heed no nightly noises! For nothing passes door and window here save moonlight and starlight and the wind off the hill-top" (LotR I 175), a statement Tom Bombadil reinforces just as they retire:

> "Sleep till the morning light, rest on the pillow! Heed no nightly noise! Fear no grey willow!" (LotR I 176)

When Pippin and Merry do experience unpleasant dreams that night, each of them remembers some fragment of Goldberry's or Tom's blessings and is quickly reassured. The efficacy of these words as help for resting prepares for the "Ho Tom Bombadil" incantation which the hobbits memorise at the end of their stay for emergency protection in the Barrow-downs.

Tom Bombadil's rune of protection summarises and identifies his realm and powers *"By water, wood and hill, by reed and willow, / By fire, sun and moon"* (LotR I 186), indicating his own benevolent accompanying presence and availability throughout the natural kingdoms of the Old Forest and Barrow-downs, a better counterpart to Old Man Willow's malicious ubiquity, whose "grey thirsty spirit drew power out of the earth and spread like fine root-threads in the ground, and invisible twig-fingers in the air, till it had under its dominion nearly all the trees of the Forest from the Hedge to the Downs" (LotR I 181). As Goldberry explains to Frodo (LotR I 174), Tom Bombadil is master of his country only in the sense of his ability to resist or counteract any other natural powers in it. He socialises with the elements and creatures, resisting their impingements when necessary, but does not arbitrate between them or rule over them. And as a nature sprite, his power is intrinsic rather than dependent (as Gandalf's would be, for instance) on the use of learned magical spells. Bombadil is "no weather-master" (LotR I 185), but he and Goldberry are able to interact personally with the elements close at hand, with Tom fending off raindrops to remain dry (LotR I 180) and Goldberry participating in the autumn rains with her songs (LotR I 179, 183-184) and facilitating the dew with her dancing (LotR I 187).

Before turning to Tom Bombadil's role in the hobbits' adventures on the Barrow-downs, we must examine the remarkable scene during the hobbits' visit, in which Tom asks to be shown the One Ring and Frodo "to his own astonishment" hands it to him.

> It seemed to grow larger as it lay for a moment on [Tom's] big brown-skinned hand. Then suddenly he put it to his eye and laughed. For a second the hobbits had a vision, both comical and alarming, of his bright blue eyes gleaming through a circle of gold. Then Tom put the Ring round the end of his little finger and held it up to the candlelight. For a moment the hobbits noticed nothing strange about this. Then they gasped. There was no sign of Tom disappearing!
> Tom laughed again, and then he spun the Ring in the air—and it vanished with a flash. Frodo gave a cry—and Tom leaned forward and handed it back to him with a smile.   (LotR I 184-185)

All of Tom Bombadil's actions with the Ring clearly show his disinterest in the artifact and his imperviousness to its lure and power. He looks through the center of the Ring, emphasizing its empty hollowness and implicitly mocking the Eye of Sauron; and he puts it only partially onto his smallest finger in order to examine it. So great is his unconcern that the hobbits take a moment to notice that he has done this without experiencing any apparent effect. He laughs and toys with it, emphasizing its insignificance by spinning it into the air, and apparently wreaks on the Ring what the Ring normally wreaks on its wearer—he makes it disappear! And then he immediately retrieves it from invisibility, hands it back to Frodo, and goes on discussing other subjects. Bombadil is so wholly dedicated to and identified with his natural realm, and has such mastery already within its bounds, that the Ring has nothing to work on with him, nothing to attract him. Because he figures forth the dynamic natural theater of Middle-earth within which the Ring's drama is being played out, it is in a way no more surprising that he remains visible while wearing the Ring than it is surprising that Bilbo, despite invisibility, cannot get his waistcoat buttons through the goblins' back door (H 95).

Bombadil however is fully aware that others are not like him, invulnerable. When Frodo puts the returned Ring on to test it, he finds that Tom is not affected by his guest's use of the Ring either; but Tom is not indifferent to Frodo's use. Rather, he enjoins Frodo to take the Ring off.

> "Hey! Come Frodo, there! Where be you a-going? Old Tom Bombadil's not as blind as that yet. Take off your golden ring! Your hand's more fair without it. Come back! Leave your game and sit down beside me! We must talk a while more, and think about the morning. Tom must teach the right road, and keep your feet from wandering". (LotR I 185)

One recalls here that this exchange over and actual handling of the Ring of Power has its beginning with a glint in Tom's eyes when hearing of Frodo's pursuit by Black Riders. Tom demonstrates in this encounter how exactly opposite his personality is to those of the Ringwraiths: he is careless about the Ring that obsesses them; he is aware of but not overly concerned with the unseen world which they choose exclusively and seek to dominate on behalf of Sauron; and he urges Frodo to take the Ring off while they seek to compel him to put it on. The Ringwraiths are quintessentially unnatural beings, having refused their humanity in search of sorcerous power and having accepted complete control by Sauron in order to prolong that power indefinitely: the glint in Tom's eyes comes not from any unhealthy interest in or collusion with the wraiths (as Frodo and the reader might fear), but from detached amusement at the wraths' alien obsession.

Tom Bombadil's power, functioning within his domain as the highest power of nature, is consistently expressed by Tom in terms of song; and it has often been noticed[8] that his discourse, whether or not printed as poetry in Tolkien's text, has a consistent lilting rhythm and considerable use of rhyme—see for instance the last two sentences of the extract just quoted, in which Tom calls Frodo back to discuss his journey: "We must talk a while more, and think about

---

8 See for example Shippey 121-122.

the morning. Tom must teach the right road, and keep your feet from wandering." These are hexameter lines with caesuras and feminine rhyme. Tom reins Frodo in to his actual task going forward with a verse-spell of implicit rhythms and significant recurring sounds; and this characteristic feature of verse and song is also, in broadest sense, at the basis of all natural life, from seasonal cycles down to diastole and systole. It is this heightened and accentuated participation in natural rhythm that the hobbits experience in the house of Tom Bombadil, with Goldberry's onomatopoeic rain and river songs and Tom "whistling like a tree-full of birds" (LotR I 187): water there goes to the heart like wine, and at each dinner the hobbits find themselves "singing merrily, as if it [were] easier and more natural than talking" (LotR I 175). The hobbits experience dinner-table revelations, one might say, of ur-art: underlying patterns of speech and tone emerge and are heartily enjoyed. As Frodo notices shortly after their first arrival at the house of Tom Bombadil, the effects of this elemental music differ significantly from the transcendently-oriented and artistic beauty of elvish song—"less keen and lofty was the delight, but deeper and nearer to mortal heart; marvellous and yet not strange" (LotR I 173).[9]

One senses clearly, in all of this, that Tom Bombadil's natural music is neither incidental nor imposed. His rhyming and singing, though truly playful, also reflect his accurate understanding of the dynamics and goals of the natural world when that world is in a state of spiritual harmony, both preternatural and supernatural. From his position within this spiritual harmony, Bombadil not only wields authority over Old Man Willow's malicious overplus of earth magic, but also has command over the unnatural incursions of the Barrow-wights, "evil spirits out of Angmar and Rhudaur" who have reanimated interred corpses of Atani warriors (LotR III 398).[10] The spell of the Barrow-wight, overheard by Frodo after his confusion and capture due to the careless lingering of the hobbits during travel through the Downs, asserts a natural magic shorn of hope, a cold pagan pride in death marked with a hoard:

> *Cold be hand and heart and bone,*
> *and cold be sleep under stone:*
> *never more to wake on stony bed,*
> *never, till the Sun fails and the Moon is dead.*
> *In the black wind the stars shall die,*
> *and still on gold here let them lie,*
> *till the dark lord lifts his hand*
> *over dead sea and withered land.* (LotR I 195)

---

9 Shippey notes that Tom Bombadil's speech, though rhythmical, is not "premeditated or artificial" (122).

10 See also LotR I 181. Shippey (126) lists other identities suggested by the wights' literary resonances.

Frodo has sufficient moral strength to attack the Barrow-wight in defense of his comrades, but not the physical or spiritual strength to defeat the monster; however, summoning help through the rune of protection memorised under Tom Bombadil's instruction earlier brings Bombadil himself to their rescue; and as Bombadil knew "the tune for" Old Man Willow (LotR I 169), he knows "stronger songs" than the Barrow-wight's (LotR I 196). Instead of the wight's cosmic vision of the Dark Lord finally ruling over a universe with all heat and light extinguished, Bombadil dismisses the wight into its own dead "black wind" in terms that recall the final exclusion of Morgoth from Middle-earth at the end of the First Age in *The Silmarillion*.[11]

> *Get out, you old Wight! Vanish in the sunlight!*
> *Shrivel like the cold mist, like the winds go wailing,*
> *Out into the barren lands far beyond the mountains!*
> *Come never here again! Leave your barrow empty!*
> *Lost and forgotten be, darker than the darkness,*
> *Where gates stand forever shut, till the world is mended.*
>
> (LotR I 197)

Bombadil's energetic dactyls answer the wight's gloomy trochees with natural magic in a still-wider frame, antithetical to the ethos of the treasure-laden barrow, anticipating a *"mended"* world, apparently a reference to the new and more immediately effectual regime of creative music expected in the *Ainulindalë* "after the end of days" (S 4). The earth responds to Bombadil's incantation by collapsing onto the wight and thus reclaiming the wight's stolen corpse, restoring the natural state of affairs in a manner that echoes the snapping closure of willow cracks after the hobbits' first rescue.

When Tom Bombadil refuses to accompany the hobbits to the Inn at Bree, observing that *"Tom's country ends here: he will not pass the borders"* (LotR I 203), he cheerfully fulfills the rule that he has been enforcing as presiding natural genius in the Old Forest and Barrow-downs; and his vigorous personal presence is never seen in the narrative again. But the natural flora and fauna of Middle-earth, the elemental energy and topography which Bombadil and Goldberry figure and mythically voice, retain a steady and dynamic presence throughout *The Lord of the Rings*. Both implicitly in the drama and explicitly in characters' thoughts and observations, the natural world is seen to perform unexpected and decisive roles, undergirding one of Tolkien's most important themes—that it is better to trust in aid unforeseen than to seize power illegiti-

---

11 "But Morgoth himself the Valar thrust through the Door of Night beyond the Walls of the World, into the Timeless Void; and a guard is set forever on those walls, and Eärendil keeps watch upon the ramparts of the sky" (S 306).

mately in order to ensure success. Bombadil's own recognition of his sphere and its boundaries provides this theme with an important case-in-point.

I will conclude with a few brief representative examples of natural interventions in the ensuing narratives of *The Lord of the Rings*, considering first the encounters with Fangorn and the Ents, most noticeably cognate of all the romance's episodes to the scenes with Tom Bombadil, and also the most extensive and important natural intervention in the plot at large.

Merry and Pippin, the two hobbits captured earlier by Old Man Willow, become the guests of Fangorn in his forest; and when Merry asks Fangorn the Ent "which side you are on," meaning to ascertain which faction he intends to support in the approaching War of the Ring (LotR II 86), Fangorn explains, "I am not altogether on anybody's *side*, because nobody is altogether on my *side*, if you understand me: nobody cares for the woods as I care for them, not even Elves nowadays" (LotR II 93). But hearing of the hobbits' plight as prisoners of orcs out of Isengard inclines him to consider more carefully the character of Saruman: "He has a mind of metal and wheels; and he does not care for growing things, except as far as they serve him for the moment" (LotR II 96). Fangorn calls an Entmoot and then leads the Ents to Isengard, where Saruman's engines and munitions are destroyed. When some of the Ents and their *huorns* help Théoden of Rohan to defeat Saruman's forces, Gandalf accurately disclaims any agency in recruiting their help: "It is a thing beyond the counsel of the wise," he says. "Better than my design, and better even than my hope the event has proved" (LotR II 189). When Saruman on the other hand attempts to use the situation to intimidate Théoden, saying, "You have won a battle but not a war—and that with help on which you cannot count again" (LotR II 236), he incidentally betrays his own exclusive interest in help over which one also has power and control, a way of thinking that noticeably differs from Elrond's advising the Company of the Ring to expect "friends upon your way when you least look for it" (LotR I 360; see also LotR II 385). Just as revealing is the Mouth of Sauron's claim that "Gondor and its deluded allies ... have wantonly destroyed" Isengard (LotR III 204): Mordor, apparently, is either ignorant of the Ents' role in recent events or has presumed a power-oriented alliance where no such thing existed.

Of course, as the Old Forest and Barrow-downs episodes would indicate, not all of nature's spontaneous interventions in *The Lord of the Rings* are initially friendly or beneficent. One remembers Tom Bombadil's uncomforting exposure of "the lives of the Forest" (LotR I 180-181) and Fangorn's accounts of *huorns* in the darker regions of his own wood (LotR II 89). The stone giants of the Misty Mountains, named in *The Hobbit* (H 65-66, 99-100) but only indicated in *The Lord of the Rings*, elicit some concern from Boromir and clarification from Aragorn during the Company's attempt on the passes of Caradhras:

> The Company halted suddenly, as if they had come to an agreement without any words being spoken. They heard eerie noises in the darkness round them. It may have been only a trick of the wind in the cracks and gullies of the rocky wall, but the sounds were those of shrill cries, and wild howls of laughter. Stones began to fall from the mountain-side, whistling over their heads, or crashing on the path beside them. Every now and again they heard a dull rumble, as a great boulder rolled down from hidden heights above. "We cannot go further tonight," said Boromir. "Let those call it the wind who will; there are fell voices on the air; and these stones are aimed at us."
> "I do call it the wind," said Aragorn. "But that does not make what you say untrue. There are many evil and unfriendly things in the world that have little love for those that go on two legs, and yet are not in league with Sauron, but have purposes of their own. Some have been in this world longer than he".
> (LotR I 377-378)

The natural world in Hollin and around Moria seems skewed toward darkness and malice by werewolves and the Watcher in the Water, Saruman's patrolling crows and Sauron's malevolent enhancement of winter cold; and one begins to feel that the region still bears some marks of Sauron's presence during the making of the Rings of Power.[12] But even these malicious deformations of nature, which drive the Company of the Ring into Moria and indirectly cause Gandalf's fall at the Bridge of Khazad-dûm, have an outcome arguably positive for the War of the Ring, as Gandalf's final victory over the Balrog deprives Sauron of a potential ally against the Elves of Lórien.

Many more of the passing circumstances in the romance could be enlisted to instance nature's independent or supporting role in the Quest of the Ring—the woodcraft of the Woses (LotR III 129-132), the water-shielded refuge of Henneth Annûn (LotR II 357-358), the brief incursion of a stream of water into the Morgai to refresh Sam and Frodo (LotR III 238-242)[13]; but two final illustrations should suffice to conclude. First, the dark moment at dawn in the Battle of the Pelennor Fields when the trumpets of Rohan first are heard—a scene Tolkien himself retrospectively claimed as one of his favorites (L 221):

---

12 The lands of Rhudaur show signs of earlier evil regimes even more obviously, as Aragorn notes (LotR I, 270).
13 Sam's gratitude to Galadriel in this vignette may be the clearest glimpse into Tolkien's specifically Roman Catholic sensibility in LotR.

> And in that very moment, away behind in some courtyard of the
> City, a cock crowed. Shrill and clear he crowed, recking nothing
> of wizardry or war, welcoming only the morning that in the sky
> far above the shadows of death was coming with the dawn.
> And as if in answer there came from far away another note. Horns,
> horns, horns. In dark Mindolluin's sides they dimly echoed. Great
> horns of the North wildly blowing. Rohan had come at last.
> (LotR III 126)

This incident, which transpires at the moment the Lord of the Nazgûl triumphantly enters the battered gates of Minas Tirith to confront Gandalf alone astride Shadowfax, marks the point at which Sauron's incursion on the West begins to be successfully turned back; and the announcement of the change comes not from Gandalf as representative of the Valar and Lords of the West, but from the natural sound of cock-crow, undisturbed by the military incursion or even by the natural deformation of induced ash cloud emanating from Mount Doom.

Second and last, a moment somewhat earlier: Frodo's discovery of the head of an ancient statue of a king as the sun sinks to penetrate the newly-emerging ash cloud of Mordor.

> Suddenly, caught by the level beams, Frodo saw the old king's
> head: it was lying rolled away by the roadside. "Look, Sam!" he
> cried, startled into speech. "Look! The king has got a crown again!"
> The eyes were hollow and the carven beard was broken, but about
> the high stern forehead there was a coronal of silver and gold. A
> trailing plant with flowers like small white stars had bound itself
> across the brows as if in reverence for the fallen king and in the
> crevices of his stony hair yellow stonecrop gleamed.
> "They cannot conquer forever!" said Frodo. And then suddenly
> the brief glimpse was gone. The sun dipped and vanished, and as
> if at the shuttering of a lamp, black night fell.
> (LotR II 395)

Despite the ominous sunset, the independent persistence of the natural world provides the Ring-bearer with an emblem of hope, a floral antecedent to the cockcrow at dawn.

Bibliography

Carpenter, Humphrey, Ed. with assistance of Christopher Tolkien. *The Letters of J.R.R. Tolkien*. Boston: Houghton-Mifflin, 1981

Hargrove, Gene. "Tom Bombadil." *J.R.R. Tolkien Encyclopedia: Scholarship and Critical Assessment*. Ed. Michael D.C. Drout. New York/London: Routledge, 2007, 670-671

Hesser, Katherine. "Goldberry." *J.R.R. Tolkien Encyclopedia: Scholarship and Critical Assessment*. Ed. Michael D.C. Drout. New York/London: Routledge, 2007, 244-246

Petty, Anne C. *One Ring to Bind Them All: Tolkien's Mythology*. Tuscaloosa: University of Alabama Press, 1979

Shippey, Tom. *The Road to Middle-earth*, revised edition. Bury St. Edmunds, Suffolk: HarperCollins, 2005

Tolkien, John Ronald Reuel. *The Fellowship of the Ring*. New York: Ballantine Books, 1965

---. *The Hobbit*. New York: Ballantine Books, 1966

---. *The Return of the King*. New York: Ballantine Books, 1965

---. *The Silmarillion*. Ed. Christopher Tolkien. London: HarperCollins, 2013

---. *The Two Towers*. New York: Ballantine Books, 1965

Melian's Girdle —
Boundaries and hidden Thresholds in Arda

Guglielmo Spirito (Assisi)

1. Introduction

> 'Is there no end to this accursed forest?' said Thorin.
> 'Somebody must climb a tree and see if he can get his head above the roof and have a look round. The only way is to choose the tallest tree that overhangs the path.'
> Of course 'somebody' meant Bilbo. They chose him because to be of any use the climber must get his head above the topmost leaves, and so he must be light enough for the highest and slenderest branches to bear him.
> In the end he poked his head above the roof of leaves. Bilbo's eyes were nearly blinded by the light. He could only hold on and blink. The sun was shining brilliantly, and it was a long while before he could bear it. When he could, he saw all round him a sea of dark green, ruffled here and there by the breeze; and there were everywhere hundreds of butterflies. (H 145f)

This scene is quite well shown in the *Desolation of Smaug*, Jackson's Movie. Bilbo crossed a rather stupendous threshold.Very seldom anything is rushed in nature. The beauty of nature insists on taking its time. The rhythm of emergence is a gradual, slow beat; always inching its way forward, change remains faithful to itself until the new unfolds in the full confidence of true arrival. Because nothing is abrupt, the beginnig of spring or autumn nearly always catches us unawares. It is there before we see it; and then we can't look anywhere without seeing it.

Change arrives in nature when time has ripened. There are no jagged transitions or crude discontinuities. It is as though one season succeeds another, moving forward in a rythm set from within a continuum. We are also often surprised by change that seems to arrive out of nowhere. We find ourselves crossing some new threshold we had never anticipated. Like spring secretly at work within the heart of winter, below the surface of our lives huge changes are in fermentation. We never suspect a thing.

At any time, you can ask yourself: at which threshold am I now standing? What am I leaving? Where am I about to enter? What is preventing me from crossing my next threshold? A threshold is not simply an accidental line that happens to separate one region from another, nor is it a mere boundary; it is a frontier that divides two different lands, rhythms and atmospheres.

> *When near the end of day, life has drained*
> *Out of light, and it is too soon*
> *For the mind of night to have darkened things,*
>
> *No place looks like itself, loss of outline*
> *Makes everything look strangely in-between,*
> *unsure of what has been, or what might come.*
>
> *In this wan light, even trees seem groundless.*
> *In a while, it will be night, but nothing*
> *Here seems to believe the relief of dark.*
>
> *You are in this time of the interim*
> *Where everything seems withheld.*
>
> *The path you took to get here has washed out;*
> *The way forward is still concealed from you.*
>
> *You cannot lay claim to anything;*
> *In this place of dusk,*
> *your eyes are blurred;*
> *and there is no mirror* (O'Donohue 134)

In the end, this border country and what it brings must remain elusive, like the mists and the everchanging colours. It will speak to each of us differently, and it will say different things at different times. It will strike chords and bring glimpses—but it can never be possessed or fully understood.

In Middle-earth, the cliffs are as fantastic as the clouds. The sky seemed to fall down towards the hills; the hills took hold upon the sky. In the sumptuous sunset, gold and purple and peacock green cloudlets and islets are the same. J.R.R. Tolkien seems to have lived like a man walking on a borderland, the borderland between this world and another.

> The next day at the hour of sunset Aragorn walked alone in the woods… And suddenly … he saw a maiden walking on a green-sward among the white stems of the birches; and he halted amazed, think-ing that he had strayed into a dream, or else that he had received the gift of the Elf-minstrels, who can make the things of which they sing appear before the eyes of those that listen.
> (LotR 1095)

The world though, is always the same, for it is always unexpected.

The vastness of Arda is gorgeous, the placing or spacing of things within a *cosmos*—that is, an order and harmony—shaped by the music of the Ainur, in different *forms* which designate the limits of the things, and *places* which designate the limit of the surrounding environs. Place presses in from without; it delimits and contains, as mountains with valleys.

> *In order to come to birth*
> *In a clean line of form,*
> *That claims from time*
> *A rhythm not yet heard*
> *That calls space to*
> *A different shape* (O'Donohue 36)

Alas, for Melkor—mightier among the Ainur—, put discord in the music, and violence and wrath, and from splendor he fell through arrogance to contempt for all things save himself, and became Morgoth, the Dark Enemy. He coveted Arda and all that is in it, and he was not alone. Among the Maiar, Sauron was his servant, and walked in malice behind him on the same ruinous path down into the Void. And the *cosmos* was wounded with *trauma*, like scars on a beloved face.

We shall go into these landscapes: a spotty trajectory, to be sure, and one with many gaping omissions to be filled in. As in the Shire's and Rivendell's maps, many parts shall remain blank beyond their edges, and those which are drawn, will be blurred, wrapped in *mist above seas of foam that sighed upon the margins of the world.*

Place has to do with both closing-in-on and opening-out-to, with concealing and unconcealing, with delimiting and going-out-beyond, with drawing-near and surpassing. And all these refuse to behave in the way that Euclidean space behaves: they also have a symbolic meaning which likewise refuses to behave in a uniform, static, abstract or punctuate manner. They have the freedom of one released from restrictive confines, the freedom of Poetic Diction, in which vastness and enclosure, distance and intimacy also coinhere. In Middle-earth we are continually crossing boundaries...

> *As the ocean absolves itself*
> *Of the expectation of land,*
> *Approaching only*
> *In the form of waves*
> *That fill and pleat and fall*
> *With such gradual elegance*
> *As to make of the limit*

> *A sonorous threshold*
> *Whose music echoes back along*
> *The give and strain of memory.*
> *Thus may your heart know the patience*
> *That can draw infinity from limitation* (O'Donohue 48)

2. Leaving a safe, well-known Place

> "You must now make haste, and neither stay nor turn back; for the Shire is no longer any protection to you", said Gildor. "Others dwelt here before hobbits were; and others will dwell here again when hobbits are no more. The wide world is all about you: you can fence yourselves in, but you cannot for ever fence it out."
> "I know – and yet it has always seemed so safe and familiar."
> (LotR 97)
> They were, in fact, sheltered, but they had ceased to remember it. (LotR 17)

Leaving the *cozy* Shire in two steps is emblematic:

> The ferry-boat moved slowly across the water. The Buckland shore drew nearer. Sam was the only member of the party who had not been over the river before. He had a strange feeling as the slow gurgling stream slipped by: his old life lay behind in the mists, dark adventure lay in front. (LotR 113)
> They saw the Hedge looming suddenly ahead. It was tall and netted over with silver cobwebs. "How are you going to get through this?" asked Fredegar. "Follow me!" said Merry, "and you will see." He turned to the left along the Hedge, and soon they came to a point where it bent inwards, running along the lip of a hollow. A cutting had been made, at some distance from the Hedge, and went sloping gently down into the ground under the Hedge and came out in the hollow on the other side. It was dark and damp. "There!" said Merry. "You have left the Shire, and are now outside, and on the edge of the Old Forest." (LotR 125)

Then, between the edges of the Old Forest and the Barrow-downs, the threshold of a *house* stands: Tom Bombadil's.

And the hobbits stood upon the threshold, and a golden light was all about them. The four hobbits stepped over the wide stone threshold, and stood still, blinking. They were in a long low room, filled with the light of lamps swinging from the beams of the roof. "Have peace now," Goldberry said, "until the morning! Heed no nightly noises! For nothing passes door and window here save moonlight and starlight and the wind off the hill-top." (cf LotR 137-140)

Note the recurring word "to pass", already echoing its deeper meaning in Galadriel's words "I shall pass into the West", and Frodo's passing into the West as well, foreshadowed by a sweet dream in Tom's bedchamber.
This whole strange world is possibly homely, because in the heart of it there is a home.
German has a word, rather difficult to translate, to express this dimension of a warm, wrapping, prottective hospitality, actually felt: *Geborgenheit*.

A rather powerful hospitality, beyond the walls of the house but within the land settled limits:

> Tom stooped, removed his hat, and came into the dark chamber, singing:
> Get out, you old Wight! Vanish in the sunlight!
> Out into the barren lands far beyond the mountains!
> Lost and forgotten be, darker than the darkness,
> Where gates stand for ever shut, till the world is mended.
> (LotR 157-158)

"Tom's country ends here: he will not pass the borders. Tom has his house to mind, and Goldberry is waiting!" As Gandalf said, "now he is withdrawn into a little land, within bounds that he has set, though none can see them, waiting perhaps for a change of days, and he will not step beyond them." (cf. LotR 163.283)

3. Dry Frontiers on a wet Land, dry Streams across wet Earth (Williams 42)

Streams, fords, rivers, waterfalls easily draw clear cut limits with their fingers of water:

> One day they found their path blocked by a running water. It flowed fast and strong but not very wide right across the way, and it was black, or looked it in the gloom. As it was they only thought of how to cross it without wetting themselves in its water [as Bombur, alas, did]. (H 140)

> Frodo heard the splash of water. It foamed about his feet. He felt the quick heave and surge as the horse left the river and struggled up the stony path. He was climbing the steep bank. He was across the Ford. But the pursuers were close behind. At the top of the bank the horse halted and turned about neighing fiercely. There were Nine Riders at the water's edge below. He knew of nothing that would prevent them from crossing as easily as he had done; and he felt that it was useless to try to escape over the long uncertain path from the Ford to the edge of Rivendell, if once the Riders crossed. (LotR 230)

The ridge upon which the companions stood went down steeply before their feet. Below it, there was a wide and rugged shelf which ended suddenly in the brink of a sheer cliff: the East Wall of Rohan. So ended the Emyn Muil, and the green plains of the Rohirrim stretched away before them to the edge of sight. It swelled like a green sea [*The liliput countless armies of the grass, the heat, the showers, the measureless pasturages...the winds' free orchestra* (Whitman 118).] The falling stream vanished into a deep growth of creses and water-plants, and they could hear it tinkling away in green tunnels. They seemed to have left winter clinging to the hills behind (cf. LotR 443f).

> In a chill hour they came to the end of the water-course. The banks became moss-grown mounds. Over the last shelf of rotting stone the stream gurgled and fell down into a brown bog and was lost. On either side and in front wide fens and mires now lay, stretching away southward and eastward into the dim half-light. Mists curled and smoked from dark and noisome pools. Far away, the mountain-walls of Mordor loomed, like a black bar of rugged clouds floating above a dangerous fog-bound sea.
> (LotR 650)

> They stood on a wet floor of polished stone, the doorstep, as it were, of a rough-hewn gate of rock opening dark behind them. But in front a thin veil of water was hung, so near that Frodo could have put an outstretched arm into it. It faced westward. The level shafts of the setting sun behind beat upon it, and the red light was broken into many flickering beams of ever-changing colour. It was as if they stood at the window of some elven-tower, curtained with threaded jewels of silver and gold, and ruby, sapphire and amethyst, all kindled with an unconsuming fire. 'This is the Window of the Sunset, Henneth Annûn, fairest of all the falls of Ithilien, land of many fountains'. (LotR 700)

4. Dark Paths

An oppressive sense of weight, of lack of space to breathe, of solid void is described in paths that are as black as black holes in the irrevocable deep dark shadow around them. Shelob's Lair, the Paths of the Dead, the crown of the pass of Cirith Ungol, among others:

> It may indeed have been daytime now, as Gollum said, but the hobbits could see little difference, unless, perhaps, the heavy sky above was less utterly black, more like a great roof of smoke; while instead of the darkness of deep night, which lingered still in cracks and holes, a grey blurring shadow shrouded the stony world about them. Some way ahead, a mile or so, perhaps, was a great grey wall, a last huge upthrusting mass of mountain-stone. Darker it loomed, and steadily it rose as they approached, until it towered up high above them, shutting out the view of all that lay beyond. Deep shadow lay before its feet.
> Drawing a deep breath they passed inside. In a few steps they were in utter and impenetrable dark. Not since the lightless passages of Moria had Frodo or Sam known such darkness, and if possible here it was deeper and denser. There, there were airs moving, and echoes, and a sense of space. Here the air was still, stagnant, heavy, and sound fell dead. They walked as it were in a black vapour wrought of veritable darkness itself that, as it was breathed, brought blindness not only to the eyes but to the mind, so that even the memory of colours and of forms and of any light faded out of thought. Night always had been, and always would be, and night was all. (LotR 744f)

The light was still grey as they rode, for the sun had not yet climbed over the black ridges of the Haunted Mountain before them. A dread fell on them, even as they passed between the lines of ancient stones and so came to the Dimholt. And so they came at last deep into the glen; and there stood a sheer wall of rock, and in the wall the Dark Door gaped before them like the mouth of night. Signs and figures were carved above its wide arch too dim to read, and fear flowed from it like a grey vapour. Then Aragorn led the way, and such was the strength of his will in that hour that all the Dunedain and their horses followed him and Legolas passed in. And there stood Gimli the Dwarf left all alone. But it seemed to him that he dragged his feet like lead over the threshold; and at once a blindness came upon him, even upon Gimli Glóin's son who had walked unafraid in many deep places of the world. (cf. LotR 817f)

Even more daring—out of love for his Master—Sam trespasses the most dangerous border: for the moment he could drive himself no further. He felt that if once he went beyond the crown of the pass and took one step veritably down into the land of Mordor, that step would be irrevocable. He could never come back (cf. LotR 932).

5. When *the stretching light-hung Roof of Clouds* is not enough (Whitman 118)

There is barely anything more deep and wonderful than really impenetrable pinewoods where the nearer trees show against the more shadowy further trees; a tracery of silver upon grey and of grey upon black.

> Day was waning. Darkness had already crept beneath the murmuring fir-woods that clothed the steep mountain-sides. The king rode now slowly at the end of the day. Presently the path turned round a huge bare shoulder of rock and plunged into the gloom of soft-sighing trees. Down, down they went in a long winding file. When at last they came to the bottom of the gorge they found that evening had fallen in the deep places. The sun was gone. Twilight lay upon the waterfalls. Merry looked out in wonder upon this strange country, of which he had heard many tales upon their long road. It was a skyless world, in which his eye, through dim gulfs of shadowy air, saw only ever-mounting slopes, great walls of stone behind great walls, and frowning precipices wreathed with mist. He sat for a moment half dreaming, listening to the noise of water, the whisper of dark trees, the crack of stone, and the vast waiting silence that brooded behind all sound.
> He loved mountains, or he had loved the thought of them marching on the edge of stories brought from far away; but now he was borne down by the insupportable weight of Middle-earth. He longed to shut out the immensity in a quiet room by a fire.
> (LotR 822)

He longed to shut out the immensity in a quiet room by a fire. Need of *Geborgenheit*: how dear, how *normal* is poor Mery!

6. *Hortus conclusus*

Much larger and higher—and older—than hobbit-size proportions on shelters, there are other havens, other places to find refuge. 'The wide world is all about you: you can fence yourselves in, but you cannot for ever fence it out', said Gildor from Rivendell to Frodo. Elrond knew it well. And Turgon discovered that as well, though to late. We need to mention, in passing at least, the Encircling Mountains which surrounded Gondolin. The Hidden Kingdom would have deserved truly a fuller attention:

> Turgon by the guidance of Ulmo discovered the hidden vale of Tumladen in the Encircling Mountains, and sent forth all his people; and they passed away, company by company, secretly, under the shadows of Ered Wethrin, and they came unseen to Gondolin, and none knew whither they had gone. And last of all Turgon arose, and went with his household silently through the hills, and passed the gates in the mountains, and they were shut behind him. (S 150)

But it is in special *gardens* that we are about to enter: and we shall linger for a little while in two of them: Lórien and Doriath.

A garden enclosed is my sister, my spouse, a spring shut up, a mountain sealed (Song 4:12).

An engraving from 1615, now in the Bayerische Staatsbibliothek, Munich, shows some Dominican saints tending a rosary-tree in a walled garden, for the *Garden Enclosed* is one of the Virgen Mary's epithets: *hortus conclusus* (Wilkins 117).

The ability of the term "Rosenkranz" to draw upon the body of popular spiritual rose-garden imagery helped to create an ethos that benefited its growth. Works like Ulrich Pinder's *Der beschlossene Gart des Rosenkrantz* (Enclosed garden of the Rose-Chaplet, 1489-1505: it is shown as a circular wall, with a gate—shut—that surrounds a rose-garden in which Mary is seated) show the continuing influence of the image, as well as Vincentius Hensberg's *Viridarium Marianum* (Marian garden, 1615) (Winston-Allen 109; Wilkins 118). In fact, as Guardini has pointed out, the rosary has the character of a sojourn. Its essence is the sheltering security of a quiet, holy word that envelops the person who is praying. The rosary is not a road, but a place, and it has no goal but a depth (Guardini 44f).

A garden is a secret place, at once closed, alive with a concentration of natural forces, and open to the sky. Its secrecy may result from its being a small place between high walls, or for its being surrounded by a forest, or simply from its being difficult to find. It is the image of primal harmony, as the abode of bliss now lost, an image as old as Eden. It is amusing, in connection with the Ave-Maria garden, that the Latin for "birds" is *aves*. In the rose-garden the singing-birds, the robin and the death-and-resurrection bird, the goldfinch, make music, and so do angels.

Lórien

Grieved after Moria, the exhausted Company arrived at the outskirts of the Golden Wood.

> "We hear that Lórien is not yet deserted, for there is a secret power here that holds evil from the land", said Legolas.
> Before them a wide grey shadow loomed, and they heard an endless rustle of leaves like poplars in the breeze. "Lothlórien!" cried Legolas. "Lothlórien! We have come to the eaves of the Golden Wood. Alas that it is winter!" Under the night the trees stood tall before them, arched over the road and stream that ran suddenly beneath their spreading boughs. In the dim light of the stars their stems were grey, and their quivering leaves a hint of fallow gold. (LotR 356)

In Cerin Amroth, Frodo looked and saw, still at some distance, a hill of many mighty trees, or a city of green towers: which it was he could not tell. Out of it, it seemed to him that the power and light came that held all the land in sway. Then he looked eastward and saw all the land of Lórien running down to the pale gleam of Anduin, the Great River. He lifted his eyes across the river and all the light went out, and he was back again in the world he knew. Beyond the river the land appeared flat and empty, formless and vague, until far away it rose again like a wall, dark and drear. The sun that lay on Lothlórien had no power to enlighten the shadow of that distant height (cf. LotR 370).

> The sun was sinking behind the mountains, and the shadows were deepening in the woods, when they went on again towards the dwelling place of the Galadhrim. Their paths now went into thickets where the dusk had already gathered. Suddenly they came out into the open again and found themselves under a pale evening sky pricked by a few early stars. There was a wide treeless space before them, running in a great circle and bending away on either hand. Beyond it was a deep fosse lost in soft shadow, but the grass upon its brink was green, as if it glowed still in memory of the sun that had gone. Upon the further side there rose to a great height a green wall encircling a green hill thronged with mallorn-trees taller than any they had yet seen in all the land.
> (LotR 372)

Galadriel led Frodo and Sam, "and passing through a high green hedge they came into an enclosed garden" (LotR 380), where her Mirror was...

But this is only a faint echo of the other Lórien, the dwelling place of the Vala Irmo in Valinor:

Melian was the name of a Maia who served both Vána and Estë; she dwelt long in Lórien, tending the trees that flower in the gardens of Irmo, ere she came to Middle-earth. Melian was a Maia, of the race of the Valar. Among all his people there were none more beautiful than Melian, nor more wise, nor more skilled in songs of enchantment. Nightingales went always with her, and she taught them their song; and she loved the deep shadows of the great trees. She was akin before the World was made to Yavanna herself; and in that time when the Quendi awoke beside the waters of Cuiviénen she departed from Valinor and came to the Hither Lands. Melian was Thingol's Queen; and their hidden halls were Menegroth, the Thousand Caves, in Doriath. Greatly though he had desired to see again the light of the Trees, in the face of Melian he beheld the light of Aman as in an unclouded mirror, and in that light he was content. And of the love of Thingol and Melian there came into the world the fairest of all the Children of Ilúvatar that was or shall ever be (cf. S 34.64-68).

Doriath

Recently Timothy Radcliffe OP, old friend of Tolkien's family, wrote me that he loves "the sense of place" and that he "was struck by the link between place and name. Tolkien is fascinated by names. Is it part of being a place that it is named. The wide world is a wild world because it has no name? Names delineate."

> Southward lay the guarded woods of Doriath, abode of Thingol the Hidden King, into whose realm none passed save by his will. Its northern and lesser part, the Forest of Neldoreth, was bounded east and south by the dark river Esgalduin, which bent westward in the midst of the land; and between Aros and Esgalduin lay the denser and greater woods of Region. Upon the southern bank of Esgalduin, where it turned westward towards Sirion, were the Caves of Menegroth; and all Doriath lay east of Sirion save for a narrow region of woodland between the meeting of Teiglin and Sirion and the Meres of Twilight. By the people of Doriath this wood was called Nivrim, the West March; great oak-trees grew there, and it also was encompassed within the Girdle of Melian,

> that so some portion of Sirion which she loved in reverence of Ulmo should be wholly under the power of Thingol. In the southwest of Doriath where Aros flowed into Sirion, lay great pools and marshes on either side of the river, which halted there in his course and strayed in many channels. That region was named Aelinuial, the Twilight Meres, for they were wrapped in mists, and the enchantment of Doriath lay over them.
>
> (S 144f)

Now Melian had much foresight, after the manner of the Maiar; and when the second age of the captivity of Melkor had passed, she counselled Thingol that the Peace of Arda would not last for ever. He took thought therefore how he should make for himself a kingly dwelling, and a place that should be strong, if evil were to awake again in Middle-earth. And ere long the evil creatures came even to Beleriand, over passes in the mountains, or up from the south through the dark forests. But it came to pass at last that the end of bliss was at hand, and the noontide of Valinor was drawing to its twilight. And when Thingol came to Menegroth he learned that the Orc-host in the west was victorious, and had driven Círdan to the rim of the sea. Therefore he withdrew all his people that his summons could reach within the fastness of Neldoreth and Region, *and Melian put forth her power and fenced all that dominion round about with an unseen wall of shadow and bewilderment: the Girdle of Melian, that none thereafter could pass against her will or the will of King Thingol, unless one should come with a power greater than that of Melian the Maia.* And this inner land, which was long named Eglador, was after called Doriath, the guarded kingdom, Land of the Girdle. Within it there was yet a watchful peace; but without there was peril and great fear, and the servants of Morgoth roamed at will, save in the walled havens of the Falas (cf. S 109-114).

> Galadriel remained in the Hidden Kingdom, for in Doriath dwelt Celeborn, kinsman of Thingol, and there was great love between them. And abode with Melian, and of her learned great lore and wisdom concerning Middle-earth. (S 136)

The inside of the wood was full of shattered sunlight and shaken shadows. They made a sort of shuddering veil which enmeshed in shadows, confusion and oblivion the wanderers and trespassers. Something in the filtered light set the mind drifting on certain borderlands of thought, with the first white daybreak before the coming of colour, and all that mystery which is alternately veiled and reveiled in the symbol of doors ajar and of mazes.

7. Enmeshed in Enchantment: a Shield stronger than any Barrier

There are thresholds rather difficult or impossible to pass through: the Fog in the Barrow-downs, the shifting quagmires with the hungry Neekerbreekers (as Sam called them), the victorious cruel Caradhras, the Rapids of Sarn Gebir, the Dead Marshes, the dreary parched plain of Gorgoroth...

There are other thresholds, though, even more challanging, because other powers besides nature are at work, for evil or good, in fallen Middle-earth.

"The wide world is all about you: you can fence yourselves in, but you cannot for ever fence it out". But it is also the case for many other things, that can't be fenced out always or for ever more.

> 'Now for it!' He drew Sting and ran towards the open gate. But just as he was about to pass under its great arch he felt a shock: as if he had run into some web like Shelob's, only invisible. He could see no obstacle, but something too strong for his will to overcome barred the way.
> Hardening his will Sam thrust forward once again, and halted with a jerk, staggering as if from a blow upon his breast and head. Then greatly daring, because he could think of nothing else to do, answering a sudden thought that came to him, he drew slowly out the phial of Galadriel and held it up. Its white light quickened swiftly, and the shadows under the dark arch fled. He sprang past them. (LotR 936f)

The smallest light defeats the thicker darkness. What is a blessing? A blessing is a circle of light drawn around a person to protect, heal and strengthen: *May nothing destructive ever cross your threshold.* Life is a constant flow of emergence. To be in the world is to be distant from the homeland of wholeness. We are confined by limitation and difficulty.

The city of Cologne in 1474 was miraculously saved from attack by Burgundian troops, and this was believed to be the result of the advice given by Jakob Sprenger, the Dominican prior of the city, which was to pray the Psalter of Our Lady—or *Rosenkranz*—, such as weaving a protective wall around the city. In 1571 Christendom's victories over the Turks at Lepanto—and in 1683 at Vienna—, were also attributed to the efficacy of the rosary, and Mary celebrated as Our Lady of Victory (cf. Wilkins 42; Chesterton).

In a similar way, Elbereth was invoked in peril and distress, and she answered helping those who ask it from her (cf. Mohammadi); others are turned back by the *Girdle of Melian*, the invisible but powerful shield that surrounds Doriath:

Melian put forth her power and fenced all that dominion round about with an unseen wall of shadow and bewilderment, that none thereafter could pass.

> 'Into Doriath shall no Man come while my realm lasts, not even those of the house of Bëor who serve Finrod the beloved'. Melian said nothing to him at that time, but afterwards she said to Galadriel: 'Now the world runs on swiftly to great tidings. And one of Men, even of Bëor's house, shall indeed come, and the Girdle of Melian shall not restrain him, for doom greater than my power shall send him; and the songs that shall spring from that coming shall endure when all Middle-earth is changed'. (S 173)

So it came to pass that Melian's Girdle revealed itself a shield stronger than any barrier...except unselfish love.

8. Landscape of Love and Doom

Beren escaping through great peril came over the Mountains of Terror into the hidden Kingdom of Thingol in the forest of Neldoreth. Terrible was his southward journey. Sheer were the precipices of Ered Gorgoroth, and beneath their feet were shadows that were laid before the rising of the Moon. Beyond lay the wilderness of Dungortheb, where the sorcery of Sauron and the power of Melian came together, and horror and madness walked. None know how he found a way, and so came by paths that no Man nor Elf else ever dared to tread to the borders of Doriath. And he passed through the mazes that Melian wove about the kingdom of Thingol, the unseen wall of shadow and bewilderment, that none could pass, unless one should come with a power greater than that of Melian, even as she had foretold; for a great doom lay upon him.

It is told in the *Lay of Leithian* that Beren came stumbling into Doriath grey and bowed as with many years of woe, so great had been the torment of the road. But wandering in the summer in the woods of Neldoreth he came upon Lúthien, daughter of Thingol and Melian, at a time of evening under moonrise, as she danced upon the unfading grass in the glades beside Esgalduin. And he fell helplessly in love. (cf. S 197)

One should come with a power greater than that of fear: *true love*. Beren successfully penetrated the Girdle with a *doom of love* upon him...

The most profound threshold is that between the inner and the outer, between going deeper into the interior self and emerging to meet the world beyond the self without protective defenses, as a friend not as a foe. It is from this firm internal center that the external can be greeted and welcomed, however strange, even challenging it might appear: so did Lúthien out of unselfish love, unlike her parents, harness her force to cross the boundaries that would have confined her. She had the courage to change, welcoming the voice that called her beyond herself, beyond the familiar field blind with the weeds of fear and the old walls of small security.

Out of love, Beren and Lúthien were not hindered by the wall of shadow and bewilderment, for *love* gave them light and direction…perhaps from (and towards) the Secret Fire that was sent to burn at the heart of the World?

Thinking of T.S. Eliot's words in *Burn Norton* "the door we never opened/Into the rose-garden", one may be reminded of a work that his generation knew in childhood, a work not of great literature but remarkable as a piece of psychological symbolism. I mean E. Hodgson Burnett's novel *The Secret Garden*. This story is a variation on that of Briar Rose, la Belle au bois dormant, and of her hundred years' sleep, and of the prince who breaks his way through the high enclosing thorny hedges (which turn to roses as he comes) and, entering that hortus conclusus, wakes her with a kiss. So too Siegfried crashes through the hedge of flame round sleeping Brunhilde and wakes her with a kiss. "And", as Eliot wrote elsewhere, "the fire and the rose are one" (Wilkins 124f).

Crossing can often mean the total loss of all you enjoyed while on the other side; it becomes a dividing line between past and future. More often than not, the reason you cannot return to where you were is that you have changed; you are no longer the one who crossed over. Originally, *threshold* related to the word *thresh*, which was the separation of the grain from the husk or straw when oats were flailed. To cross a threshold is to leave behind the husks and arrive at the grain. Lúthien—made free by Beren's love as a bird soars high in the free holding of the wind, clear of the certainty of ground, can not return to live within the narrow inner space of her former abode.

What were these hidden chosen places designed for, if not to be crossed at some point by human drama, through human hopes and true human love? There these were somehow welcomed, honored, protected and fulfilled, in unpredictable ways, bringing at last—for all Middle-earth—, rescue and salvation, as the unfolding of the Tales of Tuor—and Eärendil, the Morning Star—, and that of Beren and Lúthien—and Aragorn and Arwen—, increasingly show.

The king was slain. Upon Doriath a heavy change had fallen. For Melian was of the divine race of the Valar, and she was a Maia of great power and wisdom; but for love of Elwë Singollo she took upon herself the form of the Elder Children of Ilúvatar, and in that union she became bound by the chain and trammels of the flesh of Arda. In that form she bore to him Lúthien Tinúviel; and in that form she gained a power over the substance of Arda, and by the Girdle of Melian was Doriath defended through long ages from the evils without. But now Thingol lay dead, and his spirit had passed to the halls of Mandos; and with his death a change came also upon Melian. Thus it came to pass that her power was withdrawn in that time from the forests of Neldoreth and Region, and Esgalduin the enchanted river spoke with a different voice, and Doriath lay open to its enemies.

Thereafter Melian sent word speedily to Beren and Lúthien in Ossiriand; and she vanished out of Middle-earth, and passed to the land of the Valar beyond the western sea, to muse upon her sorrows in the gardens of Lórien, whence she came, and this tale speaks of her no more (cf. S 282f).

9. Conclusion: the Sense of Beyondness at the Heart of Things

Going out, leaving, departing is often a painful adventure (young Bilbo would have agreed wholeheartedly with this); there is an *elvish side* in our resistence to letting-go, and perhaps a *hobbit side* in it, if lazyness is involved. But *the road, as life, goes on and on...*

May the Valar enable us to stand on the true thresholds, at ease with our ambivalence, and drawn in new directions through the glow of our contradictions, and carry ourselves with careful kindness, until this winter pilgrimage leads us towards the gateway to spring.

> The rippling waters bore them slowly away. On the green bank near to the very point of the Tongue the Lady Galadriel stood alone and silent. As they passed her they turned and their eyes watched her slowly floating away from them. For so it seemed to them: Lórien was slipping backward, like a bright ship masted with enchanted trees, sailing on to forgotten shores, while they sat helpless upon the margin of the grey and leafless world. Suddenly the River swept round a bend, and the banks rose upon either side, and the light of Lórien was hidden. (LotR 397f)

Trully are we left in a *leafless* world? At least *one* single leaf remained...

It had begun with a leaf caught in the wind, and it became a tree; and the tree grew, sending out innumerable branches, and thrusting out the most fantastic roots. Then all round the Tree, and behind it, through the gaps in the leaves and boughs, a country began to open out; and there were glimpses of a forest marching over the land, and of mountains tipped with snow.

> For now he saw that the Forest was there too, opening out on either side, and marching away into the distance. The Mountains were glimmering far away.

> After a time Niggle turned towards the Forest. As he walked away, he discovered an odd thing: the Forest, of course, was a distant Forest, yet he could approach it, even enter it, without its losing that particular charm. He had never before been able to walk into the distance without turning it into mere surroundings. It really added a considerable attraction to walking in the country, because, as you walked, new distances opened out; so that you now had doubled, treble, and quadruple distances, doubly, trebly, and quadruply enchanting. You could go on and on, and have a whole country in a garden, or in a picture (if you preferred to call it that). You could go on and on, but not perhaps forever. There were the Mountains in the background. They did get nearer, very slowly. They did not seem to belong to the picture, or only as a link to something else, a glimpse through the trees of something different, a further stage: another picture. (N 110-113)

> He found the Spring in the heart of the Forest; only once long ago had Niggle imagined it, but he had never drawn it. Now he perceived that it was the source of the lake that glimmered, far away and the nourishment of all that grew in the country. He came right through the distances to the Edge. It was not visible, of course: there was no line, or fence, or wall; but he knew that he had come to the margin of that country. He saw a man, he looked like a shepherd; he was walking towards them, down the grass-slopes that led up into the Mountains.
> Beyond that I cannot guess what became of him. Even little Niggle in his old home could glimpse the Mountains far away, and they got into the borders of his picture; but what they are really like, and what lies beyond them, only those can say who have climbed them. (N 115f)

Attention, wonder are close to mystery—what Bishop John V. Taylor used to call "the sense of beyondness at the heart of things" (De Waal 157).

"Behold! we are not bound for ever to the circles of the world, and beyond them is more than memory" (LotR 1100).

> *Oh! till Thou givest that sense beyond,*
> *To shew Thee that Thou art, and near,*
> *Let patience with her chastening wand*
> *Dispel the doubt and dry the tear;*
> *And lead me child-like by the hand*
> *If still in darkness not in fear.* (Hopkins 48)

> *And, for all this, nature is never spent;*
> *There lives the dearest freshness deep down things.* (Hopkins 84)
>
> *Somewhere, out at the edges, the night*
> *Is turning and the waves of darkness*
> *Begin to brighten the shore of dawn.*
> *The heavy dark falls back to earth*
> *And the freed air goes wild with light,*
> *The heart fills with fresh, bright breath*
> *And thoughts stir to gave birth to colour.* (O'Donohue 25)

"But it did not look like this then, not *real*". "No, it was only a glimpse then; but you might have caught the glimpse, if you had ever thought it worth while to try" (cf. N 115).

> Slowly the ship slipped away down the long grey firth; and the light of the glass of Galadriel that Frodo bore glimmered and was lost. And the ship went out into the High Sea and passed on into the West, until at last on a night of rain Frodo smelled a sweet fragrance on the air and heard the sound of singing that came over the water. And then it seemed to him that as in his dream in the house of Bombadil, the grey rain-curtain turned all to silver glass and was rolled back, and he beheld white shores and beyond them a far green country under a swift sunrise.
> (LotR 1068f)

Bibliography

Chesterton, G.K. *Lepanto*. San Francisco: Ignatius Press, 2003
Guardini, Romano. *The Rosary of Our Lady*. Manchester: Sophia Institute Press, 1994
De Waal, Esther. *Lost in Wonder. Rediscovering the Spiritual Art of Attentiveness*. Norwich: Canterbury Press, 2003
Hopkins, Gerard Manley. *La freschezza più cara. Poesie scelte*. Milano: BUR, 2008
Mohammadi, Farid. "In search of the Holy Presence of the Blessed Mary in Tolkien's Middle-earth". *International Journal of Applied Linguistics & English Literature* 2,4 (2013): 1-12
O'Donohue, John. *Benedictus. A Book of Blessings*. London: Bantam Press, 2007
Tolkien, J.R.R. *The Hobbit*. London: HarperCollins, 1993
---. *The Lord of the Rings*. London: HarperCollins, 1993
---. *The Silmarillion*. London: HarperCollins, 1994
---. *Tree and Leaf*. London: HarperCollins, 2001
Whitman, Walt. *Canto una vita immensa*. Milano: Ancora, 2009
Winston-Allen, Anne. *Stories of the Rose. The Making of the Rosary in the Middle Ages*. Pennsylvania: The Pennsylvania State University Press, 2005
Williams, Rowan. *La dodicesima notte*. Milano: Ancora, 2008
Wilkins, Eithne. *The Rose-Garden Game. The Symbolic Background to the European Prayer-Beads*. London: Victor Gollancz LTD, 1969

Sympathetic Background in Tolkien's Prose
Annie Birks (Angers)

Over the centuries, literature has reflected man's visions of and attitudes towards nature. Whether it be purely conventional, ornamental, symbolical or a refuge where the romantics sought solace for the afflictions of humanity, nature has always pervaded prose and poetry and never ceased to be a source of reflection, inspiration and expression.

Considering Tolkien's poetic sensitivity and love of nature, it is no wonder that his fiction abounds with natural images and landscape descriptions. More often than not, these references to the environment appear to be connected to the events or to the structure of the story. In other words, Tolkien seems to be resorting to this old universal device usually referred to as 'sympathetic background', whereby nature in Middle-earth, for example, mirrors, mimics, is in harmony with or reacts to the characters' deeds, emotions or states of mind.

This paper will examine Tolkien's portrayal of nature—via descriptions of the environment and manifestations of the elements—in an attempt to contribute to previous and current studies on nature in Tolkien's prose and gain more insight into the use of 'sympathetic background' not only as a literary device but also as a vector of applicability.

I.

> "There are more things in heaven and earth, Horatio,
> Than are dreamt of in your philosophy."
> Shakespeare, *Hamlet* (Act I, 5, 166-7)

Let us first have a look at the etymology of the adjective 'sympathetic'. This compound word is formed with the Greek preposition *syn* (*sun*), meaning 'with, together with' and *pathos* which refers to notions of feeling, emotion and suffering. 'Sympathetic' therefore refers to one's, in this particular case: nature's, capacity to understand and share somebody's feelings (joy or suffering). The same roots are found in the word 'compassion' which is formed with the Latin preposition *cum*, meaning 'with', and the verb *pati*, 'to suffer'. The substantive 'sympathy' is usually synonymous with notions of natural affinity and community of feelings or impressions.

Thus in Shakespeare's *Macbeth*, when the Scottish King, Duncan, is murdered by his friend and host, Macbeth himself, the night is "unruly", "chimneys are blown down", "the obscure bird clamors", "the earth is feverous and shakes" (Act II, 3, 53-60) and strange unnatural things occur: a falcon is killed by an owl and the king's beautiful and swift horses turn wild in nature; some report that they even eat each other (Act II, 4, 14-18).

In this particular example, sympathetic background serves to intensify the atmosphere and to broaden it, as if not only the characters in the story were affected but also the whole universe. As the British author and editor Norman T. Carrington points out, "the strife and turmoil in nature echoes the strife and turmoil in" the characters and events (Carrington 18). The natural order of things is disturbed by the characters' choices and deeds and the disturbance eventually leads to sickness, chaos and disorder, as is the case of Scotland after the regicide.[1]

Macbeth himself is aware of the horror and consequences of such infamy. While bracing himself for the murder, he even invokes the stars to lighten his torturing conscience (I, 4, 50-51):

> Stars, hide your fires;
> Let not light see my black and deep desires.

These famous lines have a clear resonance as stars are often associated with the presence of the divine and also represent the eyes of the night. As for light, which is also generally a manifestation of the divine, it traditionally symbolises life, truth and the source of goodness (Cooper 96).

II.

> "More servants wait on man
> Than he takes notice of."
>
> George Herbert, *Man*

Anyone having explored the history of Middle-earth has undoubtedly identified constant interaction or correspondence between nature and the characters. For example, just a few chapters after the beginning of *The Fellowship of the Ring*, when Frodo, Sam and Pippin leave Hobbiton to go to Buckland, the night is clear, cool and starry, and smoke-like wisps of mist are creeping up the hillsides from the streams and deep meadows (104). The three Hobbits have crossed the Water (the stream in the Shire which runs through Needlehole and Bywater)—symbolically passing from one phase of their life to another—and they are starting on a journey which is subtly announced as being both under divine protection and exposed to peril.

The presence of the stars—manifestations of the divine, eyes of the night—can be perceived by a well-versed Tolkienian reader not only as a reference to the Elves, the Eldar, the 'People of the Stars', but also as a reference to the divine Valië Varda/Elbereth who created these constellations and provided

---

[1] By means of these images, Shakespeare reflected his contemporaries' views of the laws of the Universe.

Middle-earth with light. The "creeping" "smoke-like wisps of mist" may suggest a dark, threatening, surreptitious presence, Melkorian ingredients even, if one mentally associates the mist, in this particular context, to the geographical Misty Mountains, the great Mountain Chain originally raised by Melkor.[2] Traditionally mist symbolises a state of error and confusion (Cooper 106) and its disappearance symbolises the return of a clear vision. In any event the subtext seems to epitomise both an atmosphere of reassurance and a call to vigilance due to potential danger.

In case the reader wonders whether such assumptions may be figments of his imagination, the following day's events distinctly point towards such an interpretation. Here, the Hobbits are faced with the terrifying appearance of a Black Rider and in the evening, the West wind sighs in the branches, the leaves whisper, a star comes out above the trees, and gradually, as the stars grow thicker and brighter, the feeling of disquiet leaves the three companions.

By sheer 'coincidence' they are rescued from the nearly fatal reappearance of the Black Rider, by the arrival of the Elves themselves, singing a song dedicated to Varda/Elbereth (LotR I 114). The Hobbits notice the starlight glimmering on the Elves' hair and in their eyes. Frodo bows to Gildor and utters a few words in High-Elven speech: "A star shines on the hour of our meeting" (116). Before parting, Gildor wishes Frodo well: "I name you Elf-Friend, and may the stars shine upon the end of your road!" (121)

The reader might even feel that the West wind evokes the presence of the Valar, the Powers of the West and more precisely that of Manwë, Varda's spouse, surnamed Súlimo, Lord of the Breath of Arda. Such an assumption would appear all the more legitimate as, just to quote another example, after the war of the Ring, Manwë's presence as Lord of the winds and the clouds, is strongly felt at the death of Saruman (LotR III 355):

> About the body of Saruman a grey mist gathered, and rising slowly to a great height like smoke from a fire, as a pale shrouded figure it loomed over the Hill. For a moment it wavered, looking to the West; but out of the West came a cold wind, and it bent away, and with a sigh dissolved into nothing.

Here the image of Saruman trying to obtain forgiveness from the Powers of the West is easily detectable. And judging by the cold wind from the West which dissolves his figure and by his sigh of despair, it seems too late for him to benefit from their clemency.

---

2   The smoke can also be reminiscent of Mordor.

To go back to the beginning of the story, although the Hobbits seem to benefit from nature's benevolence at the outset of their journey, they soon discover other, less benevolent, aspects of the natural environment. After their stay at Crickhollow, they ride their ponies into the mist which seems to open "reluctantly" before them and close "forbiddingly" behind them (LotR I 152). Merry notices that the Old Forest is queer and that the trees are unfriendly. The Hobbits get the feeling that they are being watched with disapproval, deepening to dislike and even to enmity (155). And it is not just an impression as the air becomes hot and stuffy and the trees draw actually close again. The companions can feel the ill will of the wood pressing on them. A large branch even falls on them and the trees seem to close in before them as Frodo challenges the menace of the woods in a song in which he says: "For east or west all woods must fail".

As soon as Frodo realises the awkwardness of his message and regrets singing such words, the whole situation changes: the dark trees draw aside, the path becomes clear, a green hill-top rises ahead of them and the air is gleaming (157). The process is easily explainable as is pointed out by Tolkien in his *Letters*: "The Old Forest was hostile to two legged creatures because of the memory of many injuries" (L 419-420). But Frodo is not just any two-legged creature and as the American essayist and poet Ralph Emerson (1803-1882) wrote in his essay on Nature: "At the call of a noble sentiment, again the woods wave, the pines murmur, the river rolls and shines" (Emerson 13).

When the four Hobbits stay at Tom Bombadil's house, the rain turns out to be a welcome ally as it cuts them from the Old Forest and from the rest of the world and delays their departure: "Behind its deep curtain the Forest was completely veiled" (LotR 177). In his heart Frodo is glad and blesses "the kindly weather" which allows him and his companions to enjoy the privilege of listening to Goldberry's songs and Tom Bombadil's tales (178).

Although the characters themselves might not always be aware of it, nature in Middle-earth becomes an open book and Tolkien summons subtle and vital expositors to make this plain. In his essay on nature, Emerson observed that "particular natural facts are symbols of particular spiritual facts" (Emerson 10) and that we are "assisted by natural objects in the expression of particular meanings" (11). We can even talk of the language of Nature, providing man with "the dictionary and the grammar" of life. Emerson wrote that "by degree we may come to know the primitive sense of the permanent objects of nature so that the world shall be to us an open book, and every form significant of its hidden life and final cause" (14). He also stated that "a life in harmony with nature, the love of truth and of virtue, will purge the eyes to understand her text". Any well-versed Tolkienian reader could add: "therefore offering recovery or the regaining of a clear view, one of Tolkien's essential attributes of fairy-stories."

III.

"Pollution, defilement, squalor are words that never would have been created had man lived conformably to Nature."
John Muir

Tolkien's Middle-earth abounds with descriptions of the natural environment which, to quote Emerson again, make the universe become "transparent", and allow "the light of higher laws than its own", to shine through it (Emerson 14). Tolkien's presentation of nature clearly shows that the natural background is indeed part and parcel of the history of Middle-earth. In *Defending Middle-earth*, Patrick Curry echoes what Tolkien readers feel all along the story, namely the fact that Middle-earth itself appears as a character in its own right. In "Tolkien's Imaginary Nature: An Analysis of the Structure of Middle-earth", Michael Brisbois observes that "the entirety of Middle-earth's nature is an expression of divine will" (Brisbois 201)[3], thus linking Tolkien's conception of Middle-earth to medieval theology according to which "the notion of nature as the result of providential design and control was an essential tenet. Nature was an expression of God's laws..." (Brisbois 202-203)

In Christina Scull and Wayne Hammond's *Reader's Guide*, reference is made to Claudia Riff Finseth who stresses the fact that nature being a sentient character in Tolkien's writings, other characters reveal themselves through their attitudes to the natural environment (Scull/Hammond 653).

In *Tolkien in the Land of Heroes: Discovering the Human Spirit*, Anne C. Petty comments that the destruction of nature in Tolkien's tales "serves as a grand symbol for what he felt was wrong with society... He creates champions and personifications of nature who can take up the crusade for him, righting the wrongs inflicted on hill and tree by those who mar the landscape with evil intent... The dismantling of Isengard by Ents and Huorns is one of the most satisfying acts of retribution committed to paper" (Petty 219-220).

Tolkien's persistent defence of trees assuredly echoes the American naturalist and author John Muir (1838-1914) who wrote:

> Any fool can destroy trees. They cannot run away; and if they could, they would still be destroyed,—chased and hunted down as long as fun or a dollar could be got out of their bark hides, branching horns, or magnificent bole backbones... God has cared for these trees, saved them from drought, disease, avalanches, and a thousand straining, leveling tempests and floods; but he cannot save them from fools—only Uncle Sam can do that.
>
> <div align="right">(Muir, <i>Our National Parks</i>, 382)</div>

---

3   Michael Brisbois bases his arguments on Random Helms's identified laws in Middle-earth and expands on the first law: "The cosmos is providentially controlled". See Helm 72-98.

In *Defending Middle-earth*, Patrick Curry devotes a whole chapter to the vital role of trees in our Primary World and in Michael Drout's *J.R.R. Tolkien Encyclopedia,* Curry comments that Tolkien's "fictional Middle-earth is a site of struggle against ecological, as well as social and political, disaster, just as is our own" (165).

The "eco-centric" dimension of Tolkien's work has never ceased to be relevant to human society, especially contemporary society, which is increasingly criticised for its unsustainable economic exploitation of nature and natural resources.

IV.
"All things move in music and write it."

John Muir

However Tolkien's use of "sympathetic background" goes beyond mere ecology. Once John Muir wrote to a friend "All things move in music and write it. The mouse lizard and grasshopper sing together on the Turlock sands, sing with the morning stars" (Muir 203).

If nature in Tolkien's Middle-earth can be read like an open book and can reawaken senses, it is precisely because all the characters, nature included, are actively involved in the ongoing process of writing, or should one say of composing, Ilúvatar's Great Music.

The original themes propounded by Ilúvatar and elaborated on by the Ainur are still running through Middle-earth. In that world, all things come to pass but not Ilúvatar's themes. They might evolve but they are still unfolding as manifestations of both the harmonious composition of the faithful Ainur and the discordant notes of Melkor. The whole of Middle-earth is suffused with this ambivalent rendering of the divine themes and all the characters have to position themselves in this universal composition. Nature in its own way both acts as a mirror and provides feedback.

For example, the Elves who have a strong sense of the sacred rarely fall under the sway of Melkorian discordance. Wherever they become involved, things often have a tendency to improve. Tolkien wrote that they "represent, as it were, the artistic, aesthetic, and purely scientific aspects of the Humane nature raised to a higher level than is actually seen in Men. That is: they have a devoted love of the physical world, and a desire to observe and understand it for its own sake and as 'other'—sc. as a reality derived from God in the same degree as themselves—not as a material for use or as a power-platform." (L 236)

At Lothlórien Frodo can feel the Elves' close connection to nature and therefore to something larger than nature as he realises that "never before he had been so suddenly and so keenly aware of the feel and texture of a tree's skin and the life within." When the fellowship leaves Lórien in their boats, the surroundings are in harmony with what goes on in their hearts—a striking illustration of Tolkien's poignant and powerful style:

> The breeze died away and the River flowed without a sound. No voice of bird broke the silence. The sun grew misty as the day grew old, until it gleamed in a pale sky like a high white pearl. Then it faded into the West, and dusk came early, followed by a grey and starless night ... (LotR I 493)

The description of the sun first growing misty and then gleaming like a white pearl before fading into the West symbolically reactivates memories of Galadriel. The pearl is traditionally associated to "the power of the waters" (Cooper 128), which unfailingly recalls Nenya, Galadriel's ring of Water made of mithril and containing the white stone of adamant (S 347). As an adjective, "adamant" is usually used to describe somebody who is unshakable in purpose, determined, resolute and unyielding. This is a fitting reference to the Lady who has just proven her resolve by both passing the test of the ring and accepting the relinquishment of Lothlórien.

Gimli is so moved by his encounter with the Lady of Lothlórien that his opinion of the Elves has totally altered. He realises that "Elves may see things otherwise" (LotR I 492) and he now appears very different from his fellow Dwarves.

As we all know, the relation of the Dwarves with nature is sometimes more a question of exploitation than respect. By trying to wring the last ounce from the soil, by digging the mountains too deeply, too greedily and too shortsightedly, they attracted the "greedy, strong and wicked worm" Smaug in the Lonely Mountain (H 23) and they awoke the Balrog at the root of the mithril-vein in Kazad-dûm (LotR I 413). Just as the forests in Middle-earth may bear evil will to those who mistreat or destroy them, so may the Mountains of Middle-earth behave in their own way—by means of Balrogs or Dragons or "champions" as Anne Petty calls them. This might be viewed as fair retribution.

All along Tolkien seems to be advocating balance. There is nothing wrong with digging for mithril if it is done with reason or with moderation; after all Frodo is saved from the Troll in Moria thanks to his mithril corset. It is obvious that the peoples of Middle-earth each have a role to play with respect to nature. Both the Elves and the Hobbits offer an illustration of a harmonious relationship with their environment.

The description of the Shire at the beginning of the story could be seen as a manifesto for successful husbandry. It could almost be regarded as a practical compendium in prose of Keats' beautiful ode *To Autumn* when the poet exalts this season of "mellow fruitfulness" conspiring with "the maturing sun" in order "to bend with apples the moss'd cottage-trees", and "set budding more, and still more, later flowers for the bees", "for summer has o'er-brimmed their clammy cells" (Bewley 682).

> The Shire had seldom seen so fair a summer, or so rich an autumn: the trees were laden with apples, honey was dripping in the combs, and the corn was tall and full. (LotR I 99)

The Hobbit-grown corn crops would fit in perfectly in Keats' sensuous portrayal of autumnal nature.

There is no doubt that Tolkien advocates "stewardship over dominion" and that "stewardship implies husbandry" as Michael Brisbois observed (203). The Hobbits seem to know this principle inherently: "They love peace and quiet and good tilled earth: a well-ordered and well-farmed countryside was their favourite haunt", as the reader is told in the *Prologue* (17).

Increasingly, scientific research in our primary world shows the positive effects of sensible husbandry. For example, the Scottish Natural Heritage has communicated on the fact that "well-managed" estates deliver positive biodiversity benefits.[4] Nevertheless one also notices that political, social and economic discourse has a tendency to shy away from this side of reality. The reasons seem obvious: on the one hand, sound stewardship might imply putting aside large areas of land that are relatively free from economic exploitation and, on the other hand, one might have to accept the fact that predator control, deer management, heather burning, shooting, hunting and fishing can all play a positive role. All too often, our 'modern' society adopts a simple and Manichaean attitude towards these kinds of things when it advocates either leaving nature alone or unashamedly exploiting its resources.

V.

> "[What is the] extinction of a condor to a child who has never seen a wren?" Robert Michael Pyle (Louv 146)

In Middle-earth, it appears that being disconnected from nature rimes with being disconnected from certain aspects of the Great Music. Similarly, in his essay on *Smith of Wootton Major*, Tolkien bemoaned the risk of disconnection with Faery that is threatening the village. Although Wootton Major is a comfortable, commercially successful and self-satisfied village, the artistic quality of its products is declining and therefore its prosperity is jeopardised. Tolkien wrote: "If the thread between the villagers and Faery was broken it would go back to

---

4   See The Scottish Natural Heritage's 2010 leaflet on "Farmland and Lowland Ecosystems Group: Biodiversity and sporting enterprises".

its squalid beginnings." (Flieger 92) In the same vein, therefore, nature used as a sympathetic background in Tolkien's Middle-earth can help the characters to maintain a link with certain aspects of Ilúvatar's themes.

Tolkien regretted that Hobbits' feelings for wild creatures were "not alas! very commonly found among the nearest contemporary parallels" (L 197). Indeed not only do we notice that, in our primary world, mainstream society is not particularly conducive to good husbandry but we are also beginning to notice that many people (especially the younger generations) seem to be suffering from what the American author and journalist Richard Louv calls "nature-deficit disorder". People seem to be increasingly disconnected from their natural environment and academics/scientists/researchers are paying more attention to investigating the consequences of this disconnection. Even those that question Louv's use of the term "deficit disorder", are willing to admit that we increasingly lack what would be more accurately described as a series of "benefits" that can come from exposure to nature (reduction of stress, enhancement of positive mood, improvement of cognitive skills...)[5].

Didn't Tolkien write in *Leaf by Niggle* that Niggle's living picture, his real tree, "a true part of creation", is indeed used as a therapy, proving "very useful", "as a holiday, and a refreshment", "splendid for convalescence", and "for many the best introduction to the Mountains"? (TL 103) However Niggle's living picture is a far cry from his initial attempt in his shed before he had to start on his great journey. In the meantime he too had to apply some sort of internal husbandry to his seemingly neglected garden.

It is perhaps not surprising therefore to note that, in our primary world, extensive research on the subject shows how essential (and not optional) nature is to human life (Beatley 3), a fact which is easy to understand as the American biologist, researcher and author E.O. Wilson from Harvard University wrote in *The Biophilia Hypothesis*:

> For more than 99 percent of human history people have lived in hunter-gatherer bands totally and intimately involved with other organisms… In short, the brain evolved in a biocentric world, not a machine-regulated world. It would be therefore quite extraordinary to find that all learning rules related to that world have been erased in a few thousand years, even in the tiny minority of peoples who have existed for more than one or two generations in wholly urban environments. (Wilson 32)

---

5   See for example the article "What are the Benefits of Interaction with Nature?" (http://www.ncbi.nlm.nih.gov/pmc/articles/PMC3709294/)

Conclusion

Sympathetic background in Tolkien's work is in fact no mere literary device used to set the mood or emphasise a point as can not only be found in literature but also in films, or even in modern advertising, in political or economic rhetoric and so forth. It goes far beyond than that. For example, when the West wind blows on Saruman's body, one may feel the presence of the Powers of the West; when the wind comes from the East, one might suspect a manifestation of Sauron, as Aragon remarks to Gimli: "In Minas Tirith they endure the East Wind, but they do not ask it for tidings." (LotR II 18); when a brook gently murmurs, who knows whether the Vala Ulmo is not reaching forth in what is essentially his domain and whether he is not transmitting a message.

After all, in the First Age, this Lord of Waters did cause a mist to arise from the great River Sirion to protect Huor and Húrin from the Orcs before the two Eagles carried them to Gondolin; when the Fox passes "through the wood on business of his own" and ponders about the Hobbits sleeping out of doors at the beginning of their journey (LotR I 105), one might wonder whether he could be a Maia in disguise... Many examples permeate the history of Middle-earth. Some seem easy to decipher and others call for more subtle interpretations and in any event can be viewed differently in virtue of applicability.

Therefore, in Tolkien's narrative, it appears that the use of what could be broadly described as a 'literary device' in relation to our Primary World could in many instances be considered *accurate descriptions of reality* in his Secondary World. In the history of Middle-earth, Tolkien's use of sympathetic background is not restricted to merely enriching the style. It takes on a different dimension and can be perceived by the reader as conveying a more profound description of *real* events that make perfect sense within this Secondary World.

Furthermore what appears as sympathetic background provides the reader with a key to understanding Middle-earth's original music by offering a materialization of some of its ambivalent aspects, i.e. good and evil — good in so far as the music emanates from Ilúvatar's themes and evil in so far as discordant notes have invested it. However Tolkien was no Manichaean as some critics try to make him appear. Admittedly in Middle-earth, the actions towards nature of Wizards, Elves, Men, Dwarves and Hobbits are put alongside the 'workings' of Melkor and Sauron, for the reader to observe. Yet, it is important to note that attentive readers are more likely to be concerned with the potentially 'evil' actions of Wizards, Elves, Men, Dwarves and Hobbits, than with the 'obvious workings' of the two aforementioned and easily identifiable villains. This precludes any simple Manichaeism.

Finally nature, when it is presented in this way can therefore possess Tolkien's "arresting strangeness", and provide a similar experience to that of Charles Dickens' Mooreeffoc (or Coffee Room seen backwards) which is conducive to the regaining of a clear or refreshed view of things (TL 50, 59). How terrible it would be to live in a world resembling Niggle's society with people like Councillor Tomkins who regards flowers as *merely* "digestive and genital organs of plants"! But to a certain extent are we not already partaking in such a world? Isn't nature all too often regarded purely as an economic, political or aesthetic commodity?

Readers sensitive to Tolkien's use of nature as sympathetic background will no doubt return to our Primary World with different perspectives and they will perhaps find Emerson's views of nature not quite so distant, outlandish or excessive when he expressed his feeling that "every object rightly seen, unlocks a new faculty of the soul" (Emerson 14).

Bibliography

Beatley, Timothy. *Biophilic Cities*, Washington: Island Press, 2011

Bewley, Marius (Ed.). *The English Romantic Poets: An Anthology with Commentaries*. New York: The Modern Library, 1970

Brisbois, Michael J. "Tolkien's Imaginary Nature: An Analysis of the Structure of Middle-earth". *Tolkien Studies* II, eds. Douglas A. Anderson, Michael D.C. Drout, Verlyn Flieger. Morgantown: West Virginia University Press, 2005, pp. 197-216

Carpenter, Humphrey (Ed.). *The Letters of J.R.R. Tolkien*. London: Allen & Unwin, 1981

Carrington, Norman T. *Shakespeare: Macbeth*, London: James Brodie Ltd, 1983

Cooper, J.C. *An Illustrated Encyclopaedia of Traditional Symbols*. London: Thames and Hudson, 1978

Curry, Patrick. "Environmentalism and Eco-criticism"; "Nature". *J.R.R. Tolkien Encyclopedia*, ed. Michael D.C. Drout. New York: Taylor & Francis, 2007, pp. 165; 453-454

Emerson, Ralph Waldo. *Nature and Other Essays*. New York: Dover Publications, 2009

Flieger, Verlyn (Ed.). *J.R.R. Tolkien: Smith of Wootton Major*, London: HarperCollins, 2005

Guifford, Terry (Ed.). *John Muir: His Life and Letters and Other Writings*. London: Bâton Wicks, 1996

Hammond, Wayne G. and Scull, Christina. *The J.R.R. Tolkien Companion and Guide*. New York: Houghton Mifflin Company, 2006

---. *The J.R.R. Tolkien Companion & Guide*. New York: Houghton Mifflin Company, 2006

Helms, Randel. *Myth, Magic and Meaning in Tolkien's World*. London: Thames and Hudson, 1974

Louv, Richard. *Last Child in the Woods*, Chapel Hill: Algonquin Books, 2008

Muir, John. *Our National Parks*. Kindle, 1901

Petty, Anne C. *Tolkien in the Land of Heroes*. New York: Cold Spring Press, 2003

Shakespeare, William. *Macbeth*. Paris: Aubier, Éditions Montaignes, 1937

Tolkien, Christopher (Ed.). *The Silmarillion* [1977]. London: Allen and Unwin, 1979

Tolkien, J.R.R. *The Hobbit: or There and Back Again* [1937]. London: Allen and Unwin, 1981

— . *The Fellowship of the Ring* [1954]. London: HarperCollins, 1993

—. *The Two Towers* [1954]. London: HarperCollins, 1993

—. *The Return of the King* [1955]. London: HarperCollins, 1993

—. *Tree and Leaf* [1964]. London: Allen and Unwin, 1964

Wilson, Edmund O., Ed. with Stephen R. Kellert. *The Biophilia Hypothesis*. Washington D.C.: Island Press, 1993

Webography

"What are the Benefits of Interacting with Nature?" in: *International Journal of Environmental Research and Public Health*, 6 March 2013, Keniger, Lucy E., Gaston Kevin J., Irvine Katherine N., Fuller Richard A.
(http://www.ncbi.nlm.nih.gov/pmc/articles/PMC3709294)

Romantische Landschaften in Tolkiens Werk

Julian Tim Morton Eilmann (Aachen)

Die Betrachtung der Landschaft in Tolkiens Werk vor dem Hintergrund der Romantik findet im Folgenden vor der Prämisse statt, dass es nicht nur gewisse Spuren der romantischen Denkart bei Tolkien gibt, sondern dass die Romantik einen wesentlichen Schlüssel bietet, um Tolkiens Werk und dessen andauernde Faszination zu verstehen. Meiner Ansicht nach ist gerade das Romantische in Tolkiens Werk dafür verantwortlich, dass dieses so viele Generationen von Lesern begeistert. Die Ergebnisse des folgenden Artikels sind Teil einer umfassenderen Studie zum Dichter und Romantiker Tolkien, die in den nächsten Jahren vorgelegt werden soll.

Eine Schwierigkeit an einer Lesart Tolkiens als Romantiker liegt u.a. daran, dass hier mit einem Begriff operiert wird, der terminologisch schwer fassbar ist und in der Literatur- und Kulturgeschichte immer wieder anders und neu definiert wurde (vgl. Hoffmeister 177ff). Umso wichtiger ist es, kurz darzulegen, inwiefern Tolkien als Romantiker bezeichnet werden kann. Der zentrale Verbindungspunkt zwischen Romantik und Tolkien besteht in der Rolle, die Phantasie und Kunst innerhalb des romantischen Diskurses einnehmen und die sich in vielen Punkten auch bei Tolkien findet. Um dies zu verdeutlichen, müssen wir uns die wesentlichen Grundgedanken der romantischen Poetologie vor Augen führen, was angesichts der gebotenen Kürze hier entsprechend bündig ausfallen muss.

Die Rolle der Phantasie im romantischen Diskurs

Natürlich haben Dichter und Philosophen sich bereits in anderen Epochen der Geistesgeschichte mit der menschlichen Phantasie beschäftigt, aber es sind die Romantiker Ende des 18. Jahrhunderts, die die Phantasie als eine regelrecht existentielle Kraft ins Zentrum ihres Schaffens setzen (vgl. Beil 938). Die Glorifizierung der Phantasie ist dabei eine Folge des neuen philosophischen und poetologischen Denkens im Zuge der geistigen Umwälzungen, wie sie durch die Philosophie des Deutschen Idealismus insbesondere von Johann Gottlieb Fichte und Friedrich Schelling im Zeitalter der Romantik vollzogen wurden. Wir wissen, dass die Romantiker der ersten Generation in kaum zu überschätzendem Maße durch die Philosophie Fichtes beeinflusst wurden. Hier sollen Fichtes Gedankengänge nicht in Breite ausgeführt werden. Das Entscheidende ist, dass Fichte in Radikalisierung Kants die tradierten philosophischen Vorstellungen der menschlichen Wahrnehmung und Erkenntnisfähigkeit vehement infrage stellt. Ein Ergebnis von Fichtes explosiven Gedanken ist die These, dass das, was der Mensch gemeinhin als Wirklichkeit auffasst, als Produkt oder zumindest Teilprodukt des menschlichen Verstandes aufzufassen sei (vgl. Zeltner 123). Die menschliche Wahrnehmung, die die Grundlage unserer Wirklichkeitskonstruktion bildet, findet demnach kein Fundament mehr in der vermeintlich realen Welt. Die Romantiker verstanden Fichtes Gedanken derart, dass bereits der Akt menschlicher Wahrnehmung als schöpferischer Akt verstanden werden kann, wird die Welt doch erst im menschlichen Geiste *Wirklichkeit* – bzw. das, was das Individuum dafür hält. Indem auf diese Weise bereits das menschliche Denken als kreativer Akt geadelt wird, ist es aus Sicht der Romantik nur ein logischer Schluss, dass zwischen dem quasi-schöpferischen Denken und Wahrnehmen sowie dem Akt des Phantasierens und Dichtens kein grundlegender Unterschied besteht (vgl. Korff 246).

Galten die Phantasie und damit das Dichten in der Geistesgeschichte im Vergleich zum rationalen Denken oftmals als etwas regelrecht Anrüchiges, so erfuhr das Dichten in der Romantik eine immense Aufwertung. Mehr noch: Im Zuge der romantischen Poetologie wurde nicht nur die menschliche Phantasie gänzlich vom Makel des im Vergleich zum Denken vermeintlich Minderwertigen befreit. Indem die Romantiker glaubten, den grundlegend schöpferisch-kreativen Charakter des menschlichen Daseins erkannt zu haben, konnte man den Dichter zum vollkommensten Repräsentanten des Menschengeschlechts stilisieren. Im Künstler findet die Phantasie, das Element des Lebens, seinen vollendetsten Ausdruck (vgl. Korff 265).

Exakt diesen Gedanken hat Novalis, einer der Vorreiter der romantischen Poetologie, in seinem Romanfragment *Heinrich von Ofterdingen* zum Ausdruck gebracht. Dort wendet sich der Dichter Klingsohr mit folgendem Hinweis an den jungen Titelhelden:

> Es ist recht übel, daß die Poesie einen besonderen Namen hat, und die Dichter eine besondere Zunft ausmachen. Es ist gar nichts besonderes. Es ist die eigentümliche Handlungsweise des menschlichen Geistes. Dichtet und trachtet nicht jeder Mensch in jeder Minute? (Novalis, *Werke* 335).

Das schöpferische Element ist jedoch nicht allein für den Menschen als Gattungswesen charakteristisch. Vielmehr ist im romantischen Denken die gesamte Schöpfung selbst von der Poesie durchdrungen und es kommt nur auf das einzelne Individuum an, ob es diesen Zauber erkennt oder ahnungslos daran vorbeigeht. Dabei verwenden die Romantiker immer wieder andere Begriffe, um das transzendente Element des Kosmos zu umschreiben. Manchmal wird es als Poesie oder Zauber bezeichnet, manchmal werden klassische philosophische oder religiöse Begriffe herangezogen wie das Göttliche oder das Unendliche. Letztgenannten verwendet etwa Ludwig Uhland bei seiner Umschreibung des transzendenten Gehalts der materiellen Welt:

> Das Unendliche umgibt den Menschen, das Geheimnis der Gottheit und der Welt. Was er selbst war, ist und sein wird, ist ihm verhüllt. Süß und fruchtbar sind diese Geheimnisse... Der Geist des Menschen aber, wohl fühlend, daß er nie das Unendliche in voller Klarheit in sich auffassen wird und müde des unbestimmten Verlangens, knüpft bald seine Sehnsucht an irdische Bilder, in denen ihm doch ein Blick des Überirdischen aufzudämmern scheint... Dies Ahnen des Unendlichen in den Anschauungen ist das Romantische. (Uhland 8)

Für uns ist besonders der letzte Satz des Zitats ausschlaggebend, schließt sich doch damit fürs Erste der Gedankengang der romantischen Poetologie. Der empfindsame Mensch spürt, dass ihn etwas umgibt, das sein rein materielles Dasein übersteigt. Diese Ahnung des Unendlichen wiederum befeuert die Sehnsucht des Romantikers, denn zwar wird das Ersehnte in immer neuen Variationen und Spielarten erahnbar, aber eben nicht unmittelbar und ständig erfahrbar. Hieraus resultiert auch die für die Romantik charakteristische Sehnsucht, auf die ich in Bezug auf Tolkien gleich noch zu sprechen kommen werde. Die sicherlich bekannteste Formulierung dieser romantischen Perspektive hat Joseph von Eichendorff in seinem Gedicht *Wünschelrute* gefunden. Dort spricht er von einem schlafenden Lied, das uns umgibt, und das mithilfe der Poesie, also durch das magische Zauberwort des Poeten, geweckt und zum Klingen gebracht werden solle:

> Schläft ein Lied in allen Dingen
> Die da träumen fort und fort
> Und die Welt hebt an zu singen
> Triffst du nur das Zauberwort. (Eichendorff 112)

In diesen Worten kristallisiert sich die Sehnsucht des Romantikers heraus, das ihn umgebende Geheimnis der Welt – besonders der Natur – zu enträtseln, hinter den Schleier der vermeintlich prosaischen Wirklichkeit zu schauen.[1] Aus

---

1 Hier sei kurz darauf hingewiesen, dass das schlummernde Geheimnis, das Uhland das Unendliche nennt, im Rahmen eines christlichen Diskurses mit Gott identifiziert werden würde. In der Tat haben viele Romantiker den Bezug zu Gott explizit in ihren Erzählungen und Gedichten zum Ausdruck gebracht, u.a. auch Eichendorff. Dennoch ist es für die Romantik charakteristisch, dass das transzendente Element, auf das sich die romantische Sehnsucht richtet, oftmals vage und nicht genauer definiert bleibt. Dies

dem hier skizzierten Konzept romantischer Poetologie resultiert der wichtigste und sicherlich bekannteste Anspruch der romantischen Kunst, das so genannte Prinzip der Romantisierung, wie es Novalis in der für ihn typischen aphoristischen Art formuliert hat:

> Die Welt muss romantisiert werden. So findet man den ursprünglichen Sinn wieder. Romantisieren ist nichts als eine qualitative Potenzierung. Das niedere Selbst wird mit einem bessern Selbst in dieser Operation identifiziert... Indem ich dem Gemeinen einen hohen Sinn, dem Gewöhnlichen ein geheimnisvolles Ansehen, dem Bekannten die Würde des Unbekannten, dem Endlichen einen unendlichen Schein gebe, so romantisiere ich es – Umgekehrt ist die Operation für das Höhere, Unbekannte, Mystische, Unendliche – ... Es bekommt einen geläufigen Ausdruck. Romantische Philosophie... Wechselerhöhung und Erniedrigung.
> (Novalis, *Schriften* 545)

Romantisieren bedeutet demnach, die Welt neu und eben romantisch zu sehen. Hieraus folgt, dass all das, was der Mensch im Alltag als gegeben und bekannt vorausgesetzt hat, »die Würde des Unbekannten« zurückerhält, wie es Novalis ausdrückt. Das Bekannte wird wieder geheimnisvoll und kann für den Romantiker zum Mittel der Offenbarung des Unendlichen werden, was ja, wie ausgeführt, überall latent gegenwärtig sein soll.

Entscheidend ist demnach eine Veränderung des Betrachterblicks. Tendenziell ist jedes Individuum zu einer solch romantischen Sichtweise fähig, aber die meisten Menschen verbleiben allzu sehr in den gewohnten alltäglichen Denkweisen. Dies sind jene ›Philister‹, gegen die sich die Kritik vieler Romantiker richtet. Entsprechend finden wir zahlreiche romantische Romane und Erzählungen, in denen der Gegensatz zwischen der philiströsen Lebensart des Spießbürgers und den existentiellen Ambitionen des Romantikers, zum Kern der Dinge vorzustoßen, thematisiert wird.

Aus dem bisher Gesagten wird auch ersichtlich, weshalb das Phantastische in der Literatur der Romantik eine so große Rolle spielt. Denn das Phantastische kann dem Romantiker ideal als Vehikel dienen, um dem Protagonisten und letztlich auch dem Leser spielerisch die Augen für das Wunderbare zu öffnen, das ihn umgibt.

---

ist dem Wunsch vieler Romantiker geschuldet, ihre poetologischen Vorstellungen mit neuen und unbekannten dichterischen Bildern zum Ausdruck zu bringen.

Die Rolle der Natur in der romantischen Poetologie

Aus dem bisher Gesagten lässt sich schlussfolgern, dass die Natur in der Romantik zum eigentlichen Resonanzraum des romantischen Individuums avanciert. Der Romantiker ist immer auf der Suche nach Momenten, in denen sich ihm das Geheimnis des Kosmos offenbart, und hierfür scheint sich nichts besser zu eignen als die belebte Flora und Fauna, die ihm transzendierende Erfahrungen ermöglicht. Der Germanist Paul Böckmann hat den inneren Zusammenhang zwischen romantischer Sehnsucht und Natur sehr zutreffend auf den Punkt gebracht und betont dabei den Bezug zwischen Naturerfahrung und Musikalität:

> Die Sprache der Natur redet zwar nicht in deutlichen Worten zum Menschen, sondern nur als Klang und Musik; aber der Künstler weiß sie vernehmbar zu machen. Damit wird die Musik zum Vereinigungsmittel zwischen Mensch und Natur... Die Aufmerksamkeit richtet sich deshalb auf all jene Naturerscheinungen, die mit Geräuschen und Klängen verbunden sind oder sich der Musik vergleichen lassen: Das Rauschen des Waldes, der Ströme und Brunnen oder die Geräusche der Mühle, die Stimmen der Vögel, der Widerhall der Jagdhörner werden zu bevorzugten Motiven, um auf die Sprache der Natur hinzuweisen. (Böckmann 105)

Wir finden in diesem Zitat bereits einige der bekannten – und aus heutiger Sicht – stereotypen romantischen Motive: geheimnisvoll rauschende Wälder, schwermütig plätschernde Bäche und der Klang ferner Jagdhörner. All dies gehört heute zum Klischeebild einer romantischen Szenerie. Tolkien selbst hat, wie weiter unten deutlich wird, besonders in seinen frühen Texten vielfach von solchen Motiven Gebrauch gemacht. Charakteristisch für eine solche romantische Naturwahrnehmung ist, dass die Natur eben mit den ihr zur Verfügung stehenden Mitteln – visuell oder akustisch – zum Menschen spricht. Die Natur ist von einem ihr inhärenten Geheimnis, dem sprichwörtlichen schlafenden Lied, belebt, mehr noch, sie scheint im Sinne des Romantikers sich selbst nach ihrer Erweckung durch ein poetisch begabtes Individuum zu sehnen.

Aus diesem Eindruck, es mit der belebten Natur quasi mit einem empfindsamen Gegenüber zu tun zu haben, resultiert die selige Beglückung, die der Romantiker in der Begegnung mit der Natur verspürt, denn seine Sehnsucht scheint in romantischen Naturerfahrungen auf ein Echo zu stoßen, das ihm Antwort gibt. Das Bild des andächtig Lauschenden ist demnach typisch für die Romantik und von Künstlern wie Caspar David Friedrich immer wieder in Szene gesetzt worden.

Weiterhin charakteristisch ist, dass das Naturbild des Romantikers häufig von einer latenten Melancholie und Schwermut geprägt ist, denn zwar sehnt sich das Subjekt nach einer beglückenden Einheitserfahrung mit dem Kosmos, und die Ahnung des schlummernden Geheimnisses stellt sich auch phasenweise ein, allerdings ist es selten von Dauer. Und die für Eichendorff und andere so typischen Waldhörner sind überhaupt nur deshalb romantisch, weil sie aus weiter Ferne erklingen und so das Fernweh und die Sehnsucht anregen. Aus nächster Nähe geblasen, wäre das Waldhorn nur ein einfaches und wahrscheinlich auch im Ohr des Romantikers nicht besonders angenehm klingendes Instrument. Es ist demnach die räumliche Distanz, die den Hörnerklang zu einer romantischen Erfahrung macht. Ohne diese Entfernung zwischen lauschendem Subjekt und dem Objekt der Sehnsucht wäre die romantische Szenerie eben gar keine solche, sondern vielmehr eine bloße Idylle.

An dieser Stelle sei noch einmal betont, dass es sich bei dem hier gezeichneten Bild um eine generelle Charakterisierung des Romantischen handelt, bei dem Manches ausgeklammert wird. Auch wird sich das skizzierte Erfahrungsschema nicht in jeder Naturschilderung der Romantik finden. Dennoch verweist der hier aufgezeigte Zusammenhang zwischen romantischer Poetologie – Sehnsucht nach dem Unendlichen – und Naturwahrnehmung nach meiner Deutung auf den Kern der Romantik. Dieser bildet dementsprechend auch die Grundlage für den Bezug zu Tolkiens Werk, auf den ich nun eingehen möchte.

Romantische Landschaft in Tolkiens Frühwerk

Im vorliegenden Artikel möchte ich mich auf das *Buch der verschollenen Geschichten* beschränken. Denn romantische Naturschilderungen finden sich vor allem in dieser Frühphase von Tolkiens Mythologie. In späteren Werken wie dem *Herrn der Ringe* finden sich hiervon nur noch wenige Spuren. In den *Verschollenen Geschichten* hingegen ist der romantische Geist von Tolkiens Werk am stärksten spürbar, sodass ich mein Augenmerk auf die entsprechenden Passagen richte.

In einem früheren Aufsatz bin ich bereits darauf eingegangen, dass Eriol oder Ælfwine, wie er auch genannt wird, die Hauptfigur der *Verschollenen Geschichten*, als Romantiker im Feenland bezeichnet werden kann (vgl. Eilmann). Wie die Protagonisten in zahlreichen romantischen Romanen und Erzählungen wird auch in Tolkiens Buch ein Sterblicher in ein fantastisches Reich entrückt, in dem er wundersame Erfahrungen macht, die die ihn auszeichnende Sehnsucht nach dem Unendlichen zeitweise stillen. Bekanntlich verschlägt es Eriol zu Beginn der Geschichte nach Tol Eressea, der Einsamen Insel der Elben. Dort findet er Unterkunft in der Hütte des Vergessenen Spiels, einem magischen Ort. Auch erfahren wir, dass Eriol und seine Vorfahren romantische Gemüter mit einer Sehnsucht nach Transzendenz und dem Fantastischen sind. Der Grund für dieses Verlangen entstand in Eriols Familie, da einer seiner Vorfahren als Seefahrer bereits die Elbeninsel erreichte, in der Hütte lebte und durch seine Erlebnisse zeitlebens mit einer unstillbaren Sehnsucht erfüllt wurde:

> Then Eriol said: »… It had long … been a tradition in our kindred that one of our father's fathers would speak of a fair house and magic gardens, of a wondrous town, and of a music full of all beauty and longing—and these things he said he had seen and heard as a child, though how and where was not told. Now all his life was he restless, as if a longing half-expressed for unknown things dwelt within him« (LT I 20)

Angesichts des bisher Gesagten fällt es nicht schwer, diese Sehnsucht, von der Eriol hier spricht, als eine romantische zu bezeichnen, und dies wird noch deutlicher, wenn wir uns gleich seine Naturwahrnehmung vor Augen führen. Auch das im Zitat erwähnte magische Haus und der verwunschene Garten werden hierbei eine zentrale Rolle spielen. Bevor ich darauf näher eingehe, möchte ich den Blick direkt auf den Anfang der Erzählung richten, denn bereits dort finden sich erste stimmungsvolle Landschaftsschilderungen, die darauf hindeuten, dass es sich bei der Landschaft in dieser Fassung der Mythologie nicht einfach um Natur handelt, die das Individuum passiv umgibt. Im Gegenteil, Tolkien nutzt Naturschilderungen geschickt, um bereits durch die Gestaltung des Ortes jene romantische Stimmung zu erzeugen, die für die Eriol-Rahmenhandlung der *Verschollenen Geschichten* so wichtig ist:

> Now as he stood at the foot of the little hill there came a faint breeze and then a flight of rooks above his head in the clear even light. The sun had some time sunk beyond the boughs of the elms that stood as far as eye could look about the plain, and some time had its last gold faded through the leaves and slipped across the glades to sleep beneath the roots and dream till dawn. (ebd. 13)

Das Bild einer Sonne, die ihren letzten goldenen Schimmer durch ein Ulmenwäldchen sickern lässt, während sie sich metaphorisch unter den Wurzeln der Bäume zur Ruhe legt, erinnert nicht von ungefähr an romantische Landschaftsszenen, wie sie im 19. Jahrhundert immer wieder dargestellt wurden. Die Zeit der auf- und besonders der untergehenden Sonne ist ohnehin die Tageszeit, die sich für romantische Landschaftsbilder anbietet, markiert der Sonnenuntergang doch jene Phase des geheimnisvollen Zwielichts, in der sich wesentliche Gegensätze wie Tag und Nacht, Himmel und Erde visuell beeindruckend begegnen und verschmelzen. Dementsprechend ist es auch nicht verwunderlich, dass Tolkien das Zwielicht in seinem Werk immer wieder mit den Elben in Verbindung bringt, sind die Eldar doch jene Wesen in Mittelerde, die für die Sterblichen selbst zur Verkörperung des Wunderbaren werden können. Man denke nur an die Begegnung der Gefährten mit der Macht der Eldar in Lothlórien. Ich werde später noch auf andere Stellen aus den *Verschollenen Geschichten* eingehen, in denen das Zwielicht als Metapher eine wichtige Rolle spielt.

Natürlich macht ein Sonnenuntergang allein noch keine romantische Szenerie, ganz im Gegenteil. Der Kontext, die Atmosphäre und der weitere Erzählrahmen sind wie bei jedem literarischen Werk auch in diesem Falle dafür ausschlaggebend, dass beim Leser ein bestimmter Eindruck entsteht, der sich in diesem Falle nicht anders als romantisch bezeichnen lässt. So hebt Eriol die magische und viele Geheimnisse versprechende Atmosphäre des ihn umgebenden Ortes hervor: »To me it [this place] has the air of holding many secrets of old and wonderful and beautiful things in its treasuries and noble places and in the hearts of those that dwell within its walls« (ebd. 14).

Die Hütte des Vergessenen Spiels ist der zentrale Handlungsort in der Eriol-Rahmenhandlung und gleichzeitig ein dezidiert romantischer Ort, bei dessen Schilderung Tolkien auch die Landschaft in hohem Maße zur Ausgestaltung der träumerisch-stimmungsvollen Atmosphäre nutzt:

> There was a place of fair gardens in Valinor besides a silver sea. Now ... there was a light there as of summer evening, save only when the silver lamps were kindled on the hill at dusk, and then little lights of white would dance and quiver on the paths, chasing black shadow-dapples under the trees. (ebd. 19)

Wie sieht der Ort aus, der hier beschrieben wird? Wir hören von lieblichen Gärten am Rande eines silbrigen Sees, d.h. es wird das Bild einer entrückten friedlichen Parklandschaft evoziert. Dort herrschte eine Lichtstimmung wie an einem ununterbrochenen Sommerabend. Mit wenigen Pinselstrichen wird hier also ein romantisches Landschaftsbild gezeichnet, das den Rahmen für den Aufenthalt der Sterblichen im Elbenland bietet. Mit unserem Wissen um die romantische Landschaftsschilderung überrascht es uns nicht, dass an diesem Ort eine dauerhafte Abendstimmung herrscht. Wie erwähnt ist das abendliche Zwielicht ein romantischer Topos par excellence. Dies ist die Zeitphase, in der sich die Gegensätze auflösen, die das Dasein der Menschen bestimmen.

Vor dem Hintergrund des romantischen Denkens ist es nicht erstaunlich, dass genau zu der Zeit, in der Tag und Nacht sich verbinden, aus der Welt der Menschen neue Kameraden über den Pfad der Träume zu den menschlichen Kindern ins Feenreich gelangen. Es handelt sich um Individuen, die der prosaischen Welt in eine poetische Sphäre entfliehen möchten, und dieser poetische Ort wird, wie wir sehen, mit einem sternenbeschienenen Garten im Dämmerlicht assoziiert. Die Kinder gelangen ins Feenreich über den so genannten Pfad der

Träume, mit elbischem Namen Olórë Mallë. Dieser Weg, der die Menschenwelt mit dem Überirdischen verbindet, ist ein Pfad der Verheißung, denn er ist von einer hohen Böschung mit überhängenden Bäumen umgeben, d.h. einer dichten – aber natürlichen – Grenze. Aber diese landschaftliche Grenze ist kein Ort des Schreckens, wie der Alte Wald im *Herrn der Ringe*, der auch nur durch ein Tor in einer Hecke betreten werden kann, sondern ein Ort der Verlockung, denn es lebt ein immerwährendes Geflüster in ihm, große Glühwürmchen erhellen das Dunkel und verströmen ein geheimnisvolles elbisches Licht. Wer über diesen Pfad geht, wird also schon unterwegs vom Feenland gelockt und sanft hinübergezogen:

> This was a time of joy to the children, for it was mostly at this hour [dusk] that a new comrade would come down the lane called Olórë Mallë or the Path of Dreams. It has been said to me, though the truth I know not, that that lane ran by devious routes to the homes of Men, but that way we never trod when we fared thither ourselves. It was a lane of deep banks and great overhanging hedges, beyond which stood many tall trees wherein a perpetual whisper seemed to live; but not seldom great glow-worms crept about its grassy borders. (ebd. 18)

Dieser Pfad der Träume führt zum »schönsten aller Gärten« (»the fairest of all the gardens«, ebd.), in dem die Hütte des Vergessenen Spiels auf die Menschenkinder wartet. Die Kinder verbringen ihre Zeit in diesem Garten wie in einem nie enden wollenden romantischen Traum einer erfüllten Jugend. Sie tollen herum, bauen sich aus den Schösslingen einer mächtigen Eiche Pfeil und Bogen (vgl. ebd.). Der zauberhafte Charakter dieses landschaftlichen Idylls der Träumer wird auch dadurch betont, dass sich im eigens hervorgehobenen Fliederbusch die Vögel mit den schönsten Stimmen sammeln und fortwährend singen: »But in the lilacs every bird that ever sang sweetly gathered and sang« (ebd.).

In einem solchen romantischen Setting wie dem hier geschilderten Parkgarten ist die Präsenz der schönsten Singvögel natürlich kein Zufall. Im Gegenteil, immer wieder symbolisiert in romantischen Gedichten und Erzählungen der Gesang des Vogels die romantische Sehnsucht selbst, denn aufgrund seiner Flugfähigkeit erscheint dieses Tier weniger an das irdische Dasein gebunden zu sein als der Mensch. So wie die Vögel im Herbst in die Ferne ziehen, würde auch der Romantiker gerne den prosaischen Alltag verlassen. Weiterhin zeugen die Vögel mit dem Wohlklang ihres Gesangs von der Verbundenheit der Natur mit der poetischen Seite des Menschen. Ein typisches Beispiel für diese Sichtweise des Vogels in der Romantik ist Eichendorffs Gedicht *Nachklänge*:

> Lust'ge Vögel in dem Wald,
> Singt, solang es grün,
> Ach wer weiß, wie bald,
> wie bald Alles muss verblühn!
>
> Sah ich's doch vom Berge einst
> Glänzen überall,
> Wußte kaum, warum du weinst,
> Fromme Nachtigall.
>
> Und kaum ging ich über Land,
> Frisch durch Lust und Not,
> Wandelt' alles, und ich stand
> Müd im Abendrot.
>
> Und die Lüfte wehen kalt,
> Übers falbe Grün,
> Vöglein, euer Abschied hallt –
> Könnt' ich mit euch ziehn! (Eichendorff 243f)

Steht der Flug des Vogels für das Fernweh und die romantische Sehnsucht, ist ein Ort wie der von Tolkien beschriebene Garten, an dem sich die Vögel mit dem schönsten Gesang niederlassen, natürlich ein besonders romantischer Ort.[2]

Warum lassen sich die Singvögel im magischen Garten ausgerechnet auf einem Fliederbaum nieder? Nach der tradierten Symbolsprache kündigt der Flieder nicht nur den Frühling an, er steht auch für die zarten Bande zwischen zwei Herzen. Auch steht der duftende Flieder für die Treue des Partners. Warum Tolkien auf das Symbol des Flieders, noch dazu des weißen Flieders, zurückgreift, wird ersichtlich, wenn wir uns vor Augen führen, dass in den *Verschollenen Geschichten* viele Kinder im Elbengarten Gefährten werden und sich später im erwachsenen (prosaischen) Menschenleben als Liebende wieder begegnen. Die Träumer sind also bei Tolkien von einer zauberhaften Parklandschaft umgeben, in denen betörende Singvögel wie die Nachtigall sich auf weißen Fliederbüschen niederlassen – eben dem Symbol ewiger Liebestreue. Wir sehen, dass selbst ein

---

[2] Auch in dem Gedicht »You & Me and the Cottage of Lost Play«, entstanden im Kontext der *Verschollenen Geschichten*, umgibt die Protagonisten der ständige Gesang eines Vogels. Passend zur romantischen Liebesbegegnung, die im Gedicht geschildert wird, liefert die Nachtigall den akustischen Rahmen für den Aufenthalt im romantischen Garten: »While all about the nightingales / Were singing in the trees« (LT I 28).

auf den ersten Blick unscheinbares Detail einer Landschaftsschilderung im Textganzen bedeutungsvoll aufgeladen sein kann.

In dieser Textstelle geht es romantisch weiter: Wie wir erfahren, wollen die Elben die Kinder davor bewahren, noch weiter ins Elbenland vorzudringen, da der Eindruck der Bezauberung für die Sterblichen zu groß sein könnte. Einige Träumer jedoch werden von Sehnsucht getrieben, hinter den paradiesischen Garten Eldamars zu blicken und einen Blick auf die verzauberten Küsten zu erhaschen. Am Strand vernehmen sie die ferne Musik der Solosimpi, der elbischen Flötenspieler, wodurch erneut die Sehnsucht in ihren Herzen geweckt wird (vgl. LT I 19).

Es wird deutlich: Zwar betreten die Glücklichen, die Garten und Hütte erreichen, einen verwunschenen Ort, an dem sie Glück und Harmonie erfahren, dennoch ist hiermit nicht jene elbische Vollkommenheit erreicht, wie sie den Menschen im Klang der Musik vernehmlich wird. Tolkien gestaltet hier ganz typisch für die Romantik eine Szenerie von sich immer neu öffnenden Horizonten: So wie dem Sterblichen, der wundersamerweise den Pfad der Träume beschreitet, bereits der elbische Zaubergarten mit seiner herrlichen Vogelmusik und den betörenden Pflanzen als Paradies erscheinen muss, so wird auch hier die unstillbare Sehnsucht erneut geweckt, wenn der poetische Weckruf erklingt und sich der Blick auf das richtet, was jenseits der dämmrigen Baumschatten auf den Wanderer wartet. Die Wanderung durch das Zauberreich kann also von demjenigen, der den Sehnsuchtsruf der elbischen Flöten vernimmt, fortgesetzt werden. Angesichts des romantischen Gehalts dieses Kapitels ist auch der nächste Gedankenschritt, den Tolkien aus dieser Szenerie ableitet, nicht weiter verwunderlich. Denn, so informiert uns der Erzähler, kehren diejenigen, die noch weiter nach Valinor vorgedrungen sind, voller Staunen zurück:

> they [the dreamers] strayed into *Kôr* and became enamoured of the glory of Valinor... Yet some there were who... heard the Solosimpi piping afar off, or others who straying again beyond the garden caught a sound of the singing of the Telelli on the hill, and even some who reaching *Kôr* afterwards returned home, and their minds and hearts were full of wonder. Of the aftermemories of these, of their broken tales and snatches of song, came many strange legends that delighted Men for long and still do, it may be; for of such were the poets of the Great Lands. (ebd.)

»[T]hey became enamoured«: Der für Tolkien so wesentliche Begriff der Bezauberung, *enchantment*, liegt hier nahe, um diese Erfahrung des Wunderbaren begrifflich zu fassen. Aber, und dies ist die entscheidende Folgerung, diese verzauberten Wanderer im Feenreich sind es auch, die später nach ihrer Rückkehr in die Gefilde der Sterblichen zu den großen Dichtern der Menschen wurden.

Typisch für das romantische Denken ist, dass die Erfahrung des Wunders, also die Erfahrung von Transzendenz, wieder in Poesie verwandelt werden muss. Anders kann sich das Gefühl der Bezauberung offenbar nicht Bahn brechen. Die Bezauberung, die in der prosaischen Wirklichkeit für den Durchschnittsmenschen nicht spürbar bzw. nur als Ahnung vernehmbar ist, wird durch ein Werk menschlichen Kunstschaffens, zumeist Poesie und Musik, erfahrbar.

Diesem Gedanken liegt demnach insgesamt das Konzept zugrunde, dass die Dichtkunst der Menschen elbische Wurzeln hat. Versteht man die Elben wiederum als Repräsentanten des Wunders und der Transzendenz, so bildet die Dichtung den Schlüssel zwischen Alltagswelt und dem, was das Alltägliche übersteigt.

Eriol im Zaubergarten

Interessanterweise ist es genau jener elbische Zaubergarten, den wir bereits kennengelernt haben, der auch für ein besonders romantisches und die Sehnsucht weckendes Erlebnis Eriols verantwortlich ist. Insgesamt lässt sich feststellen, dass sich Eriol, so lange er sich in der Hütte des vergessenen Spiels aufhält, in einem Zustand der Bezauberung und Ehrfurcht befindet, was in zahlreichen Textzitaten bereits im Eingangskapitel deutlich wird:

> Eriol is »filled with a **happy wonderment**... and his heart was **more glad** within him than it had yet been in all his wanderings, albeit since his landing in the Lonely Isle his **joy** had been great enough«.
> »... for it seemed to him that **a new world and very fair** was opening to him«

Und über die sterblichen Gäste im elbischen Heim heißt es:
> »In one thing only were all alike, that a look of **great happiness** lit with a merry expectation of **further mirth and joy** lay on every face.«   (alle ebd. 15, Hervorhebung JE)

Eriol und die anderen Menschen befinden sich also in einem Zustand der Freude, einer glücklichen Verwunderung (*happy wonderment*). Ein wunderbarer Schimmer scheint alles zu umgeben. Dieser glückliche Zauber scheint eine Form der fundamentalen Begeisterung zu sein, die über die alltäglichen Freuden der Menschenwelt weit hinausgeht. Eriol steht offensichtlich unter einem Zauber, dessen Ursprung nicht ausgemacht werden kann, ganz genauso wie es die Protagonisten im *Herrn der Ringe* immer wieder in Bezug auf ihre Begegnungen mit den Elben schildern: »If there's any magic about, it's right down deep, where I can't lay my hands on it, in a manner of speaking« (LotR 351).

Diese Freude, die das Fassungsvermögen der Sterblichen offensichtlich übersteigt, findet eine Steigerung in Eriols allererster Nacht in der *Hütte des verlorenen Spiels.* Immer noch erfüllt von einem Gefühl des überirdischen Glücks, wird Eriol von seinen Gastgebern in ein Schlafgemach geleitet, das selbst unter einem Zauberbann zu schlummern scheint und das auf ihn die Wirkung ausübt, als sei der Schlaf in eben diesem Gemach »die größte aller Freuden«.[3] Bevor sich Eriol allerdings zur Ruhe legt, übt der magische Zaubergarten vor dem offenen Fenster mit all seinen optischen und akustischen Reizen eine bezaubernde Wirkung auf ihn aus. Wir werden sehen, dass es sich hier um eine dezidiert romantische Landschaftsszenerie handelt. Schauen wir uns den Wortlaut dieser Stelle also genauer an:

> Ere he laid him down however Eriol opened the window and **scent of flowers gusted in** therethrough, and a glimpse he caught of **a shadow-filled garden that was full of trees**, but its spaces were barred with **silver lights and black shadows** by reason of the moon; yet his window seems very high above those lawns below, and **a nightingale sang suddenly in a tree** nearby. Then slept Eriol, and through his dreams there came a music thinner and more pure than any he heard before, and it was **full of longing**. Indeed it was as if pipes of silver or flute of shapes most slender-delicate uttered crystal notes and threadlike harmonies beneath the moon upon the lawns; **and Eriol longed in his sleep for he knew not what.** (ebd. 46)

Der Blick eines empfindsamen Individuums, das am geöffneten Fenster in eine malerische Landschaft hinabblickt und durch ferne Musik betört wird, ist eine urromantische Situation, die in vielen Erzählungen und Gedichten der Romantik zu finden ist. Der Fensterblick hat deshalb so vielfältigen Eingang in die Literatur und Kunst der Romantik gefunden, weil in dieser Situation Gegensätze miteinander verbunden sind, die im Alltag oftmals als getrennt wahrgenommen werden: Drinnen und Draußen, Hell und Dunkel, Mensch und Natur. Der Romantiker am Fenster ist in diesem Falle das Verbindungsglied.

Der romantischen Landschaft kommt in diesem Kontext die Aufgabe zu, auf den Protagonisten – und natürlich auch auf den Leser – eben möglichst *romantisch*, also besonders geheimnisvoll, zauberhaft und anziehend zu wirken. Eine solche Landschaft scheint dem Menschen nicht fremd zu sein, sondern vielmehr lieblich vertraut. Die Landschaft spricht den Betrachter im wahrsten Sinne des Wortes an. Deshalb sind neben den parkähnlichen optischen Elementen auch akustische Reize wichtig. Oftmals sind es die besonders bei Eichendorff ständig vernehmbaren Posthörner, die in den sprichwörtlich stillen Ländern erklingen.

---

3 »it seemed to him that sleep was the best of all delights, but that fair chamber the best of all for sleep« (LT I 46)

Aber auch Vogellaute können entsprechenden Signalcharakter haben. Deshalb verwundert es in einem solchen romantischen Setting nicht, dass in der zitierten Eriol-Passage Nachtigallgesang aus einem Baum im Garten erklingt. Was auf den ersten Blick wie ein vernachlässigbares Detail einer Landschaftsbeschreibung erscheint, ist in Wahrheit ein romantisches Referenzsymbol. Denn wie oben erwähnt, handelt es sich bei der Nachtigall um einen besonders romantischen Singvogel, der einerseits für die Liebe stehen kann, aber noch allgemeiner ein Sehnsuchtswecker ist, der mit seinem Gesang im Lauschenden ein tiefes Verlangen auszulösen vermag. Und eben dies geschieht auch mit Eriol, von dem es heißt, dass er im Schlaf von einer unbestimmten – romantischen – Sehnsucht erfüllt wird.

Für unsere Fragestellung interessant ist, dass sich Eriols Betörung durch den elbischen Zaubergarten als ähnliche Situation auch in einem anderen Werk der fantastischen Literatur findet: George MacDonalds *Phantastes*. Dieser Klassiker der modernen Fantasy stellt insgesamt einen wichtigen Referenzpunkt für ein Verständnis von Tolkien als Romantiker dar, lässt sich doch zeigen, dass die moderne fantastische Literatur allgemein in einer direkten Tradition der Romantik steht und viele Aspekte romantischen Denkens in der Fantasy des späten 19. Jahrhunderts Niederschlag gefunden haben.

Hier möchte ich jedoch nur auf eine Textstelle auf *Phantastes* eingehen, in der erstaunlicherweise eine sehr ähnliche Landschaftserfahrung geschildert wird wie bei Tolkien. Anodos, die Hauptfigur in MacDonalds Roman, gelangt zu Beginn in eine fantastische Traumwelt, in der er verschiedene Abenteuer erlebt. Am Ende des siebten Kapitels wird ihm in einem verwunschenen Schloss der Blick aus einem Turmfenster gewährt. Was Anodos sieht und was dies bei ihm auslöst, steht in deutlicher Analogie zu Eriols romantischem Landschaftserlebnis:

> But as soon as I looked out of the window, a gush of **wonderment and longing flowed over my soul** like the tide of a great sea. Fairy Land lay before me, and drew me towards it with an **irresistible attraction**. The trees bathed their great heads in the waves of the morning, while their roots were planted deep in gloom; save where on the borders the sunshine broke against their stems, or swept in long streams through their avenues, washing with brighter hue all the leaves over which it flowed; revealing the rich brown of the decayed leaves and fallen pine-cones, and the delicate greens of the long grasses and tiny forests of moss that covered the channel over which it passed in motionless rivers of light.
>
> (MacDonald, Hervorhebung JE)

Die Landschaft selbst ist im Detail natürlich eine andere. Aber das Entscheidende ist, dass die rätselhafte Verwunschenheit der Landschaft und ihre wundersame und sehnsuchtsweckende Wirkung sich mit Tolkiens Schilderung vergleichen lassen. Wenn es bei MacDonald heißt »Fairy Land lay before me, and drew me towards it with **irresistible attraction**«, dann wäre dies auch eine adäquate Beschreibung von Eriols Erleben. Auch der Zaubergarten Eldamars ist *Fairy Land* – Feenland.

Man kann demnach feststellen und könnte dies anhand zahlreicher anderer Werke der klassischen Fantasy wie z.B. Lord Dunsanys *Die Königstochter aus Elfenland* näher ausführen, dass die Sehnsucht des Sterblichen nach Feenland auf den Kern des Romantischen in der Phantastik verweist. Diese Verzückung durch Feenland ist im *Buch der verschollenen Geschichten* bei Tolkien noch sehr stark und, wie deutlich geworden ist, ein wesentliches Element der Geschichte.

In seinen späteren Hauptwerken treffen wir viel seltener auf solch dezidiert ausgearbeitete romantische Situationen. Die Elben haben ihre Rolle als Vermittler zwischen dem Transzendenten und dem Alltäglichen jedoch bewahrt und sind entsprechend auch im *Herrn der Ringe* immer noch in der Lage, die Sterblichen zu verzaubern. Eriols Gefühl eines großen Wunders und sein Eindruck, im elbischen Eiland eine neue und schöne Welt betreten zu haben, lässt sich auch auf die Gefährten in Lothlórien übertragen, die dort – salopp gesprochen – aus dem Staunen nicht mehr herauskommen. Auch sie sind in diesem Moment Romantiker im Feenland.

Bibliographie

Beil, Ulrich. »Phantasie«. *Historisches Wörterbuch der Rhetorik*. Hg. Gert Ueding. Bd. 6. Tübingen: Max Niemeyer, 2003. 927-943

Böckmann, Paul. »Klang und Bild in der Stimmungslyrik der Romantik«. *Gegenwart im Geiste. Festschrift R. Benz*. Hg. Walther Bulst u. Arthur v. Schneider. Hamburg 1954. 103-125

Eichendorff, Joseph v. *Ausgewählte Werke*. Hg. Paul Stapf. Wiesbaden: Emil Vollmer o. J.

Eilmann, Julian. »Romantische Sehnsucht im Werk J.R.R. Tolkiens«. *Hither Shore* 8 (2011): 242-252

Hoffmeister, Gerhard. »Forschungsgeschichte« [der Romantik]. *Romantik-Handbuch*. Hg. Helmut Schanze. Stuttgart: Kröner, 1994. 177-206

Korff, Hermann August. *Geist der Goethezeit. Versuch einer ideellen Entwicklung der klassisch-romantischen Literaturgeschichte*. Bd. 3. Leipzig: Koehler & Amelang, 1959

MacDonald, George. *Phantastes – A Faerie Romance*. http://www.gutenberg.org/files/325/325-h/325-h.htm

Novalis. *Schriften. Die Werke Friedrich von Hardenbergs*. Hg. Paul Kluckhohn u. Richard Samuel. Bd. 2. Stuttgart: Kohlhammer, 1960

---. *Werke in zwei Bänden*. Bd. 1. Hg. Rolf Toman. Köln: Könemann, 1996

Uhland, Ludwig. »Über das Romantische«. *Ludwig Uhland Werke*. Hg. Hans-Rüdiger Schwab. Bd. 2. Frankfurt, 1983

Tolkien, J.R.R. *The Book of Lost Tales*. Hg. Christopher Tolkien. (*The History of Middle-earth* 1 u. 2) London: HarperCollins, 2002

---. *The Lord of the Rings*. London: HarperCollins, 1995

Zeltner, Hermann. »Johann Gottlieb Fichte«. *Neue deutsche Biographie*. Hg. v. der Historischen Kommission bei der Bayerischen Akademie der Wissenschaften. Bd. 5. Berlin: Duncker & Humblot, 1971. 122-125

Landscape as Metaphor in *The Lord of the Rings*

Thomas Kullmann (Osnabrück)

Many readers of *The Lord of the Rings* are bewildered by the prominence and length of the book's landscape descriptions. If we enjoy reading about elves, dwarves, wizards and orcs; if we like to follow our favourite characters on dangerous quests, to witness chivalric valour and to wonder about the eternal warfare of good and evil, we may fancy that landscapes belong to a different kind of book. In fact the motifs mentioned go back to a variety of literary traditions, including ancient English and Scandinavian epic, medieval romance, folktale and fairy tale, and nineteenth-century children's literature. What all of these traditions or genres have in common is that landscapes do not feature in any remarkable way. If we place LotR in a category called "Fantasy" (as opposed to "realism") landscape certainly constitutes an alien element.

Landscapes, in fact, are central to mainstream nineteenth-century and early-twentieth-century realistic writing. They feature prominently in the novels by many of those authors who have been 'canonised' by late nineteenth- and early-twentieth-century scholars of English literature: the Brontë Sisters, Charles Dickens, Thomas Hardy, D.H. Lawrence. All of these authors provide ample descriptions of the rural (and sometimes urban) landscapes in which their novels are set: Yorkshire, London and environs, Wessex, Nottinghamshire. The tradition can be traced back to the Gothic novelists, most prominently Ann Radcliffe and Charles Robert Maturin, who sometimes give ample space to descriptions of sublime views of areas they have never seen, although they may have read about them: such as the Alps, the Pyrenees and the Apennine mountains (e.g. Radcliffe 27-48, 163-171, 224-229), and even an island off the coast of India (Maturin 272-281). The rise of this tradition certainly ties in with the emergence of tourism and travel accounts but can also be traced to some literary antecedents in the field of lyric and epic poetry, most notably Milton's *Paradise Lost* (cf. Kullmann, *Natur* 65-69). But there are hardly any examples earlier than that. Altogether the tradition is not an old one: obviously readers require a good deal of cultural training to take an interest in visual impressions based on the interplay of landscape, weather, time of year, and time of day.

Landscape description can thus be considered an integral part of so-called 'realistic' writing. It relates to the readers' own experience in a metonymic—as opposed to metaphoric—way, as landscapes are contiguous, rather than similar, to their own experiences.[1] Having said that, however, my next proposition

---

1 The dichotomy of metaphoric and metonymic narration goes back to Roman Jakobson, "Two Aspects of Language". Concerning the use of this dichotymy as an instrument of

may appear paradoxical: landscape description in authors like Ann Radcliffe, the Brontë Sisters, Thomas Hardy, and D.H. Lawrence obviously does not just serve the usual ends of realistic description, i.e. providing protagonists with a 'real-life' background and determining their social conditions. Almost invariably, landscapes assume other, i.e. metaphoric, functions: in Radcliffe (following Jean-Jacques Rousseau, cf. Kullmann, *Natur* 118), the most prominent one is that of providing a link to the deity or "Great First Cause" (*Mysteries* 114).

God in the age of enlightenment is manifested in His works rather than in Scripture. Characters in observing and admiring the sublimity of sunset, twilight, and moonshine or the glorious cliffs of the Alpine mountains arrive at a notion of divinity. Moreover, by admiring the sublimity of nature, the characters prove their own moral excellence, in opposition to people preferring the atmosphere of metropolitan opera houses and gambling-tables to the pure air of the Alps. Sometimes, however, the notion of nature's sublimity mingles with the function of providing a parallel to a character's situation and feelings, as with Emily St. Aubert in Radcliffe's *Mysteries of Udolpho* (cf. Kullmann, *Natur* 139-143):

> At length, the travellers began to ascend among the Apennines. The immense pine-forests, which, at that period, overhung these mountains, and between which the road wound, excluded all view but of the cliffs aspiring above, except that, now and then, an opening through the dark woods allowed the eye a momentary glimpse of the country below. The gloom of these shades, their solitary silence, except when the breeze swept over their summits, the tremendous precipices of the mountains, that came partially to the eye, each assisted to raise the solemnity of Emily's feelings into awe; she saw only images of gloomy grandeur, or of dreadful sublimity, around her; other images, equally gloomy and equally terrible, gleamed on her imagination. She was going she scarcely knew whither, under the dominion of a person, from whose arbitrary disposition she had already suffered so much ... (224)

In Victorian novels, such as Brontë's *Wuthering Heights* and Hardy's *Tess of the d'Urbervilles*, landscapes invariably characterise the protagonists and their interactions, visualising their mental conditions and providing a commentary on what happens. When, in *Wuthering Heights*, Heathcliff, sixteen-year-old Catherine's intimate friend, disappears, the house is struck by a thunderstorm:

---

literary scholarship cf. Kullmann, Kinder- und Jugendliteratur 21-23; Patterns 50-54, and Meaning..

> About midnight, while we still sat up, the storm came rattling over the Heights in full fury. There was a violent wind, as well as thunder, and either one or the other split a tree off at the corner of the building; a huge bough fell across the roof, and knocked down a portion of the east chimney-stack, sending a clatter of stones and soot into the kitchen fire. (84)

The storm parallels Catherine's agitation about Heathcliff's disappearance and provides a visual correlative to her mental state (cf. Kullmann, *Natur* 315-318).

In Romantic and Victorian novels, nature can interact with the characters in various ways: characters experience pleasure when looking at landscapes; landscapes can influence characters (e.g. by "soothing" them when in trouble, e.g. in *The Mysteries of Udolpho* 367); a character can feel at home in a certain natural environment; a character 'interprets' nature in a particular and subjective way; landscape and nature can mirror the plot, i.e. the characters' interactions. Descriptions of nature thus become, as Hillis Miller points out in connection with Emily Brontë's *Wuthering Heights*, "a major resource of figurative language by means of which the quality of people and of their relations are defined" (445).

As I argue in my book *Vermenschlichte Natur* (Nature Humanized), the relationship between landscape and weather descriptions and the interpersonal plots can be defined as a syntactic as well as a functional relationship (esp. 18, 161-164, 469). Certain signals, including personification and parallelism, connect a landscape and weather phenomenon to a human predicament; this connection then serves a function such as characterization, commentary or psychological analysis. A simplified version of this narrative mode of 'landscape as metaphor' might be given as follows:

interaction of nature and characters	metaphoric functions of landscape
(syntactic relationship)	(functional relationship)
viewing, perceiving	providing a link to the deity
influence	characterization
parallelism	analysis of mental condition, mood
personification	narrator's warning/ commentary

Basically any of the syntactic relationships enumerated in the left-hand column can go with any of the functions mentioned in the right-hand column.

On the level of the plot, the coincidence of weather phenomenon and human disposition is invariably an accidental one; it has been arranged by the author for the purposes of narrative. While it may be within the boundaries of verisimilitude that a thunderstorm may strike the Yorkshire moors at a certain time of year, the coincidence of the storm and a crisis among the main characters is not motivated by any logical connection. The meteorological conditions, such as sunshine or storms, do not feel or sympathise with the characters, even though these characters (and inexperienced readers) sometimes believe they do. This narrative technique can be compared to what John Ruskin called "pathetic fallacy", i.e. the habit of poets to ascribe emotions, i.e. their own emotions, to plants, winds, waves, and celestial bodies (5: 201-219).

I'd like to suggest that some of the landscape descriptions in *The Lord of the Rings* operate in the same ways and fulfil similar functions, e.g. the descriptions accompanying the boat journey down "the Great River", where the landscape can be interpreted as a visualisation of mental states of the 'questants'. After taking leave of Celeborn and Galadriel, Frodo and his companions find themselves in an environment rather different from the cosy and protective woods of Lórien:

> So the Company went on their long way, down the wide hurrying waters, borne ever southwards. Bare woods stalked along either bank, and they could not see any glimpse of the lands behind. The breeze died away and the River flowed without a sound. No voice of bird broke the silence. The sun grew misty as the day grew old, until it gleamed in a pale sky like a high white pearl. Then it faded into the West, and dusk came early, followed by a grey and starless night. Far into the dark quiet hours they floated on, guiding their boats under the overhanging shadows of the western woods. Great trees passed by like ghosts, thrusting their twisted thirsty roots through the mist down into the water. It was dreary and cold. Frodo sat and listened to the faint lap and gurgle of the River fretting among the tree-roots and driftwood near the shore, until his head nodded and he fell into an uneasy sleep. (369f, II/8)

It is only towards the end of this paragraph that any direct pronouncement is made about a character's state of mind. This is when the narrator states that "it was dreary and cold" and that Frodo slept uneasily. At the beginning of the last sentence of this paragraph, Frodo emerges as a 'focaliser'. But it is difficult to decide on whether the experience described before refers to the nine companions in general or to Frodo in particular. It seems obvious, at any rate, that the point of view is a limited one: it is not just a fact that their way is a long one and that the hurrying waters are wide but it is also their perception. This perception obviously forms a parallel to the travellers' mental condition informed by the anticipation of a long and hard journey.

The companions' perception of their environment is conspicuously marked by absences: the woods are "bare" of leaves; no glimpse of the regions beyond them can be seen, there is no breeze, there is no sound; the effect of sunshine is limited; the night is grey and starless. The absence of objects perceptible by the senses of eyesight, hearing and touch appears to indicate the absence of those mental and physical comforts the travellers have now left behind. This effect is emphasised by the personifications present in the passage quoted: the woods are "stalking" on both sides of the river, the verb carrying the connotations of stealth, stiffness, haughtiness and menace. The breeze "dies away", while dusk "comes early"; trees are compared to ghosts; their roots are "thirsty", and trees forcefully try to assuage their thirst by "thrusting" their roots into the river, the river which is "fretting".

As in nineteenth- and early-twentieth-century novels, landscape descriptions serve to visualise the characters' states of mind. What matters more than the atmospheric conditions of this part of Middle-earth is the sense of desolation experienced by the travellers. If the landscape description does indeed serve to convey the characters' state of mind, this narrative technique can only work because of the literary tradition which makes use of it. In the passage quoted traditional descriptions of sunset and starlight which in Gothic novels and Romantic poetry indicate the observer's elevated thoughts and sublime emotions are inverted. Readers need to be aware of this tradition, consciously or intuitively, in order to make sense of this description.

The tradition referred to is that of the so-called 'mainstream' nineteenth-century novel. A parallel to the passage quoted might be found in Thomas Hardy's *Tess of the d'Urbervilles* (1891), a novel about the fortunes of a young woman living and working in a region in south-west England. After her beloved husband has abandoned her, Tess finds herself doing fieldwork at a place called Flintcomb-Ash:

> Here the air was dry and cold, and the long cart-roads were blown white and dusty within a few hours after rain. There were few trees, or none ... The stubborn soil around her showed plainly enough that the kind of labour in demand here was of the roughest kind ...   (*Tess* 356)

The landscape contrasts with the idyllic one of Talbothays Dairy where Tess had met the man with whom she fell in love and hoped to share her life. The change of landscape visualises Tess's experience for those readers who cannot immediately participate in her subjective emotions of both happy love and profound despair.

Other landscape passages in LotR can be interpreted similarly: when the hobbits have crossed the Water west of Hobbiton, "the night was clear, cool, and starry, but smoke-like wisps of mist were creeping up the hill-sides from the streams and deep meadows" (70, I/3), indicating that they are in good spirits although they are aware that their quest might be beset with mysteries. When moving on from Bree, the hobbits' increasing fears are mirrored by the landscape:

> The land before them sloped away southwards, but it was wild and pathless; bushes and stunted trees grew in dense patches with wide barren spaces in between. The grass was scanty, coarse, and grey; and the leaves in the thickets were faded and falling. It was a cheerless land, and their journey was slow and gloomy.
> (194, I/12)

Things brighten up when the travellers, after passing through the mountains of Moria, approach Lothlórien and come across a little stream:

> About it stood fir-trees, short and bent, and its sides were steep and clothed with harts-tongue and shrubs of whortle-berry. At the bottom there was a level space through which the stream flowed noisily over shining pebbles. (326, II/6)

The landscape is now characterised by its variety. Visual impressions mingle with auditory ones, and with the whortleberries even the sense of taste is appealed to. The stream's noise and the pebbles' shining correspond to the recovery of spirits by the travellers who are given the chance to rest after a stage beset by difficulties.

Similar observations apply to the journey which takes Aragorn, Legolas and Gimli to the Riders of Rohan (411-420, III/2) and, of course, to Frodo's and Sam's journey to Mordor where the difficulty of the undertaking is visualised by "impassable" cliffs and "livid, festering marshes" (589, IV/1). Landscapes appear to be there to be interpreted as outside signs of an inward, or mental, state. Sometimes an interpretation of the scenery is provided in the text itself, as when Sam crosses the river west in the Ferry: "He [Sam] had a strange feeling as the slow gurgling stream slipped by: his old life lay behind in the mists, dark adventure lay in front" (97, I/5).

We see that in LotR, as in nineteenth-century realist novels, landscape and weather phenomena coincide with the plot on the level of the characters; and in the passages quoted this coincidence appears to be an accidental one, just as in novels like *Wuthering Heights* or *Tess of the d'Urbervilles*. The notion that "when it comes to modern writers, Tolkien was notoriously beyond influence", as Tom Shippey maintained in *The Road to Middle-earth* (225), should evidently be re-examined.

At the same time, I should like to contend that in Tolkien's fantasy setting the relationship between plot, characters, and landscapes can take more intimate forms. As an example I should like to quote a passage which describes the travelling hobbits' experience of twilight, set after their first encounter with a Black Rider and immediately before their first meeting with elves:

> Twilight was about them as they crept back to the lane. The West wind was sighing in the branches. Leaves were whispering. Soon the road began to fall gently but steadily into the dusk. A star came out above the trees in the darkening East before them. They went abreast and in step, to keep up their spirits. After a time, as the stars grew thicker and brighter, the feeling of disquiet left them, and they no longer listened for the sound of hoofs. They began to hum softly ... (75f, I/3)

This description of twilight can be compared to similar descriptions in Ann Radcliffe's Gothic novels, where the experience of twilight also serves to elevate the travellers' feelings. The cluster of personifications, however, appears to correspond to the hobbits' entering a new world altogether, a world foreign to them and characterised by unknown dangers as well as fabulous comforts. The description of the nightly landscape introduces the world of the elves; when they approach the elves' resting-place "the woods on either side bec[o]me denser" (80, I/3); the stars are now given Elvish names:

> Away high in the East swung Remmirath, the Netted Stars, and slowly above the mists red Borgil rose, glowing like a jewel of fire. Then by some shift of airs all the mist was drawn away like a veil, and there leaned up, as he climbed over the rim of the world, the Swordsman of the Sky, Menelvagor with his shining belt. The Elves all burst into song. (80, I/3)

The hobbits' approach to the elves' place is accompanied by an intensification of the experience of the woody landscape and the starlit sky. The unique character of the experience of meeting the elves is given a correlative in the descriptions of nature.

When the companions of the fellowship begin to climb the mountains of Moria they are caught in a blizzard. This blizzard gradually changes its character. While it starts out as a 'normal' phenomenon which happens to accompany and illustrate the travellers' state of mind, it changes into a manifestation of forces which seem to deliberately oppose Frodo's and Gandalf's quest:

> While they were halted, the wind died down, and the snow slackened until it almost ceased. They tramped on again. But they had not gone more than a furlong when the storm returned with fresh fury. The wind whistled and the snow became a blinding blizzard. Soon even Boromir found it hard to keep going. The hobbits, bent nearly double, toiled along behind the taller folk, but it was plain that they could not go much further, if the snow continued. Frodo's feet felt like lead. Pippin was dragging behind. Even Gimli, as stout as any dwarf could be, was grumbling as he trudged.
> The Company halted suddenly, as if they had come to an agreement without any words being spoken. They heard eerie noises in the darkness round them. It may have been only a trick of the wind in the cracks and gullies of the rocky wall, but the sounds were those of shrill cries, and the wild howls of laughter. Stones began to fall from the mountain-side, whistling over their heads, or crashing on the path beside them. Every now and again they heard a dull rumble, as a great boulder rolled down from hidden heights above.
> 'We cannot go further tonight,' said Boromir. 'Let those call it the wind who will; there are fell voices on the air; and these stones are aimed at us.'
> 'I do call it the wind,' said Aragorn. 'But that does not make what you say untrue. There are many evil and unfriendly things in the world that have little love for those that go on two legs, and yet are not in league with Sauron, but have purposes of their own. Some have been in this world longer than he.'
> 'Caradhras was called the Cruel, and had an ill name,' said Gimli, 'long years ago, when rumour of Sauron had not been heard in these lands.' (281f, II/3)

The first paragraph contains parallelism between landscape and character as was conventional to the nineteenth-century novel: The wind's fury depicts the travellers' toil on their arduous journey, with the physical inconveniences representing a mental state. The second paragraph features "eerie noises", "shrill cries" and "wild howls of laughter".

In a realist novel these phrases would denote imaginative personifications of natural phenomena. In the passage quoted, however, Boromir seriously asks the question if an individual is responsible for nature's fury, such as Sauron, the arch-villain. Aragorn's interpretation is more sophisticated: he connects a natural explanation with the concept of nature as endowed with a soul. Objects such as mountains can be friendly or unfriendly towards humans, hobbits, elves or dwarves. This corresponds to the memory of the mountain's 'cruelty' adduced by Gimli the dwarf, which certainly constitutes a magical and primitive concept of nature.

As with the hobbits approaching the elves, nature descriptions prepare the readers for the characters' encounter with the unknown, with elements of fantasy neither characters nor readers have met with before.

Finally, I would like to refer once more to the companions' journey down the Great River, which began with the sense of desolation and accompanying scenery discussed before. The scenery then undergoes a change, which, however, does not have a soothing effect on the travellers but introduces them to a new environment, both unfamiliar and scary:

> The weather was still grey and overcast, with wind from the East, but as evening drew into night the sky away westward cleared, and pools of faint light, yellow and pale green, opened under the grey shores of cloud. There the white rind of the new Moon could be seen glimmering in the remote lakes. Sam looked at it and puckered his brows.
> The next day, the country on either side began to change rapidly. The banks began to rise and grow stony. Soon they were passing through a hilly rocky land, and on both shores there were steep slopes buried in deep brakes of thorn and sloe, tangled with brambles and creepers. Behind them stood low crumbling cliffs, and chimneys of grey weathered stone dark with ivy; and beyond these again there rose high ridges crowned with wind-writhen firs. They were drawing near to the grey hill-country of the Emyn Muil, the southern march of Wilderland. (375f, II/9)

Like the passages discussed before, this description introduces an encounter with creatures strange and frightening. This time it is orcs (377, II/9), who will indeed soon contribute to the dissolution of the company and the dispersal of its members. In the meantime, however, another intensification of fear caused by nature leads up to the revelation of another world as strange to the hobbits as it is to the readers:

> Sheer rose the dreadful cliffs to unguessed heights on either side. Far off was the dim sky. The black waters roared and echoed, and a wind screamed over them. Frodo crouching over his knees heard Sam in front muttering and groaning: 'What a place! What a horrible place! Just let me get out of this boat, and I'll never wet my toes in a puddle again, let alone a river!'

> 'Fear not!' said a strange voice behind him. Frodo turned and saw Strider, and yet not Strider; for the weatherworn Ranger was no longer there. In the stern sat Aragorn son of Arathorn, proud and erect, guiding the boat with skilful strokes; his hood was cast back, and his dark hair was blowing in the wind, a light was in his eyes: a king returning from exile to his own land. (383f, II/9)

As in the previous examples, extraordinary nature phenomena introduce a new area of experience; what happens here, however, is not an encounter with strange creatures (as with elves, mountain monsters or orcs) but a recognition, as Strider sheds his identity as lonesome ranger or scout and assumes that of a king. The cliffs, the black waters and the wind illustrate the strangeness of this transformation, as does the archaic imperative: "Fear not!" (which may, of course, remind us of Luke 2.10). The world of warlike heroism connected with Aragorn is as remote from the world of the hobbits as are the elves and the mountain monsters.

Tolkien makes use of the nineteenth-century novelistic device of landscape as metaphor and adapts it to a context informed by fantasy. One of the purposes of his landscape descriptions appears to be to introduce transitions to fantastic environments. Rather than stepping over a threshold into the world of the elves, the travellers as well as the readers are gradually prepared for it by nature phenomena which appear increasingly metaphoric. The narrative device of metaphoric landscape obviously establishes a link between the 'real world' and the worlds of fantasy, and thus enables the readers to suspend disbelief in the fantastic world. Moreover, the metaphoric quality of landscape descriptions ties in easily with the metaphoric character of LotR in general. As I argue in my article on "Metaphorical and Metonymical Meaning in *The Lord of the Rings*", Frodo's quest, Aragorn's kingship, the end of Sauron, and the elves' departure can be interpreted as referring to real life in a metaphoric way. Landscapes and their figurative meanings partake of this metaphoric narrative and may thus provide hints as to the interpretation of the fantasy motifs attached to them.

Bibliography

The Bible: Authorized King James Version. Eds. Robert Carroll & Stephen Prickett. Oxford: Oxford University Press, 1997

Brontë, Emily. *Wuthering Heights*. Ed. Ian Jack. Oxford: Oxford University Press, 1995

Hardy, Thomas. *Tess of the d'Urbervilles*. Ed. David Skilton. Harmondsworth: Penguin, 1978

Jakobson, Roman. "Two Aspects of Language and Two Types of Aphasic Disturbances." *Selected Writings, vol. 2: Word and Language*. Den Haag, Paris: Mouton, 1971, 239-259

Kullmann, Thomas. *Englische Kinder- und Jugendliteratur: Eine Einführung*. Berlin: Erich Schmidt, 2008

---. "Intertextual Patterns in J.R.R. Tolkien's *The Hobbit* and *The Lord of the Rings*". *Nordic Journal of English Studies* 8.2 (2009): 37-56 (http://ojs.ub.gu.se/ojs/index.php/njes/article/viewRST/338/335)

---. "Metaphorical and Metonymical Meaning in *The Lord of the Rings*". *Transitions and Boundaries in the Fantastic* Eds. Christine Lötscher et al. Zurich: LIT, 2014: 53-62

---. *Vermenschlichte Natur: Zur Bedeutung von Landschaft und Wetter im englischen Roman von Ann Radcliffe bis Thomas Hardy*. Tübingen: Niemeyer, 1995

Maturin, Charles Robert. *Melmoth the Wanderer*. Ed. Douglas Grant. Oxford: Oxford University Press, 1989

Miller, J. Hillis. "Nature and the Linguistic Moment". *Nature and the Victorian Imagination*. Eds. U.C. Knoepflmacher & G.B. Tennyson. Berkeley, Ca.: University Press, 1977, 440-451

Radcliffe, Ann. *The Mysteries of Udolpho*. Ed. Bonamy Dobrée. Oxford: Oxford University Press, 1980

Ruskin, John. *Works*. London: George Allen, 1903-1912

Shippey, Tom. *The Road to Middle-earth*. London: George Allen & Unwin, 1982

Tolkien, John Ronald Reuel. *The Lord of the Rings*. London: HarperCollins, 2002

The Influence of medieval Storytelling, and more particularly of *Sir Degaré*, on Tolkien's Portrayal of the Wilderness in *The Lord of the Rings*

Tatjana Silec (Paris)

In a review for the *Times Literary Supplement* published after the release of *The Two Towers* by Peter Jackson, Thomas Shippey suggested that Tolkien's "narrative structures" were "part of his world view". This remark holds true for his view on literature as well. Thus, while the influence of Old English literature has long been recognised in Tolkien's works, together with that of Scandinavian sagas or the Finnish *Kalevala*, on a formal as well as a thematic level[1], it has taken a little more time for scholars to recognise other influences: Classical mythology or Celtic folklore, for instance, mainly because Tolkien's professed dislike of them. As far as English medieval literature is concerned, we all know that Tolkien's heart went to the poets who aimed at reviving the native tradition of alliterative verse, like the anonymous author of *Sir Gawain and the Green Knight*, rather than to those who tried to mimic Continental prosody and vocabulary; but we also know that he could make an exception (or two, or three) of course: after all, Tolkien translated *Sir Orfeo*, which is a short romance in the style of the *Lais de Marie de France* (even though his translation was published only after his death by his son).—And judging from his poems, he liked rhyming couplets!

What I will try to show in this paper is that Tolkien did not find his inspiration for his depiction of the wilderness in LotR in the best works of Middle English literature only, but that he also lifted some elements from minor works, for instance *Sir Degaré*, a romance he must have known since it is found in the same manuscript as *Sir Orfeo* and which contains a passage from which Tolkien might have part of his inspiration for the hobbits' adventures in the Old Forest and later in the Barrow-downs, and more precisely for his representation of the wild as something that is not just a place one might have to go through, but as something that can crop upon one unawares, at certain times, much like the Old Man Willow. I will also try to show that while much has been made, and justly so, of Tolkien's love of *Gawain and the Green Knight*, his storytelling

---

1 Even though, as Carl Phelpstead remarks, most scholars have focused on the "thematic connections" and overlooked the "formal" ones, an oversight which his own paper goes toward correcting as far as the Scandinavian sagas and their "mixing of verse and prose" are concerned (23).

owed at least as much to the tried techniques of the anonymous authors of popular medieval romances like *Sir Degaré* for instance, whose audience would not always have been particularly cultured, as to the refined and extremely gifted Gawain-poet who lived at a time when orality was slowing giving way to literacy,—romances were beginning to be composed with a reader in mind as well as a listener, so that their authors had to be able to please both.

Anyone who has ever heard extracts of LotR, read out loud by a professional storyteller knows that Tolkien did that as well, probably intentionally given the prominent place given to oral literature in LotR, in which, among Elves and Men alike, many works of literature seem to have begun as lays. Lays were poems meant to be sung, which may later be written down by the people who heard it, with the imperfections which later recollection might entail (we have one good example in the first book, when Sam sings Bilbo's rendition of the *Fall of Gil-galad* but has to stop after a few stanzas because he has forgotten the rest (185-186). In fact, LotR as whole may be seen as a "written version of the Song of Nine-Fingered Frodo sung by the bard at Cormallen" (Prozesky, 22; one may also see Blaszkiewicz on the topic).

When telling a story to a listening audience, there is one basic rule: the people who are listening be able to follow the story without having to concentrate too much. This means that in a language based on word order—and English had become such a language by the time lays began to be composed—it is safer to keep such word order simple; it also helps to use stock-phrases at appropriate times, to make it easier for the audience to identify the characters and follow the action, especially if your audience is not paying attention,—and we know this must have been the case given the number of addresses to the audience, asking them to be quiet and listen to the tale, that pepper Middle English romances! The result is an extremely compact kind of storytelling in most Middle English romances, which often focus on action rather than description, for in that type of poem, the depiction of the setting must be brief, lest the audience lose track of the main story. Most romances are pretty straightforward in that respect: their protagonists are usually on a quest, which means that they are on the move all the time. When they stop, for whatever reason, the narrator or poet then gives some information on the scenery, usually from the point of view of the protagonist (at least in the later romances). Action generally follows the description of the surroundings, and the two rarely mingle, unless they are one and the same[2].

The description of a natural landscape usually remains very sketchy in a romance: the protagonist may see a pavilion in a meadow, or may come by a ford, or even stop under a tree to eat something. Most of the time it only

---

2   As is the case when Nature itself becomes the enemy, something which occurs regularly in Tolkien's Middle-earth, especially in the forest or in the mountains.

takes a couple of lines at most for the poet to set the scene, and there is rarely more than one modifier attached to the nouns that appear in the description, which is often little more than a formula. Of course, Tolkien's descriptions of landscapes[3] are much more detailed than your average medieval romances, and there are none of the incongruities one finds in medieval romances[4]. However, as is the case in the romances, they are often kept to the minimum, contrary to what may be observed in most of the more recent works of fantasy, in which the writers seem to think that they must describe everything in minute detail.

As Steve Walker showed in the book he devoted to Tolkien's prose, the "velocity" of which he says is much to be admired (88)[5], Tolkien invites the reader to fill in the landscapes he sketches with elements taken from his or her own experience (8); indeed "despite all the detail he puts in, Tolkien leaves more out" (93); a technique which "fits well with Tolkien's personal and literary concern that things should grow naturally" (94). But what Tolkien also does, just like the medieval composers of the lays and romances, is allow us to see the landscape through the eyes of his protagonists, who are on a journey[6] and who, most of the time, are only scanning their surroundings to find the safer, shorter route from A to B; it shows in the straightforward manner of the description, and explains why the description of a particular landscape usually precedes any kind of action (and here I mean any other action than the simple act of moving on). Usually the time of day also figures in the description, for the same reason. Here are two examples taken at random from the first book of LotR:

> The sun had gone down red behind the hills at their backs, and evening was coming on before they came back to the road at the end of the long level over which it had run straight for some miles. At that bent it bent left and went down into the lowlands of the Yale making for Stock; but a lane branched right, winding through a wood of ancient oak-trees on its way to Woodhall.
>
> (77)

---

3 I should probably say here that there are different types of description of landscapes in LotR: the vista—in which a character sees the landscape from a vantage point and is therefore able to see much further than is generally possible; the brief description of a place as the scene of action, and the longer one, usually when the place itself is the source of action (and most often than not dangerous). While the first type of description is rarely found in medieval works of fiction (exceptions that come to mind would be the description of the fairy castle in *Sir Orfeo* or that of the castle of Lady Fame in Chaucer's *House of Fame*), the other two are, which is why this discussion will not include the vista.
4 ...In which faraway places are often portrayed as being exactly like England or France (cf. Bevis of Hampton, for instance.)
5 And is found in medieval romances as well, one might add, with their quasi-absence of punctuation and quick sequences of action.
6 Walker devotes a whole chapter in his book ("The Road goes ever on an on") to the concept of the journey in Tolkien's work, from which the quotations above are extracted.

> They found a passage between two hills that led them into a valley
> running south-east, the direction that they wished to take; but
> towards the end of the day they found their road again barred
> by a ridge of high land; its dark edge against the sky was broken
> into many bare points like teeth of a blunted saw.
>
> (p. 203)

In most medieval romances, the general movement of the story, which closely follows the tribulations of the main character so that the poet is like an invisible servant dogging the footsteps of his master, remains the same. The purpose of the descriptions that are interspersed in the narrative also does, which is to allow the audience to realise what kind of space the hero(ine) has entered, and what (s)he is to expect in it: either solace and comfort, or danger and deceit. In medieval terms, this usually translates as being in a civilised environment, one that bears the mark of man, or at least in an open space, which allows you to see your enemy form afar.

This explains why adventures of the kind pursued by the knight-errant happen in the wild, a territory which is heralded in various ways in the poems: either by way of a stock-phrase that introduces an element only found in such a landscape: an "old" (or "deep", or "thick") "forest" ("holtes hore", *Sir Orfeo*, l. 214, p. 31; "holtwodez", *Gawain, Passus II*, p. 20), "high fells" (*Gawain, ibid*), the moor ("heth", *Lay le Freine*, l. 147, p. 72), or simply, by use of the modifier "wild" before any given noun. Even in *Gawain and the Green Knight*, in which descriptions of the Welsh country Gawain goes through on his way to the Green Chapel are detailed enough to allow the audience to understand that the hero has left civilisation, this word occurs regularly.

Each time it serves as a signal that Gawain is going to have an adventure, or even a series of adventures: in this poem, an adventure of the lesser kind (i.e. the fight with a monster or an enemy knight), which is not told in detail and merely serves as a reminder that Gawain is the best of Arthur's knights and that the wilderness is a dangerous place, where you will have to fight for your life, not just because wild beasts abound, but also because the weather itself can kill you. This kind of danger is not taken lightly by the poet, who tells us that Gawain feared the cold season, "[f]or were wrathed hym not so much þat winter nas wors" ("For war did not worry him as much as winter, which was worse", *Passus II*, p. 21), and then moves onto a vivid description of the knight shivering in his armour in the icy rain.

Generally speaking, the people of Middle-earth interact with their environment in ways that are defined by the nature of that environment, like the men and women of the Middle Ages, who were not protected from its effects the way we are today. In *The Lord of the Rings* the wilderness too is as a testing ground for heroes, knights and rangers and hobbits alike[7], as several scholars have shown over the years. A brief summary of what has already been said about the wilderness by J.S. Ryan and others will suffice here.

As J.S. Ryan shows, while the wilderness, and especially the forest, is the obvious *locus* for the adventures of a knight-in-armour, the landscapes that fall in that category can be more or less undomesticated, and therefore, more or less dangerous (*Nameless* 9 and 22f; *Wild* 219f); there are degrees, which can be more or less apparent, and this, of course, mirrors the experience that medieval men and women had of their environment: while high mountains and moors were considered inhospitable and therefore mostly left untouched, the forest for instance would not have been assimilated to a wild place *de facto*, as it was owned by the king and kept by his foresters and gamekeepers. It may have been dangerous, because of the odd encounter with a wolf, a boar, or a thief, but part of it at least was not really wild.

In many ways, in fact, it was only one step removed from the fields and orchards of the countryside, while the safest, most civilised landscape was that of the garden inside the walls of the castle. This being said, the forest can also be portrayed as a haven sometimes, for the Fellowship of the Ring and for the heroes and heroines of medieval romances alike: Frodo and his friends find shelter in the forest of Lothlórien, Tristan and Yseult hide their love in the forest, a wounded Lancelot is taken care of there by a saintly hermit, etc (Jardillier, 165). In LotR however, the forest-as-refuge, "havre de paix à l'abri des âges"[8] (Hoët, 225) is the domain of the Elves, for instance Galadriel whose benevolent influence is felt everywhere in her kingdom[9].

Humans and hobbits, on the other hand, do not make such a good job of taking care of their forests, since they mostly make them smaller by cutting trees down, which is why the Old Forest near Hobbiton is full of hate toward two-legged creatures; a feeling which Tom Bombadil later "lays bare", speaking of "the hearts of trees and their thoughts, which were often dark and strange, and filled with a hatred of things that go free upon the earth, gnawing, biting, breaking, hacking burning: destroyers and usurpers" (130).

Medieval knights are tried by their time in the wilderness just as much as they are by the monsters or enemies they meet there. For you do not remain civilised for long if you live in the wild: unless you are a hermit and protected by your faith and God. Foresters are always described as being close to wild

---

7 However, the weather is only rarely an enemy as fearsome as the winter Gawain worries about, unless it is made fouler by magic, as is the case when the Fellowship approaches Caradhras. This might reflect Tolkien's own experience, as British weather, while often wet and unfriendly, is only rarely deadly!
8 "A peaceful haven outside time and decay"
9 In medieval romances, the wild is usually represented as the natural habitat of fairies as well, but only because they are just as inhuman and, most often than not, savage.

beasts in medieval tales, and as such they count among the knight errant's natural foes, as Gawain or Tristan for instance both learn. This is mentioned in passing in *Gawain and the Green Knight*, where "wodwos" or "wild-men of the woods" (*Nameless* 24) appear alongside wolves, dragons and giants as the kind of beasts that the hero has to fight on his way to the Green Chapel (*Passus II* 20)[10], while Tristan is tormented by foresters during his episode of madness (which Malory includes in his *Morte Darthur*). In medieval texts, only mad men (or saints) desire to live in the woods, because madness and bestiality were closely associated in the romances. This finds a dim echo in LotR, when Merry contradicts Fredegar, who believes that no-one ever goes in the Old Forest by saying that "[t]he Brandybucks go in—occasionally when the fit takes them" (107; emphasis mine). Of course, the "fit" Merry alludes to is no more than a sudden impulse felt by a Brandybuck—a family notoriously famous in the Shire for being more than a little crazy—, but it mirrors, in a much lighter and less dramatic way, that of the mad knight whose frenzy takes him to the forest[11].

In the Middle Ages, a man or a woman who dwelt in the wild could therefore not be trusted; in *The Lord of the Rings*, one finds this kind of ingrained suspicion of "outlandish folk" (85) in the hobbits and the people of Bree. Verlyn Flieger, who studies Turin Túrambar and Gollum as prime examples of "Tolkien's wild men", includes Aragorn in her list, justifiably so, as, upon first meeting Aragorn (as Strider), even Frodo fears that "he had fallen in with a rascal" because of his strange looks and unkempt appearance (163), even though it is Sam who voices the strongest opposition to taking advice from the stranger, on the grounds that "[h]e comes out of the Wild, and I never heard no good of such folk" (165) (Flieger, *Wild*, 100-101; see also Ryan, *Nameless*, 6f). Hobbits like their surroundings to be in good order and neat, and people's general appearance to be the same. When they first come across Tom's patch of land after their misadventure with the Old Man Willow, what they notice right away, with obvious relief, is the fact that it is well looked after, and that nature there looks perfectly domesticated: "The grass under their feet was smooth and short, as if it had been mown or shaven. The eaves of the Forest behind were clipped, and trim as a hedge. The path was now plain before them, well-tended and bordered with stone" (121).

In the Middle Ages, especially towards the end of the period, the wilderness, which was objectively dangerous for many reasons, also became the symbol of other forces: forces that threatened civilisation from within and were almost always expressed in symbolic terms. To medieval men and women, especially

---

10 Shippey shows that these "woodwos" must have been the source of inspiration for his own wild men in his essay on the Tolkien and the *Gawain*-poet, as Honegger remarks (*Gawain* 550).
11 For instance Ywain, who, like a man possessed ("wilde and wode"; l. 1649-50) goes into the forest "als it wore a wilde beste" ("as if he were a wild beast", l. 1654).

of the higher sort, it was absolutely essential the people should tame the chaos that was always threatening to engulf civilisation from within and without.

The hobbits, with their instinctive dislike of strangers and of anything that lies beyond the borders of the Shire are quite similar. The difference between medieval literature and *The Lord of the Rings*, however, is of course that while the poets and writers of the romances all endorsed (or at least seemed to endorse) the general view regarding life in the wilderness and its negative influence on a man, Tolkien clearly takes a stand against it. His foresters are the Ents, not the Dunlendings, and they cannot do much more than try and mitigate the harm done by men on trees. Tolkien was writing after the Industrial Revolution; he had been through one World War and was witnessing a second when he wrote most of LotR. His landscapes are no longer metaphors of the old fight between chaos and order, they are affected by it. Wild Nature is not bad simply by virtue of being untamed. As Ryan says, his "neo-mediaeval and fable-like forests have become the century's great metaphor for the way mankind chooses to treat the world" (*Nameless* 29).

To sum up, if Tolkien borrowed many elements from medieval representations of the wilderness in general, he inserted these elements in an ethos that was resolutely at odds with the medieval view on nature. What I should like to do now, as an addendum to this study, is show that, while Tolkien undoubtedly derived many of these elements from the best Scandinavian sagas and English romances, such as *Gawain and the Green Knight* or *Sir Orfeo*, whose tremendous influence on Tolkien's fantasy writings has been studied[12], he also drew on some lesser works which are not as well known to readers for instance, *Sir Degaré*, another Breton lay of the *Auchinleck Manuscript*, and one which, despite not being as good in terms of form and content as *Sir Orfeo*—which was also compiled in the same book—, must have been very popular given the number of version that have come down to us.

The story of Degaré is of particular interest because in this text, it does not take much to cross the boundary between the forest as a safe environment and the forest as a wild place: leaving the road is enough and such is also the case in LotR, in which the protagonists are sometimes lulled into a false sense of security by the apparent harmlessness of their surroundings. This is nowhere more apparent than at the very beginning of the book, when the hobbits set on their trip and get lost in the Old Forest. The comparison between their adventures in the woods is worth making with what happens to one of the main characters in *Sir Degaré*. This romance begins as a Catskin Cinderella story: with a fair princess whose widowed father loves her a little too much. Every year, father and daughter go on a pilgrimage to the queen's grave, and the

---

12 See Honegger, *Gawain* for an overview of the text's importance, as well as his paper on *Sir Orfeo*..

road they take goes through a forest. At the beginning of the lay, they set out on their usual trip to the abbey where the queen is buried and, at first sight, it seems as though nothing bad could ever happen to the lady, surrounded as she is by her father's knights.

At some point during the journey however, the princess has to leave the road because she needs to relieve herself[13], and she takes a couple of ladies-in-waiting with her. Soon enough they are lost: "The wode was rough and thikke, iwis/ And thai token the wai amys"[14] but instead of turning back, they unwittingly go deeper into the woods: "Thai moste souht and riden west/Into the thikke of the forest" (ll. 61-62 and 63-64, p. 102)[15]. Their experience of the wood is quite similar to that of the hobbits once they leave the road for the Old Forest: "On the far side was a faint path leading up on to the floor of the Forest, a hundred yards and more beyond the Hedge; but it vanished as soon as it brought them under the trees... Looking ahead they could see only tree-trunks of innumerable sizes and shapes... all the stems were green or grey with moss and slimy, shaggy growths" (110-111). Very soon, they too find themselves going deeper into the forest rather than out: "They were being headed off, and were simply following a course chosen for them—eastward and southwards, into the heart of the forest and not out of it" (114).

The ladies in the forest in *Sir Degaré* soon begin to feel drowsy because of the heat and they fall asleep under a tree a little before noon: Degaré's mother is the only one who stays awake, but we are given to understand that she is under a spell that leads her further away from her companions (whose sleep is also unnatural, for they elected to rest under a chestnut tree,—an unfortunate choice as this tree was deemed to be magical in Celtic folklore):

> The weder was hot bifor the non;
> Hii leien hem doun upon a grene,
> Under a chastein tre, ich wene,
> And fillen aslepe everichone
> Bote the damaisele alone.
> She wente aboute and gaderede floures,
> And herknede song of wilde foules.

---

13 A very mundane reason indeed, which was probably chosen not only because it justified the lady leaving the road, but also because there was nothing out of the ordinary about it, making the appearance of the uncanny later on even more shocking and sudden. In LotR, while Tolkien never alludes to such issues, his hobbits spend a great deal of time talking about food and drink and the pleasures afforded by a comfortable bed, thus creating a realistic, down-to-earth background against which their encounters with the moving willow and the ghosts in the Barrow-downs stand out particularly vividly.
14 "the wood was overgrown and thick, I think/and they lost their ways"
15 "They rode west, into the heart of the forest". That they should go west is also of note, because in Celtic folklore, this is the direction one should take to go to Fairyland.

> So fer in the launde she goht, iwis,
> That she ne wot nevere whare se is.
> To hire maidenes she wolde anon.
> Ac hi ne wiste never wat wei to gon.[16]
>
> (ll. 73-82, p. 103)

In the Old Forest too, the weather turns hot, and the begin to feel sleepy (even though Tolkien first introduces this feeling, and its probably unnatural origins, by making it exude from the environment, rather than signalling the intrusion of magic the way the medieval—and not extremely gifted—composer of *Sir Degaré* does by mentioning the type of tree under which the ladies choose to take a nap):

> A golden afternoon of late sunshine lay warm and drowsy upon the hidden land between. In the midst of it there wound lazily a dark river of brown water, bordered with ancient willows[17], arched over with willows, blocked with fallen willows, and flecked with thousands of faded willow-leaves... there was a warm and gentle breeze blowing softly...   (115; emphasis mine)

Not soon after this, the hobbits fall asleep under (or rather against) the willow-tree which has magically appeared where they stopped, and which seems to be "singing about sleep" (117). They are saved from danger by Tom Bombadil; the lady in *Sir Degaré* is not so fortunate: she comes across a male fairy who rapes her before letting her go back to her ladies-in-waiting.

In another lay, *Sir Orfeo*, Heurodis also falls asleep under a tree (this time at midday and under a grafted tree), and then she has a terrible dream. In both lays, a tree works as a gateway to the uncanny, but the time at which the incident happens is noteworthy, for the land changes with the hour: there are periods of the day which are more dangerous than others, and night time is

---

16 "The weather was hot before noon;/They lay down on a green under a chestnut tree, I think,/and they all fell asleep,/except the young lady./She wandered away, gathering flowers/and listening to the song of wild birds./She went so far, indeed,/that she could not tell where she was./She wanted to go back to her ladies-in-waiting but did not know which way to go".

17 While the willow-tree was associated to the underworld in Greek and Roman mythology, and especially to Proserpina and Hecate, few people remember it now as having anything supernatural about it, unlike the chestnut tree or the rowan tree, so that its description would not tingle the reader's memory; instead, Tolkien chooses to repeat the name of the tree several times, and it is that repetition which, conjoined with all the adverbs and adjectives conveying an impression of general indolence and the soft alliterations of the passage, which convinces the reader that something is amiss. The whole passage is of course a lovely example of Tolkien's interest in "phonosemantics" (for more on the topic, see Smith).

not the worse, even though it may be the scariest[18]. The hobbits are kept awake by night-time noises on many occasions during their journey, but it is often around noon and toward the evening that danger lurks, especially, supernatural danger. This again is something that Tolkien might have derived from medieval literature and folklore: the "curious incident" (to use Flieger's expression) of the Barrow-downs with the ghosts is very similar to what happens to Heurodis, and in both cases it takes place in broad day-light, around noon, in a place that was deemed to be safe either because it was not far from civilization (the abbey, the garden) or because it was an open space, which traditionally in medieval romances, is a place where the knight can finally relax because he will see his enemies long before they can harm him.

To me therefore, the whole episode has as much to do with medieval romances, in which reincarnated beings sometimes crop up[19], as with the personal feelings Tolkien might have harboured on the concept of reincarnation itself and which Flieger studies in her paper (*Incident*, 99f).

Here again, it seems to me that he derived his inspiration from his knowledge of medieval literature, but rewrote it to make it fit his aim, which was to spin a good yarn, much like a medieval storyteller would have done.

Bibliography

Blaszkiewicz, Bartomiej. "Orality and Literacy in Middle-earth". *O what a Tangled Web. Tolkien and Medieval Literature: A View from Poland*. Ed. Barbara Kowalik, Zurich/Bern: Walking Tree Publishers, 2013

Flieger, Verlyn. "The Curious Incident of the Dream at the Barrow: Memory and Reincarnation in Middle-earth". *Tolkien Studies* 4 (2007): 99-112

---. "Tolkien's Wild Men: from medieval to modern". *Tolkien the Medievalist*. Ed. Jane Chance, 95-105

---. "'The Story of Kullervo' and essays on *Kalevala*". *Tolkien Studies* 7 (2010): 211-278

Friedman, John Block. "Eurydice, Heurodis and the Noon-Time demon". *Speculum* 41.1 (Jan. 1966), 22-29

Gay, David Elton. "J.R.R. Tolkien and the *Kalevala*: Some Thoughts on the Finnish Origins of Tom Bombadil and Treebeard". Ed. Jane Chance. *Tolkien and the Invention of Myth: A Reader*. Lexington: University Press of Kentucky, 2004, 295-304

Laurent Guyénot. *La mort féerique. Anthropologie du merveilleux XIIe –XVe siècle*. Paris: Gallimard, 2011

---

18 See Friedman's brilliant study of the reasons why people are more susceptible to be attacked by supernatural demons at certain times of the day.
19 For more on the topic, see Laurent Guyénot. *La mort féerique. Anthropologie du merveilleux XIIe–XVe siècle*. Paris: Gallimard, 2011, esp. p. 74f.

Hoët, Sébastien. "Forêts". *Dictionnaire Tolkien*. Ed. Vincent Ferré. Paris: CNRS Éditions, 2012, 224-226

Honegger, Thomas. "Fantasy, Escape, Recovery, and Consolation in *Sir Orfeo*: The Medieval Foundations of Tolkienian Fantasy". *Tolkien Studies* 7 (2010): 117-136

---. "Sire Gauvain et le Chevalier Vert". Ed. Vincent Ferré. *Dictionnaire Tolkien*. Paris: CNRS Editions, 2012, 548-551

Jardillier, Claire. "Les échos arthuriens dans Le Seigneur des Anneaux". *Tolkien et le Moyen-Âge*. Ed. Leo Carruthers. Paris : CNRS éditions, 2007, 143-169

Lay le Freine. *The Middle English Breton Lays*. Eds. Anne Laskaya & Even Salisbury. TEAMS. Kalamazoo: Western Michigan University, 2001, 61-87

Phelpstead, Carl. "With chunks of poetry in between": The Lord of the Rings and Saga Poetics. *Tolkien Studies* 5 (2008): 23-38

Prozesky, Maria . "The Text Tale of Frodo the Nine-fingered: Residual Oral Patterning in *The Lord of the Rings*". *Tolkien Studies* 3 (2006): 21-43

Ryan, J.S. "'The Nameless Wood' and 'The Narrow Path'". *In the Nameless Wood: Explorations in the Philological Hinterland of Tolkien's Literary Creations*. Cormarë Series n° 30, Zurich/Bern: Walking Tree Publishers, 2013, 3-33

----. "The Wild Wood—Place of Danger, Place of Protest". *In the Nameless Wood*. Op. cit. 219-234

Shippey, Tom A. "The Plot Unravels". *Times Literary Supplement*, 12-20-2002

---. "Tolkien and the Gawain-poet [1995]". *Roots and Branches: Selected Papers on Tolkien by Tom Shippey*. Ed. Thomas Honegger. Zurich/Bern: Walking Tree Publishers, 2007

Sir Degaré. The Middle English Breton Lays. Op. cit, 89-144

Sir Gawain and the Green Knight. Eds. J.R.R. Tolkien & E.V. Gordon. Revised by Norman Davis. Oxford: Oxford University Press, 1967. Electronic Text Center, University of Virginia (09-06-2014): http://www.luminarium.org/medlit/gawaintx.htm

Sir Orfeo. The Middle English Breton Lays. Op. cit, 15-59

Smith, Ross. "Fitting Sense to Sound: Linguistic Aesthetics and Phonosemantics in the Work of J.R.R. Tolkien". *Tolkien Studies* 3 (2006): 1-20

Stokoe, William C. Jr. "The Double Problem of Sir Degaré". PMLA 70:3 (June 1955). 518-534

Tolkien, John Ronald Reuel. *The Lord of the Rings*. 50th Anniversary Edition (based on the reset edition first published by HarperCollins, 1994), New York: Houghton Mifflin Company, 2004

Ywain and Gawain. Eds. Albert B. Friedman & Norman T. Harrington. London/New York/Toronto: Oxford University Press, 1964

Walker, Steve. *The Power of Tolkien's Prose. Middle-earth's Magical Style*. New York: Palgrave Macmillan, 2009

Man, Nature and Evil in *The Lord of the Rings* and *La saga de los Confines*

Natalia González de la Llana (Aachen)

1. Introduction

Nature, with its different landscapes and creatures, with its symbolism and the very special atmosphere in which the reader is introduced, plays, as we all know, an important role in Tolkien's *The Lord of the Rings*.

La saga de los Confines (*The Saga of the Borderlands*) by the Argentinian author Liliana Bodoc seems to give a similar importance to man's relationship to the natural world. Her fantasy novels take place, most of the time, in the Fertile Lands, which are invaded by troops coming from the Ancient Lands—a situation which reminds one strongly of precolombine America and its subsequent Spanish conquest.

Nature is not just a setting in these works, it is not only a space where events develop, but an essential feature that allows the reader to distinguish between good and bad characters.

In the following pages, we would like to analyze and compare the way in which both writers seem to establish a link between the concept of man's position in Nature, as it is presented in different characters and peoples, and their ethics. First of all, we will take a look at Tolkien's and Bodoc's protagonists' attitude towards their habitat and what this means in terms of moral values, and then we will focus on the relationship between evil and the natural.

2. Man's Relation to Nature

2.1 The Lord of the Rings

In *The Lord of the Rings* Tolkien's figures distinguish themselves, among other aspects, through their particular relationship to Nature. Elves are in this context the ones who show a better and deeper understanding of their environment, as they feel profoundly attached to trees and can communicate with animals. Hobbits love gardens and fields and they cultivate them with great care, while dwarfs, who live in mountain caves, are strongly connected to stones and ores, but have a different attitude towards the forest and its inhabitants, as their love for axes make them natural enemies of the trees.

Negative characters like the Orcs show an absolute lack of respect for Nature and, among Men and Wizards, we can also identify a contrast between those who feel near to it and those who despise it, Gandalf and Saruman being a clear example of this dualism.

In his study *Natur und Kultur in J.R.R. Tolkiens The Lord of the Rings*, Eike Kehr (31-38) points out how Nature has an indicator function in Tolkien's work, which enables the reader to come to conclusions about people and societies (like we see, for instance, in the White Tree of Gondor, closely tied to the king's destiny), but also serves as a sign, which only some characters are conscious enough to perceive (while the west wind is a herald of a happy turn of events, the east wind is usually a bad omen, which is why it blows constantly in Sauron's field of influence).

However, according to Kehr, Nature also appears as an expression of the charac-ters' emotional state, although it is not clear in most of the cases whether the external circumstances are really to be understood as the origin or the expression of the figure's feelings, but they both are shown as a unity anyway. On the other hand, Nature seems to be very alive in *The Lord of the Rings* and it even takes part in the events of the story, as is obvious with the Ents and the Eagles, and at the same time conveys a moral position, often according to the species (spiders are an example of evil creatures).

There is also a certain inherent connection between characters and landscapes, as Sam remarks when speaking about the Elves and Lothlórien: "… they seem to belong here, more even than Hobbits do in the Shire. Whether they've made the land, or the land's made them, it's hard to say" (LotR I 468). And we could add, following Tolkien's ideas, that man belongs to Nature, he is a part of it, but has no right to subjugate it. He must find a way to coexist with other living creatures in his environment without destroying it.

The consequences of the irresponsible use of unlimited power over Nature can be seen in Saruman, whose evil deeds will be finally punished by the Ents. Through modern science and technology, the world is no longer "magical". With the Hobbits, on the contrary, the reader has the possibility of perceiving the simple things of life as fascinating and full of wonder: mountains, caves and forests are regarded with awe and admiration by these characters, reminding us all of the beauty of our own world. This is the "recovery" Tolkien writes about in *On Fairy-stories*, i.e. the ability of seeing things afresh, of remembering what we, in the familiarity of our daily lives, have forgotten (Kehr 102-103).

The relationship to Nature is therefore no secondary aspect in *The Lord of the Rings*, but the sign of a "Daseinskonzept" as Christian Kölzer and Marcus Roso explain (182-184). The Elves, first born in the order of creation, have a special place in it and live in almost perfect accordance with the Being, which can be seen, for example, in their ability to communicate with other forms of existence (also plants, and even stones and rivers are thought of as animated in

Middle-earth). Men and other good creatures are somewhat further away from the ideal level of Being, and farthest away of all are the supporters of evil who either, like Sauron and Saruman, have disposed of all bonds with creation, or like the Orcs, represent themselves as the destructive perversion of it.

2.2 La saga de los Confines

Nature also plays an important role in Liliana Bodoc's *La saga de los Confines*, a trilogy that tells the story of Misáianes' attempt to conquer the Fertile Lands destroying all peoples and cultures who live therein. The first novel begins with a mystery: some ships from the Ancient Lands are coming through the Yentru Sea and nobody knows whether they are friends or enemies. Representatives from each folk have to attend a council in the city of Beleram where they will try to determine the foreigners' real purpose.

A message is sent, among others, to Dulkancellin, chosen to speak for the husihuilkes, and to Kupuka, the Earth Wizard. The latter explains how he got to receive the news:

> La noticia fue enviada por dos vías diferentes. Los mensajeros humanos anduvieron los senderos de la tierra, en tanto otros emisarios se movieron por caminos ajenos al hombre. Hasta mí llegaron los halcones. Fueron ellos los que me convocaron para referirme las novedades, más allá de la Puerta de la Lechuza. El día de la fiesta del Valle, bajé de la montaña y caminé hasta aquel sitio. Del otro lado del límite es posible entender sin reservas el lenguaje de los animales. Claro que es posible sólo para algunos.
> (Bodoc, *Venado* 58)[1]

This communication between men and animals appears more than once in Bodoc's novels, where not only animals, but also other natural elements like the wind become messengers. We get to see the direct intervention of Nature as a guide, as an interlocutor, or as an aid to help the people of the Fertile Lands against their cruel invaders.

Different creatures populate this imaginary continent, like the "lulus" with their long tails which they use as whips in battle, or "the animals with hair" brought to the Fertile Lands by the sideresios on their first arrival, and which

---

[1] The English translation of the quotes from *La saga de los Confines* is mine: The news was sent by two different means. The human messengers walked the land paths, while other emissaries moved through roads foreign to man. To me came the falcons. They were the ones that summoned me to recount the novelties beyond the Owl Gateway. On the day of the Valley's celebration, I went down the mountains and walked to that place. On the other side of the border, it is possible to understand without reservation the language of the animals. It is possible, of course, only for some.

are later used with great ability by the husihuilkes. This is, of course, a clear allusion to the horses brought to America during the Spanish conquest.

But there are also some hybrid beings in this world's creation. The Falcon Wizard was once Piukemán, Dulkancellin's son, who dared a transgression and was thus punished:

> El hombre que se aventurara a ver lo prohibido sería condenado en sus ojos. El Halcón Ahijador castigaba al hombre imprudente arrebatándole la vista. No para dejarlo en la oscuridad de la ceguera, sino para otorgarle la suya propia. A partir de ese momento, sin importar si tenía los ojos abiertos o cerrados, el hombre veía como el Halcón. Si el Halcón Ahijador devoraba su presa, el hombre veía un revoltijo de sangre. Y aunque apretara los ojos, lo seguía viendo. (Bodoc, *Venado* 203)[2]

In any case, wizards, men, animals are all part of a natural world which has to be respected and loved in all its forms. Magic was long ago divided into two groups: that of the Open Air and that of the Enclosure. The defendants of the latter believed that Magicians and their wisdom had to be kept above the creatures in order to take care of them from a higher position, while the Astronomers of the Open Air decided to stay close to all creatures and be their equal. This is, without doubt, the option that is defended in the novels and expressed with clarity by Kupuka:

> ... un brujo de los Confines no es más ni menos que un nogal; un nacimiento humano no es más ni menos que una floración, un Astrónomo escrutando las estrellas no es más ni menos que un pez desovando. El cazador no es más ni es menos que la presa que necesita para vivir; un hombre no es más ni es menos que el maíz que lo alimenta. Esto es lo que Zobralkán dijo; y es lo primordial. La Creación es una urdimbre perfecta. Todo en ello tiene su proporción y su correspondencia. Todo está hilado con todo en una trama infinita que no podrían reproducir ni mis amadas tejedoras del sur. Pobres de nosotros si olvidamos que somos un telar. Y que no importa dónde se corte el hilo, de allí Misáianes comenzará a tirar hasta deshacer el paisaje. (Bodoc, *Venado* 317)[3]

---

2 The man who ventured to see the forbidden would receive a punishment to his eyes. The Minister Falcon punished the unwise man by taking his vision away. Not to let him in the darkness of blindness, but to give him his own. From that moment on, no matter whether his eyes were open or closed, the man saw like the Falcon. If the Minister Falcon devoured his prey, the man saw a tripe of blood. And even if he pressed his eyes shut, he still saw it.

3 ... a wizard from the Borderlands is neither more nor less than a walnut tree; a human birth is neither more nor less than a flowering, an Astronomer scrutinizing the stars is neither more nor less than a spawning fish. The hunter is neither more nor less than the

Just like in *The Lord of the Rings*, the relationship that characters have towards Nature is therefore a sign of their personality and morals, and that is the reason why the husihuilkes with their simple life are the principal object of identification for the reader.

On the other end of the ethical scale, Misáianes, who never leaves the cold mountain in which he was born, creates the sideresios, beings that do not belong to the same species or speak the same language, and who have been deprived of pity or love, who have been fed on resentment, to become dutiful slaves of their master. His servant Drimus, a powerful wizard sent on a dark mission to the Fertile Lands, also breeds a pack of wild black hounds trained to kill. Evil's "creative power" is based on distortion and cruelty.

3. Evil and Nature
3.1 *The Lord of the Rings*

The landscapes where the dark forces are dominant in *The Lord of the Rings* are horrible places where nothing grows, where Nature has been destroyed and substituted, like in Isengard, by technological "progress", and where decent human labor has been exchanged for cruel slavery. The use of technology as a way of ruling over Nature and using its resources for egoistic purposes is clearly criticised in Tolkien's work through the figure of Saruman, whose lust for power makes him lose the right path:

> A strong place and wonderful was Isengard, and long it had been beautiful; and there great lords had dwelt, the wardens of Gondor upon the West, and wise men that watched the stars. But Saruman had slowly shaped it to his shifting purposes, and made it better, as he thought, being deceived-for all those arts and subtle devices, for which he forsook his former wisdom, and which fondly he imagined were his own, came but from Mordor… (LotR II 198-199)

Similar to Sauron, Saruman lives in an elevated location from where he can see the wasteland he has created. In the volcanic landscape of Mordor, the Dark Lord watches from his tower. Curiously enough, Bodoc's Misáianes also abides in a mountain from where he does not need to move to keep control over his dominions.

---

prey he needs to live on; a man is neither more nor less than the corn that feeds him. This is what Zobralkán said; and this is paramount. Creation is a perfect tannery. Everything in it has its proportion and its correspondence. All is spun with all in an infinite weft that could not be reproduced even by my beloved weavers from the south. Poor us, if we forget that we are a loom. And that it does not matter where the thread is cut, from there Misáianes will begin to pull until he has unpicked the landscape.

The mountain in its vertical form, close to the sky, participates in the symbolism of transcendence, but it can also be seen as a sign of man's delusions of grandeur and pretentiousness (Chevalier 645-649). The construction of a tower for Chevalier and Gheerbrant immediately evocates Babel, shown in the Bible as the work of human pride and the attempt of man to reach God's height (Chevalier 959-960).

This *hybris* is easy to recognise in Saruman, who is corrupted through his search for knowledge, reminiscent of Adam's and Eve's Fall, Faust or even Frankenstein. When Saruman begins to study Sauron's arts, he probably sets out to do some good, but at some point he feels tempted to take the power for himself. As Elrond says: "It is perilous to study too deeply the arts of the Enemy, for good or for ill" (LotR I 346-347).

Like all characters mentioned above, the white magician commits a transgression that goes against Nature (or even God) by trying to obtain a knowledge that does not belong to the human race. He does not accept his place in creation, but tries to deny his limits and aspires to reach divine power. The consequence for him, as for the others, is failure and often death (González de la Llana, *Transgresión* 219-251).

Saruman's search for knowledge can be compared to Frankenstein's in the sense that they both give life to new creatures with unnatural methods: Treebeard speculates that Saruman has crossbred Orcs with Men just as Frankenstein collects pieces from different corpses to build his monster. Taking God's/Nature's prerogative to create (González de la Llana, *Frankenstein*), these characters make use of modern science and technology to bring to existence horrid beings that will only cause destruction.

Adam and Eve or Faust do not share this creative wish, but they also pursue a knowledge that will earn them punishment. In all these cases, knowledge seems to have an ambivalent value, as its intrinsic positive side is put into question by the sacrilege by which it is gained and the results it brings. However, it is not knowledge in general that is being criticised, but a knowledge that separates human beings and Nature, a so-called progress that allows men to go beyond their own limits in the attempt of becoming new (and dangerous) gods.

Theodor Ziolkowski points out that Hesiod's Prometheus and the biblical story of the Fall of Man both show a very similar vision of society and human history: man used to live in a paradise or a golden age in which nothing was forbidden, except the means of progress (knowledge and fire, respectively) (Ziolkowski 31-32). Tolkien also seems to believe that there is something wrong with a certain kind of knowledge, a knowledge lacking responsibility like Frankenstein's and Saruman's (not everything that can be done, must be done) and a knowledge that fights against our own nature in its different manifestations: "Men are essentially mortal and must not try to become 'immortal' in the flesh" (Carpenter 189), says the author in one of his letters.

Like Faust, Saruman makes use of magic to his own advantage disrespecting natural laws. Tolkien agreed with C.S Lewis that modern sorcery gains its real impetus from modern science. Gandalf is a wizard whose artistic enchantments heighten our regard for the wonders and mysteries of the natural order. In our own world, by contrast, magic is never an art but always a technique of manipula-tion. No wonder that Tolkien regarded much of modern technology—precisely because it seeks to put nature under its command—as a disguised form of magic: the attempt to accomplish grand ends by instant means (Wood 29-30).

From the end of the Middle Ages until the atomic explosion, as Randel Helms (45) points out, our deepest intellectual efforts have been faustian, we have been in a search for knowledge and power over Nature which has made us like Sauron. We can rule over the natural world, but we realise at the same time that we have become corrupted. Just like Sauron we can destroy the vegetation or change and control people, but also like Sauron, we are prisoners of our own desires. Frodo is, on the contrary, an Anti-Faust as he consciously decides to destroy the ring, a symbol of every corrupting power. Hobbits with their love of a peaceful and joyful life in harmony with the natural environment represent the victory over the demanding hunger for domination.

We can affirm then that knowledge is opposed to wisdom in *The Lord of the Rings* as can be seen, for example, in Saruman's attempt to lead Gandalf into temptation like a new devilish serpent:

> 'And listen, Gandalf, my old friend and helper!' he said, coming near and speaking now in a softer voice. 'I said *we*, for *we* it may be, if you will join with me... We can bide our time, we can keep our thoughts in our hearts, deploring maybe evils done by the way, but approving the high and ultimate purpose: Knowledge, Rule, Order; all the things that we have so far striven in vain to accomplish, hindered rather than helped by our weak or idle friends. There need not be, there would not be, any real change in our designs, only in our means.'
>
> 'Saruman,' I said, 'I have heard speeches of this kind before, but only in the mouths of emissaries sent from Mordor to deceive the ignorant...
>
> 'And why not, Gandalf?' he whispered. 'Why not? The Ruling Ring? If we could command that, then the Power would pass to *us*. That is in truth why I brought you here. For I have many eyes in my service, and I believe that you know where this precious thing now lies...' As he said this a lust which he could not conceal shone suddenly in his eyes.

'Saruman,' I said, standing away from him, 'only one hand at a time can wield the One, and you know that well, so do not trouble to say *we*! But I would not give it, nay... Well, the choices are, it seems, to submit to Sauron, or to yourself. I will take neither.'
(LotR I 339-340)

While Saruman, already lost to his evil wishes, tries to convince his old friend with hackneyed arguments, like the ends justifies the means, or to provoke his will for power with promises and lies, Gandalf remains conscious of the real dangers of the Ring and, above all, keeps control over himself (whereas Saruman cannot hide his lust), since he knows well that nobody can use the Ring and not become a Dark Lord himself. Real wisdom consists in knowing one's own limits, in accepting human nature as it is and its place in a world which is not our possession.

3.2 La saga de los Confines

As in *The Lord of the Rings*, evil also destroys Nature in *La saga de los Confines*: "Misáianes se hará fuerte en las Tierras Antiguas. Luego enviará sus ejércitos a devastar este continente, porque tal es su designio: ni un solo árbol en flor, ni un solo pájaro cantando"[4] (Bodoc, *Venado* 104).

The first transgression against Nature is, however, Misáianes' birth. As Death's son, he saw the light of this world because his mother broke the Great Laws. Condemned not to beget any mortal or immortal creature, Death cried and begged, but the prohibition was absolute. Then Misáianes' mother disobeyed, molded an egg from her own saliva and took it out of her mouth. From these filthy matters the son was born, sheltered by a forgotten mountain in the Ancient Lands. When the Great Laws were disobeyed, a wound opened itself up and through it Eternal Hatred went and found a body and a voice in Misáianes.

The forbidden son came to dominate different creatures, like the sideresios, who did not exist until the Uncreated summoned them to his shadow. Misáianes' legions were recruited among all the species that populated the land at that moment. He assembled them, trained them, and, after "blowing into their ears", many swore him loyalty. Misáianes never left the mountain in which he was born, a cold and dark place: "En su territorio, el aire era de niebla. Muerte y muerte, frío y oscuridad que sin cesar extendían sus límites sobre el mundo"[5]

---

4 Misáianes will become strong in the Ancient Lands. Then he will send his armies to devastate this continent, because that is his plan: not one blooming tree, not one singing bird.
5 In his territory, the air was made of fog. Death and death, coldness and darkness that ceaselessly extended their limits over the world.

(Bodoc, *Venado* 178). And there he kept his most degraded and his most elevated vassals, the first ones to do the most miserable tasks, the second ones to carry out his intentions in the world. But many others adored him and served him because his words were so similar to the truth (his convincing whispering is reminiscent of the serpent in the Garden of Eden and of Saruman again) and they did not suspect whom they were following.

His creatures are, like in Tolkien's work, not natural beings, but the product of his evil making, and he is himself the consequence of a transgressional act. Apart from the sideresios, the people of the Ancient Lands were forced to submit to slavery under Misáianes reign, too. They were deprived of their names and separated into groups according to the work they did. Although in this case we are not facing new creatures, they have lost their essence, they have been dehumanised by the treatment they have to endure, they have lost all consciousness and have become "acting flesh" ("carne que obraba") (Bodoc, *Fuego* 177).

The search for knowledge and the dangers of hunger for power are represented in *La saga de los Confines* through the division of magic in two brotherhoods and especially through Bor's temptation. Misáianes establishes a pact with Molitzmós, aspiring king of the Lords of the Sun's people, to get him to produce a crack in the magic of the Fertile Lands. Molitzmós's mission is to try and corrupt the magician Bor by feeding his pride with skillful words, and by leading him into a position of doubt with regard to the old fight in the world of the magicians.

> —En efecto, la Cofradía del Recinto proclamó que la Magia debía regir sobre las Criaturas con su sola mano. Ellos afirmaron que el don de la Sabiduría era el atributo que los señalaba para el mando. Porque sólo para los Sabios es cosa propia y natural la consagración generosa. Y entonces la Magia, poseedora de la Sabiduría, nunca torcería los fines de su poder. No hay mejor mando que el de la Sabiduría, afirmaron, pues el Sabio halla su gloria en la generosidad. Y sin embargo, los del Aire Libre entendían las cosas de manera muy diferente —Bor hizo una pausa para espiar la reacción de Molitzmós, y luego continuó—: La Cofradía del Aire Libre abandonó las Tierras Antiguas con la esperanza de reencontrar aquí lo que creyeron que allá se había perdido: la marca de la Magia. A su entender, aquello que la Cofradía del Recinto tomaba por natural, y llamaba su "obligación de velar por las Criaturas", era una alteración de su legítimo destino de la Magia [sic]. Y lo que llamaba "consagración generosa" era, en verdad, arrogancia. La Cofradía del Aire Libre comprendió que en las Tierras Antiguas la Magia estaba alejándose de su origen; y que

un día, por esa causa, su luz se apagaría. Ese convencimiento fue
el que los decidió a cruzar el mar para empezar de nuevo en las
Tierras Fértiles, lejos de los recintos donde sus pares se recluían.
Al aire libre.[6]   (Bodoc, *Venado* 187)

In fact, though some members of the Brotherhood of the Enclosure are essential in the fight against Misáianes, there is a clear sympathy towards the more democratic ideas of the Open Air, whose members are ready to work for the Creatures and *with* them at the same time. The danger of believing that great knowledge brings superiority is obvious in this quote and in the trilogy in general. The hybris of the Wise can lead them astray and many will actually fall under Misáianes influence, this hybris that makes them think that they will be strong enough to keep faithful to their principles even if they hold their power and their knowledge over the others. The Brotherhood of the Open Air tries to maintain what for them is the real spirit of Magic looking for a new place in the Fertile Lands.

After several conversations with Molitzmós, Bor also falls into the temptation of believing himself and the magicians as superior to the Creatures, and shows opposition to the other Supreme Astronomer Zabralkán. But, unlike Saruman, Bor realises what he has done because his intentions were not evil and repents after meeting Death:

- Tú eres un buen vasallo -continuó la dueña-. Uno de los que
mucho hicieron para que nuestra victoria fuese posible.
El espíritu de Bor comenzó a desmoronarse como una torre de
arena olvidada en la costa.
- No entiendo lo que dices -balbuceó.
- Di, mejor, que no entiendes lo que hiciste.

---

6   Indeed, the Brotherhood of the Enclosure proclaimed that Magic should govern the Creatures with its only hand. They affirmed that the gift of Wisdom was an attribute that distinguished them for command. Because only for the Wise generous consecration is a proper and natural thing. And then Magic, owner of Wisdom, would never warp the ends of its power. There is no better command than Wisdom, they affirmed, as the Wise finds his glory in generosity. However, the Open Air Brotherhood understood things very differently—Bor made a pause to gauge Molitzmós' reaction and then went on. The Open Air Brotherhood abandoned the Ancient Lands with the hope to find here again what they thought that had been lost there: the mark of Magic. In their opinion, that which the Brotherhood of the Enclosure took as natural and called their "obligation to watch over the Creatures" was an alteration of their legitimate destiny. And what they called "generous consecration" was, in reality, arrogance. The Open Air Brotherhood understood that in the Ancient Lands Magic was withdrawing from its origin and that one day, for that cause, its light would fade. This conviction was what decided them to cross the sea to begin anew in the Fertile Lands, far away from the enclosures where their pars withdrew. Into the open air.

La dueña se rió que congelaba.
De pronto perdió hasta su delgadez. Y se deslizó al estanque como un reflejo, el reflejo de la Sombra en el agua. Desde aquel lugar habló con el Supremo Astrónomo durante un largo rato. Lo hizo sin burla, pero sin piedad.
- ¡Vasallo de Misáianes, tu soberbia nos ha sido valiosa! -comenzó diciendo... [7]   (Bodoc, *Sombra* 151)

As in *The Lord of the Rings*, we find here a kind of faustian figure who forgets the real sense of knowledge and wisdom, but in this case Bor sees in time his pride and his mistake, he realises how he has been the victim of the diabolical game played by Molitzmós, and discovers that the Brotherhood of the Enclosure, the one he wanted to get back to, is allied with Misáianes.

4. Conclusions

We have seen in this article how Liliana Bodoc's trilogy of the Borderlands coincides with Tolkien's *The Lord of the Rings* in the importance given to Nature and to man's relation to it. In both works, the characters' attitude towards their environment is not just a small characteristic of their personality, but a sign of their morals and spiritual height.

Nature, with the different forms that it can take in these secondary worlds, can also participate actively in the development of the events or be at least a messenger which provides news and omens.

The fact of using technology as a way of ruling over Nature and enjoying its resources for egoistic purposes is criticised in Tolkien's novels, above all through Saruman, whose search for knowledge becomes an impossible *hybris* that will mean his fall and ultimate death. His corruption is manifested in a contempt for the natural world which he destroys without much consideration and the use of his magical power to give birth to monstrous and cruel beings crossbreeding Orcs with Men. Knowledge and "progress" which alienate men and drive him away from natural laws are dangerous and evil.

---

[7] "- You are a good vassal - the mistress continued -. One of those who did much to make our victory possible
Bor's spirit began to crumble like a sand tower forgotten on the coast.
- I don't understand what you are saying - he babbled
- Better say that you don't understand what you did. The mistress gave a freezing laugh. Suddenly she even lost her thinness. And she slithered to the pond like a reflection, the reflection of the Shadows on the water. From that place she talked to the Supreme Astronomer a long time. She did it without mockery, but without pity.
- Misáianes' vassal, your pride has been valuable to us! - she began to say..."

Something similar is to be seen in *The Saga of the Borderlands*, where Misáianes is the product of a transgression against Nature and also creates unnatural beings like the sideresios. The dangers of pride in relation to knowledge and power are represented through the two magical brotherhoods and in the character of Bor, whose temptation to believe himself and the other magicians as superior to the Creatures, manifest themselves as wrong and false. Creation is a perfect tannery in which everything and everybody is equally important.

Evil occurs, therefore, in both works, when man does not respect Nature and his appropriate position in it.

Bibliography

Bodoc, Liliana. *La saga de los Confines I. Los días del Venado*. Santiago de Chile: Suma de Letras, 2012

---. *La saga de los Confines II. Los días de la Sombra*. Barcelona: Edhasa, 2006

---. *La saga de los Confines III. Los días del Fuego*. Barcelona: Edhasa, 2007

Carpenter, Humphrey (Ed.). *The Letters of J.R.R. Tolkien*. New York: Houghton Mifflin, 2000

Chevalier, Jean & Alain Gheerbrant. *Dictionnaire des simboles*. Paris: Robert Laffont & Jupiter, 1982

González de la Llana, Natalia. *Adán y Eva, Fausto y Dorian Gray: tres mitos de transgresión*. Aachen: Shaker, 2009

---. "El pecado de Frankenstein". Álabe. Revista de Investigación sobre Lectura y Escritura 7 (2013): http://revistaalabe.com/index/alabe/article/view/151

Helms, Randel. *Tolkiens Welt. Tolkien und die Silmarille*. Passau: Erster Deutscher Fantasy Club, 1986

Kehr, Eike. *Natur und Kultur in J.R.R. Tolkiens* The Lord of the Rings. Trier: Wissenschaftlicher Verlag Trier, 2011

Kölzer, Christian & Marcus Roso. »Maschineller Sündenfall. Wirtschaftssysteme und Daseinskonzepte im *Herr der Ringe*«. *Das Dritte Zeitalter: J.R.R. Tolkiens* Herr der Ringe. Tagungsband 2005. Wetzlar: Phantastische Bibliothek Wetzlar, 2006, 173-184

Tolkien, J.R.R. *The Lord of the Rings I. The Fellowship of the Ring*. London: Unwin, 1989

---. *The Lord of the Rings II. The Two Towers*. London: Unwin, 1989

---. *The Lord of the Rings III. The Return of the King*. London: Unwin, 1989

Wood, Ralph C. *The Gospel According to Tolkien. Visions of the Kingdom in Middle-earth*. Louisville/London: Westminster John Knox Press, 2003

Ziolkowski, Theodor. *The Sin of Knowledge*. Princeton: Princeton University Press, 2000

The Dead Marshes and οἰκουμένη: the Limits of a Landscape in Middle-earth

Michaël Devaux (Livarot)

Death, it is well known, is the main theme of *The Lord of the Rings*. And *The Lord of the Rings* is, obviously, the main work of Tolkien. Therefore focusing on landscape in Tolkien's work can be regarded as a central subject with the Dead Marshes. What a striking landscape of Middle-earth, indeed? "The Passages of the Marshes" (book IV, chapter II) may be among the most fascinating chapters.

But immediately there are at least two questions about such an assertion: "the Dead Marshes are a landscape of Middle-earth". 1/ Do the Dead Marshes belong to Middle-earth? 2/ Are the Dead Marshes a landscape? Answering these questions help us to think what a landscape is and what Middle-earth is.

Let's continue questioning Middle-earth first, we'll reach the Dead Marshes later. So what is Middle-earth? What is the nature or essence of such a world? There are two ways to understand this question. The first one is: what is an imaginary or secondary world? We have then to speculate about imagination, sub-creation, literature, and so on. The second question is: how a world (not a place) can be described from its own name? Maybe the second question only bears meaning for an imaginary world. There are many articles and books about the former. I want to draw attention to the latter. If we follow Tolkien, may be philology, in his imaginary toponymy will give rise to geography. Describing the world with words helps to visualise it, and for Tolkien to tell its (hi)story.

There's a paradox about Middle-earth. If Tolkien has coined the specificity of his imaginary world with that name, Middle-earth, it doesn't come from his imagination![1] Tolkien gave us a double explanation for its origin. "Middle-earth" comes from Old English *midden-erd*, and there's a Greek equivalent that Tolkien used seven times: οἰκουμένη. Is it the same idea? What are we about to accept with that equivalence? What are the different senses of these words for the earth or world? Why does Tolkien use them? When did he begin to use them? What did he find with both of them and each of them? It'll be the first part of our study. We'll continue with the analysis of the link between the Dead Marshes and Middle-earth. Does Middle-earth include every place in Arda? Is there a difference between Middle-earth and Arda, not to speak about Ambar and Eä? Being a synecdochical name of Arda, Middle-earth often took the place

---
1 L 283 "not my invention".

of the concept of Arda. Where are the boundaries of Middle-earth? Our thesis is that the Dead Marshes still belong to Middle-earth as *oikoumene* and are in its limits. So we'll have to face the consequence: beyond the Dead Marshes, we are outside Middle-earth as *oikoumene*.

I. *Middangeard* and ἡ οἰκουμένη γῆ

A. Dwelling: the incubation period of the link (1914-1937)

Tolkien seems to begin to use the expression 'Middle-earth' later that one can imagine. He didn't use it as such in *The Book of Lost Tales*, or in *The Hobbit*[2]. We can even assume that there's an incubation period of the expression 'Middle-earth' in the *legendarium*. Indeed if all came from the poem *Éalá Éarendel* (1914) then Middle-earth is already present from Old English *middangeard*[3] in the second verse, but Tolkien said at that time to translate it in English as "mid-world"[4]. And in 1930 (?), in the Old English version of the *Earliest Annals of Valinor*, we again meet *middangeard*. 'Middle-earth' occured in the late 1930s (Gilliver 164). This incubation period is due to the nodal conception of earth as home, a dwelling place. And this is the link between middle-earth and *oikoumene*. The link is given in the *New English Dictionary* (nowadays *Oxford English Dictionary*, OED).

You can see for the entry 'Middle-earth' what Tolkien borrowed from the *Dictionary*: about perversion from Old English, opposition to Fairyland, and the history of the word.

a) You can see for the entry 'Middle-earth' what Tolkien borrowed from the *Dictionary*: about perversion from Old English, opposition to Fairyland, and the history of the word.

---

2 In his correspondence, we find it first in L #131, letter to Milton Waldman, at the end of 1951 (?).
3 Entitled *Éalá Éarendel Engla Beorhtast*, this poem (24.09.1914) is edited in LT II 268 for the first draft. Since 19th June to 14th October, Tolkien loans the *Bibliothek der angelsächsischen Poesie* by Grein & Wülcker (see Garth, *Tolkien* 44 and 322). Tolkien read inside: "Eala Earendel! engla beorhtast / ofer middangeard monnum sended" (III, 5). This text comes from the *Exeter Book*, a manuscript done in 940, given by bishop Leofric to the library of Exeter Cathedral (Ms 3501). – *Middangeard* is also in *Beowulf*, v. 75, 1771; *Christ* I, 275; *Cædmon's Hymn*, 7; *The Wanderer*, 61, 75.
4 "Éarendel sprang up from the Ocean's cup / In the gloom of mid-world's rim" (LT II, 268, cf. *Parma Eldalamberon* 18, 121, 123 (fragment PF17g). In *A Middle English Vocabulary* for Kenneth Sisam's *Fourteenth Century Verse & Prose* (1921), s. v. *Myddel-erde*, Tolkien translated it as "the world". This is the first sense in the *New English Dictionary*.

New English Dictionary, vol. VI-2 (1908)	Tolkien
Middle earth. Forms: see MIDDLE and EARTH sb. **1.** [An etymologizing perversion of MIDDLE-ERD.] The earth, as placed between heaven and hell, or as supposed to occupy the centre of the universe. Now only *arch.*, sometimes applied to the real world in contradistinction to fairyland. c **1275** LAY. 7205 He þohte to bi-winne mid strengþe and mid ginne al þe middelerþes [c 1205 middel eurdes] lond. *Ibid.* 9066 Com a þisse middilherþe [c 1205 middel ærde] hone maidenes sune. *a* **1300** *Cursor M.* 8003 Bituix þe midel erth and þe lift. **1390** GOWER *Conf.* III. 94 Fro the seconde, as bokes sein, The moiste dropes of the reyn Descenden into Middilerthe. c **1440** *York Myst.* ix. 158 Fadir, what may þis meruaylle mene? Wher-to made god medilerth and man? **1522** *World & Child* (Roxb.) A v, All mery medell erthe maketh mencyon of me. **1598** SHAKS. *Merry W.* v. v. 84 But stay, I smell a man of middle earth. **1600** W. WATSON *Decacordon* (1602) 238 O monster of mankinde fitter for hell, then middle earth. **1813** SCOTT *Trierm.* I. ix, That maid is born of middle earth, And may of man be won. **1819** CRABBE *T. of Hall* x, A kind of beings who are never found On middle-earth, but grow on fairy-ground. **1860** HAWTHORNE *Transform.* xxxviii, It is difficult to imagine it [*sc.* Catholicism] a contrivance of mere man. Its mighty machinery was forged and put together, not on middle earth, but either above or below. † **2.** The middle of the earth. *Obs.* *Sea of middle earth, middle earth sea,* the Mediterranean. *Middle earth ocean,* an imaginary ocean in the middle of the earth. **1387** TREVISA *Higden* (Rolls) I. 53 Þe grete see of myddel erþe bygynneþ in þe west at Hercules pilers. **1494** FABYAN *Chron.* v. lxxvii. 36 In the South see of Myddell Erth. **1555** W. WATREMAN *Fardle Facions* I. iii. 34 The floude of Nilus ..passeth into the middle earth sea, with seuen armes. **1593** NORDEN *Spec. Brit., M'sex.* I. 8 The forme of this land is Trianguler, much like Cicilia an Island in the middle-earth sea. **1613** PURCHAS *Pilgrimage* VII. ii. 663 So would those good men drowne a great part of the African and American World..by their imagined middle-earth Ocean. p. 421 c	- (see dictionaries) is a modern alteration of medieval *middle-erde* from OE *middan-geard* (Nomenclature 774) - It is a modernization or alteration (*New Oxford Dictionary* 'a **perversion**') (L 283). - real world, in use specifically opposed to imaginary worlds (as **Fairyland**) (L 239) - modern form (appearing in the 13th century and **still in use**) (L 239) - north shores of the Mediterranean (L 376)

Middle-erd. *Obs.* exc. *dial.* Forms: see MIDDLE and ERD; also 4 myddelnerde, 2-3 middelert, 4 midulert, 5 medlert, 8 midlert, 5 middle yorde, myddell yarde. See also MIDDLE EARTH. [Formed by substitution of *middel* MIDDLE a. for *middan-* in *middaneard*, *-geard*: see MIDDENERD. There may have been an OE. **middel(*ʒ*)eard* corresponding to OS. *mittilgard*, OHG. *mittilgart*.] The world; the earth taken as situated between heaven and hell; also, the people dwelling on the earth. *c* 1175 *Lamb. Hom.* 15 Þas laʒen weren from Moyses a þet drihten com on þis middilert for us to alesnesse of deofles onwalde. *c* 1200 ORMIN 3638 Godess þeowwess blomenn aʒʒ Inn alle gode þæwess, Her i þiss middellærdess lif. *c* 1205 LAY. 25569 Lauerd drihten crist domes waldende midelarde mund. **1297** R. GLOUC. (Rolls) 9052 Me nuste womman so vair non in þe middel erde. *c* 1315 SHOREHAM VII. 580 Wy nedde hy be ine helle y-stopped For euere mo, Ac Nauʒt her in þys myddelnerde, For to maky men offerde. **13.**. *Gaw. & Gr. Knt.* 2100 More he is þen any mon vpon myddelerde. *a* 1400 *Pistill of Susan* 263 (MS. A.) Þou maker of myddelert, þat most art of miht. *c* 1460 *Towneley Myst.* iii. 100 Therfor shall I fordo All this medill-erd. ? *a* 1500 *Chester Pl.* IV. 267 Father,.. I hope for all middle-yorde you will not slaye your childe. **1513** DOUGLAS *Æneis* VI. viii. 11 Thair saw he als, with huge greit and murnyng In mydle erd most menit, thir Troianis. **1768** ROSS *Helenore* (1789) 50 This gate she could not long in midlert be. p. 421 c	- It is just a use of Middle English *middel-erde* (or *erthe*), altered from Old English *Middangeard*: the name for the inhabited lands of Men 'between the seas'. (L 220)
†**Mi·ddenerd.** *Obs.* Forms: 1 middanʒeard, -eard, 2 middanerd, middennard, midenarde, 3 middæn eard, middeneard, middenerd, middenherde, myddenerd, OE. *middangeard* (later *-eard* by association with *eard* dwelling, ERD), corresp. to OHG. *mittingart*, Goth. *midjungards.* The exact formation is obscure, but the elements are OTeut. **midjo-* MID a. + *gardo-z enclosure, tract, YARD. Cf. ON. *miðgarðr* MIDGARD, OS. *mittilgard*, OHG. *mittigart* and *mittilgart*; also MIDDLE-ERD. According to Brugmann, the first element is OTeut. **midjumo-*, superlative of **midjo-* MID a. : cf. MIDMOST.] The world; the earth as situated between heaven and hell; also, the inhabitants of the earth. *Beowulf* 75 Maniʒre mæʒþe ʒeond þisne middanʒeard. *c* 1000 *Ags. Gosp.* John iv. 42 We witon þæt he is soþ middan-eardes hælynd. *a* 1175 *Cott. Hom.* 225 Ic wille senden flod ofer alne middennard. *c* 1205 LAY. 24778 Whar þu þat mod nime a þisse middenerde. *c* 1275 *Passion our Lord* 478 in *O. E. Misc.* 50 Hit wes welneyh mydday þo þusternesse com In alle Middenherde fort þet hit wes non. *Ibid.* 544 Iesus crist .. com in-to þis myddenerd sunfulle men to ryhte. p. 419 a	- O. English *middan-geard* (L 283) - *midden-erd* > *middel-erd* (L 239) - mediæval E. *midden-erd*, *middle-erd* (L 283) - *oikoumenē*, the abiding place of Men, the objectively real world, in use specifically opposed to imaginary world (as Fairyland) or unseen worlds (as Heaven or Hell). (L 239)

b) We can see for the entry 'Middenerd' what the notice says about *middangeard* "(later *-eard* [without g] by association with *eard*, dwelling)". This is this idea that is also in *oikoumene*: dwelling. In 1923, in *A Middle English Vocabulary*, Tolkien did not focus of this idea.

Strabo of Amasia in his *Geography* said "we call 'oikoumene' the world which we inhabit and know"⁵. In Greek, *oikoumene* is the feminine of the present passive participle of οἰκέω 'I dwell'. The complete expression is *he oikoumene ge*⁶ 'the inhabited earth'.

I think Tolkien only began to make the association *middengeard*, earth, dwelling, *oikoumene* in 1937. That was the end of the incubation period, begun in 1914. There are several arguments to support it. First, the first known reference to *oikoumene* by Tolkien occurs in *The Etymologies* under the root √MBAR. As we know, *The Etymologies* (published in *The Lost Road*) is a text written in 1937-1938⁷.

Tolkien wrote in *The Etymologies*: "MBAR- dwell, ~~build~~, inhabit Q *a-mbar (ambaren)* 'oikoumenē', Earth; (...)". *In margin*: Old Noldorin *mbar* 'home'. And on title page: MBAR dwell. Quenya *mbar(d)*- home, dwelling."⁸ That's from a linguistic point of view, wanting to express 'to dwell' that Tolkien encounters or remembers the classic *oikoumene*. Then he can see it as an aspect of *middaneard*. Tolkien makes *oikoumene* a familiar place, a "home", and essentially an inhabited place, 'the great habitation'. It can then translate not only Middle-earth, in Quenya *Endor* or *Ennor*, but *Ambar*, the settlement⁹.

B. The Limits of *oikoumene*

I notice, at last, that at this time, in 1937, was published the (until now) reference study about *Oikumene*, by Friedrich Gisinger in the *Paulys Realencyclopädie der classischen Altertumswissenschaft*¹⁰. I can't say for sure that Tolkien read it, but is it just a coincidence? Maybe, or not...

---

5   See the analysis of Dueck 43.
6   Tolkien used the complete expression in *Words, Phrases and Passages in* The Lord of the Rings, *Parma Eldalamberon* 17, 163, but please correct the edited text as follows: instead of ἡ οἰκουμένη (δῆ) read ἡ οἰκουμένη (γῆ)—*corrigendum* approved by Christopher Gilson. C.S. Lewis comments the expression in his article "World": "(...) *orbis terrae* in Latin. This represents the Greek *he oikoumene* which is an ellipsis of *he oikoumene ge*, 'the inhabited earth'. So in Matt. xxiv. 14 ('preached in all the world'), or Luke ii. 1 ('that all the world will be taxed')" ('World', IV. World in biblical translation, *Studies in Words*, 2nd ed. 1967, p. 224).
7   LR 344-5; a larger period, between 1931 and 1938, is assumed in *Parma Eldalamberon* 18, 7.
8   LR 372 including "Addenda" 33.
9   See "Fate and Free Will" (1968), in *Tolkien Studies* 6, 2009, 183, about *Ambar*: "The sense 'world'—applied usually to this Earth—is mainly derived from sense 'settlement': 'the great habitation' (οἰκουμένη) as 'home of speaking creatures' esp. Elves and Men."—the reading οἰκουμένη have been approved by Carl Hostetter.
10 Gisinger 2123-2174 (I would like to thank Thomas Honegger for sending me a copy of this article). There are two incentives which do not come from working on the *legendarium* but from Tolkien's life (personal, religious and professional) for the interest of Tolkien in reading about *oikoumene*: first, from a religious point of view, he may have been excited

I'm not going to provide a presentation of a detailed evolution in conception of *oikoumene* following the ancient geographers, as Friedrich Gisinger did. And I have no intention, nor the time, to tell the history of the concept of *oikoumene* by educated scholars of the 20th Century[11]. I'll only make a few remarks to try to distinguish between logics of conception of *oikoumene* to be able to determine Tolkien's.

What is *oikoumene* for the Ancient Greeks? The paradox is that the inventor of *oikoumene*, Herodotus of Halicarnassus, is against the idea of a surrounding Ocean, that is to say that his *oikoumene* is not a *middle*-earth! With *oikoumene*, the main geographical distinction is not between earth or land and sea or water, but between the existence of inhabitants or not. *Oikoumene* is then the familiar world, the inhabited world. And Herodotus brings into conflict *oikoumene* and *ereme*, desert. We'll come back to that point at the end of this paper. The Greek Miracle is born with the ordering of the world as a two-part earth: the inner sea (Mediterranean) and the outer sea (Atlantic), the ocean being thought of as a circle. That's the representation in Homer. But Herodotus didn't think that Ocean is to be found in all directions. Almost in *all* directions (except the West[12]), Herodotus said from testimonies that there is *eremos*, desert. What lies beyond, he didn't know.

C. Middle-earth: the Middle of what?

Let's go back to Tolkien. Middle-earth is in the middle of what? There are two major ways of answering. The first one is to look at what says the dictionary, as Tolkien invites us to. We then learn that Middle-earth is 'between heaven and hell'. That's not exactly what Tolkien means when he uses the word. Even if Mordor seems to be infernal indeed, Tolkien doesn't conceive it as a place after death. Frodo and Sam try to go there alive, even if they think it should be quite impossible to survive.

The second way of answering follows Tolkien himself regarding what Middle-earth is the middle of. And he says "middle because thought of vaguely as set amidst the encircling Seas (in northern imagination) between ice of the North

---

in the 1930s by the works of the Lutheran pastor Dietrich Bonhoeffer, in London between 1933-1935, about ecumenism; secondly, Tolkien, as philologist, worked on a related subject in 1936 in his article "Sigelwara Land" about Ethiopia, at the edge of *oikoumene*.

11 This history is to be written. I only notice that William Smith's *Dictionary of Greek and Roman Geography* didn't dedicate an entry for *oikoumene*, and that Martin Heidegger never gave any attention to the greek *oikoumene*, even if he so often worked from greek concepts, and even if he wrote at least two text about dwelling: "Building Dwelling Thinking", "... Poetically man dwells...", both of 1951.

12 The Northern edge is usually seen with the Scythians, while the Southern reach the Ethiopians, Indians Eastward, and Westwards the Pillars of Hercules (Gibraltar). *Oikoumene* has an inner sea (Mediterranean) and an outer sea (Atlantic). See Shahar 9.

and the fire of the South"[13]. Tolkien is giving here a double explanation. On the one hand, this quotation is only the justification of the use of the concept of *oikoumene*, and we have already seen that there was an Ocean surrounding *oikoumene*. This middle-earth is an earth in the middle of the Ocean. On the other hand, Tolkien doesn't in fact spirit us to Greece, but to Scandinavia, referring to the northern imagination. This double explanation is external, referring to a Greek concept, and to the northern imagination. Tolkien also gives an internal explanation: "The sense is the 'inhabited lands of (Elves and) Men', envisaged as lying between the Western Sea and that of the Far East (only known in the West by rumour)" (*Nomenclature* 774).

As a main conclusion of this first aspect of our enquiry, we see that Tolkien used *oikoumene* in a sense quite different from the Greek's concept. Let's inquire into about the Dead Marshes as inside or outside Middle-earth as *oikoumene*.

II. *Oikoumenē* and the Dead Marshes

Passing through the Dead Marshes is an experience that contrasts with going elsewhere in Middle-earth. This region is the reverse, the opposite of the definition of Middle-earth. If Middle-earth is lands surrounded by an aquatic area, a marsh is water limed in soil, some earth encircling waters[14]. Becoming aware of this inversion, the question of whether the Dead Marshes belong to Middle-earth deserves to be asked.

A. The Dead Marshes and their Origin

The Dead Marshes are immediately at the North West of the Gate of Mordor, the Morannon. Frodo, Sam and Gollum began their passage on March 1st, 3019 of the Third Age. The stagnant waters are a reminiscence of the corruption of bodies, and are then a very concrete image of the physical death (not death as liberation[15]). Moreover, it's a single place: an old military cemetery. The dead warriors of the battle of Dagorlad are the only ones to rest in graves and were not buried in mounds[16]. And the cemetery became marshes! Tolkien, and that's a peculiar thing, said its origin is in the real world: "Personally I do not think that either war (and of course not the atomic bomb) had any influence upon the plot or the manner of its unfolding. Perhaps in landscape. The Dead Marshes

---

13 L 283, letter to Rhona Beare, 14.10.1958.
14 "C'est que le marais est l'eau engluée dans la terre; de plus au lieu d'être une étendue aquatique circonscrivant les terres, il est circonscrit par elles" (Jourde 31).
15 See *ibid*.
16 See Arduini/Testi 144.

and the approaches to the Morannon owe something to Northern France after the Battle of the Somme. They owe more to William Morris and his Huns and Romans, as in *The House of the Wolfings* or *The Roots of the Mountains*."[17]

Tolkien gives here two influences. The first one is physical or geographical; the second one comes from literature. Commentators already explored these two ways. Years ago (in 1982), Barton Friedman in his article "Tolkien and David Jones" and recently John Garth in his book and several articles tracked and checked the relations between the battle of the Somme and the Dead Marshes[18]. And for the literary commentaries, Robert Morse found a parallel with Eneas descent to Hades, the realm of Pluto (Morse 10-11); and Wayne Hammond and Christina Scull point out parallels with *She* by Rider Haggard[19]. Margaret Sinex in an article in *Tolkien Studies* gave recently parallels with *Bárðar Saga* and the *Will o' the Wisp* folklore. I will not follow these paths. I will try to go further from geographical thinking.

B. Three Approaches to the Dead Marshes as Landscape

The Dead Marshes are a wholly atypical and unique place. It became for Tolkien a labyrinth. Mostly because there's nothing to eat, and almost nothing is visible. Where they are coming from and where they are going to are not visible. The reason of such an isolation is not vegetation or relief, but fog. That's a landscape without the possibility to look at it. The truth is, you look at it, but you don't see anything. It leads us to the question: is every landscape a panorama? Is every place a landscape? Maybe the Dead Marshes are a place where the limit of the concept of landscape is reached. Going there requires making some experiences, much more than an open view. It gives nonetheless something to see: if it doesn't offer itself to the eyes, it offers the Dead to be seen. That's, therefore, a limit-landscape: it can only be described by parts or pieces, without an overview. What Frodo, Sam and Gollum first see of it from outside turns out to be different: that's a deceitful or lying landscape, a fantastic landscape, and almost a deadly one.

1. The Dead Marshes are first a *deceitful or lying landscape*[20] because we were first thinking it was fen or marshlands, but we find in fact pools, and ponds: "The hobbits soon found that what had looked like one vast fen was really an endless network of pools, and soft mires, and winding half-strangled watercourses" (p. 626). There's a misinterpretation of what they believe to cross. The

---

17 L 303, from a letter to Professor L. W. Forest, 31.12.1960. A few remarks from Morris' books are in Perry 158.
18 See the three works by John Garth cited in bibliography.
19 See Hammond/Scull 452.
20 See Shippey 196.

unity of a fen landscape is splintered into a network of various grounds and firmness (pools, soft mires, water-courses). Similarly, they found another lie in that land because "the Sun was riding high and golden", for the hobbits on the ground all is "bleared, pale, giving no colour and no warmth" (*ibid.*). This is definitively a lying land: even if they're not yet "in the Land of Mordor where the Shadows lie", the Shadow already makes this land lie. It lies because the reality is not seen as usual (for the Sun) and in the sense that they are waiting for something and found another (a fen/network of pools): sensations or perceptions are not right; and finally it's lying landscape in the sense of something stretched, lengthened (that's "endless").

2. The Dead Marshes are, secondly, a *fantastic place*. The lie extends indeed to the fantastic dimension of the Dead Marshes. Sam and mainly Frodo[21] saw dead people in the pools. All are mixed, good (Elves, Men) and spiteful (Orcs). What was the nobility of the battle, they are all here, side by side, "all dead, all rotten"—as Gollum says (p. 628). Nobility or glory passed out. Are the battle and the war then vain or useless? Isn't the hoax or deception, the perfidious tricks by Sauron to let them believe this precisely, when Frodo is coming close to Mount Doom? That's Frodo own hermeneutical point of view of this experience in book IV, chapter v: the power of Sauron had tried to induce him to think that all war is vain. "…it is some lying trick of the Enemy. I have seen the faces of fair warriors of old laid in sleep beneath the pools of the Dead Marshes, or seeming so by his foul arts" (p. 667).

3. Tolkien was even, thirdly, about to go further and to conceive the Dead Marshes as a *deadly place*. In the first drafts, in April 1944, the 'fantastic lie' opened more the door to despair because this place was changing into a sight of the death of the hobbits in the gleam of the waters of the pools with the light of the moon! "The moon came out of its cloud. They looked in (the pool). But they saw no faces out of the vanished past. They saw their own. Sam, Gollum, and Frodo looking up with dead eyes and livid rotting flesh at them"[22]. It is not only a landscape of death, but a deadly or lethal landscape: a place that lets one attend to the spectacle of one's own death, of its corruption *post mortem*. As Pierre Jourde in his book about *Imaginary Geographies* says: "the marsh reflects the hero in negative, giving him an image of what he fears and what he has to avoid to be"[23].

---

21 See Perry 154: "Tolkien has Frodo take the view of Spiritualists of the late nineteen-century, claiming it is possible to have contact with the dead. Sam takes a Christian position, that the faces are an evil deception."
22 WR 110, cf. 105.
23 "…le marais reflète en négatif le héros, lui donnant l'image de ce qu'il redoute et doit éviter d'être" (Jourde 32).

C. *Oikoumenē* and Desert: Dead Marshes and No man's land

There's a point deserving a last commentary. When Tolkien admits to the origin of the Dead Marshes on the battlefields of France, he did not only do it for the Dead Marshes. He completes: "The Dead Marshes and the approaches to the Morannon owe something to Northern France after the Battle of the Somme."[24] The lands between the Dead Marshes and the Black Gate of Mordor are described as "the Desolation of the Morannon"[25], or simply as a "desert"[26].

We can make three remarks about that before concluding. The first one is that with the desert we meet the word that works with *oikoumene* as a couple. When Herodotus forged *oikoumene*, he distinguished it from *ereme* or desert. The second remark is that the expression 'No man's land' was brought to common use in English with World War I. It was popularised[27] by Ernest Swinton, the father of the tank, in a text entitled *The Point of View* (1908) in that text: "Here and there in that wilderness of dead bodies—the dreadful 'No-Man's-Land' between the opposing lines—deserted guns showed up singly or in groups, glistening in the full glare of the beam or silhouetted in black against a ray passing behind."[28] Eric J. Leed, in his book *No Man's Land*, says that "Astonishing numbers of those who wrote about their experience of war designate No Man's Land as their most lasting and disturbing image. This was a term that captures the essence of an experience of having been sent beyond the outer boundaries of social life, placed between the known and the unknown, the familiar and the uncanny" (Leed 15). These two quotations lead us to think that the Dead Marshes and the No Man's Land in Tolkien convey together memories of the No Man's Land of World War I. But that's not exactly the same conception. In World War I, the No Man's Land is the land of the uncanny and non-familiar that is outside *oikoumene*. But in Tolkien's, as dreadful as the passage of the Dead Marshes and of Noman-lands[29] was, the hobbits feel that they were both different from Mordor. The Dead Marshes are inside *oikoumene* because there are still dead inhabitants below water. The Noman-lands is outside *oikoumene*: nobody inhabits there. That's a kind of dry version of the Dead Marshes.

24　L 303. Isn't it the declension of a similarly landscape, the wet one and the dry one? There are holes, a smelly malorodous place but not due to the stagnant waters. Smells can come from chemical reactions that Tolkien would once describe with the Dead Marshes. He then has translated these features to the Noman-lands, a duplication of the Dead Marshes. We know that Tolkien has reconfigured the entrance of Mordor.
25　LotR 1093, cf. p. 631.
26　"The marshes and the desert were behind them" (LotR 631, 636, cf. p. 886).
27　Middle English knows the word, meaning a place outside the city of London for executions, but that's after Christmas truce of 1914 that No Man's Land was frequently used.
28　Swinton 243.
29　This is the orthography in Tolkien's LotR 631, cf. p. 373.

Beyond, all became wholly different. "Dreadful as the Dead Marshes had been, and the arid moors of the Noman-lands, more loathsome far was the country that the crawling day now slowly unveiled to his (Frodo) shrinking eyes. Even the Mere of Dead Faces some haggard phantom of green spring would come; but here neither spring nor summer would ever come again" (LotR 631). Mordor is a *non plus ultra* in the ultimate kind of abomination, a point of no return. We see here a distinction between the Mordor and every other place, even the nearest ones. Noman-lands is/are a liminal space between the *oikoumene* and Mordor. It was physically and morally experienced by the hobbits.

Conclusions

First. Regarding the 'landscapeness' of the Dead Marshes: I think Tolkien tries to express that such a place can't be seen as a landscape. Those who pass through see nothing of it as a landscape, even if they see horrors below water. But as readers we see very well this oppressive 'landscape'.

2. Considering seriously Middle-earth as *oikoumene* implies to see clearly how Tolkien follows the sense of *oikoumene* by Herodotus. The father of *oikoumene* brings it in conflict with *ereme*, rather than the opposition of seas and lands. Tolkien doesn't exactly think the same way. Middle-earth is still surrounded by seas. But we see in *The Lord of the Rings* that Middle-earth is an *oikoumene* including the Dead Marshes, and that Noman-lands are *ereme*: like Herodotus on that point. And these two places come from the landscape of the battle of the Somme.

3. In such ways, we saw why we can assume that Dead Marshes are a limit: as a non-landscape, and as the limit, the boundary of a vanishing *oikoumene* as a dwelling place. And the Noman-lands are a boundary of Middle-earth, not in the sense of reaching the Ocean, but because that's a wholly different place from the desert itself beyond. Even the dead inhabitants in the Dead Marshes may hint at a less lethal experience than meeting an Orc in Mordor...[30]

---

30 I would like to thank David Ledanois for having emended my English.

Bibliography

Arduini, Roberto, and Claudio Testi (Eds.). *The Broken Scythe: Death and Immortality in the Works of J.R.R. Tolkien.* Zurich and Bern: Walking Tree Publishers, 2012

Dueck, Daniela. *Strabo of Amasia: A Greek Man of Letters in Augustan Rome.* London: Routledge, 2000

Friedman, Barton. "Tolkien and David Jones: The Great War and the War of the Ring". *Clio* 11/2 (1982): 115-36

Garth, John. "'As Under a Green Sea': Visions of War in the Dead Marshes". *Myth and Magic: Art according to the Inklings.* Eds. Michael Segura & Thomas Honegger. Zürich and Bern: Walking Tree Publishers, 2007, 285-313

---. *Tolkien and the Great War.* London: HarperCollins Publishers, 2003

---. "Tolkien and the Great War". *The Lord of the Rings 1954-2004.* Eds. Wayne G. Hammond & Christina Scull. Milwaukee: Marquette University Press, 2006, 41-56

Gilliver, Peter et al. *The Ring of the Words: Tolkien and the Oxford English Dictionary.* Oxford: Oxford UP, 2006

Gisinger, Friedrich. "Oikumene", *Paulys Realencyclopädie der classischen Altertumswissenschaft.* Stuttgart: 1937, vol. 17/2, cols. 2123-74

Hammond, Wayne G., and Christina Scull. *The Lord of the Rings. A Reader's Companion,* London: HarperCollins, 2014

Heidegger, Martin, "Building Dwelling Thinking". *Poetry, Language, Thought,* translated by Albert Hofstadter. New York: Harper and Row, 1971, 145-61

---. "... Poetically man dwells...". *Poetry, Language, Thought,* translated by Albert Hofstadter. New York: Harper and Row, 1971. 209-27

Jourde, Pierre. *Géographies imaginaires de quelques inventeurs de mondes au xxe siècle: Gracq, Borges, Michaux, Tolkien,* Paris: José Corti, 1991

Leed, Eric J. *No Man's Land: Combat and Identity in World War I.* New York: Cambridge UP, 1979

Morse, Robert E. *Evocation of Virgil in Tolkien's Art: Geritol for the Classics.* Oak Park: Bolchazy-Carducci Publishers, 1986

Perry, Michael W. *Untangling Tolkien: A Chronology and Commentary for* The Lord of the Rings. Seattle: Inkling Books, 2003.

Shahar, Yuval. *Josephus Geographicus: The Classical Context of Geography.* Tübingen: Mohr Siebeck, 2004

Shippey, Tom. *The Road to Middle-earth.* London: Grafton, 1992

Smith, William. *Dictionary of Greek and Roman Geography.* London: Walton and Maberly, 1854 (2nd ed. 1870)

Swinton, Ernest. *The Green Curve and Others Stories,* Garden City NY: Doubleday, Page & Company, 1914

Tolkien, J.R.R. "Addenda and Corrigenda to the *Etymologies*", *Vinyar Tengwar* 45 (2003): 3-38

---. "Fate and Free Will". *Tolkien Studies* 6 (2009): 183-8.

---. "Nomenclature of *The Lord the Rings*". In Hammond/Scull, 2014, 750-82

---. *The Lord of the Rings,* 50th anniversary edition. Boston: Houghton Mifflin, 2004

---. *Parma Eldalamberon* 17 (2007)

---. *Parma Eldalamberon* 18 (2009)

Appendix

Condordances of the quotations of Tolkien about οἰκουμένη, sorted in chronological order:

1. 1931-1938: "MBAR- dwell, ~~build~~, inhabit. Q *a-mbar* (*ambaren*) '**oikoumenē**', Earth; (...)" (*The Etymologie*, LR 372).
2. September, 18th, 1954: "Middle-earth is just an archaic English for ἡ[31] οἰκουμένη, the inhabited world of men. It lay then as it does, round and inescapable. That is partly the point. (letter to Hugh Brogan, L 186).
3. September, 25th, 1954: "But the whole 'legendarium' contains a transition from a flat world (or at least an **οἰκουμένη** with borders all around it) to a globe..." (letter to Naomi Mitchison, L 197).
4. 1955: *Ambar* "This may be translated 'world'–meaning this Earth as the place (by destiny) inhabited by Elves and Men, the Children of Eru. It thus resembles ἡ οἰκουμένη (γῆ[32]), but was not limited either to the parts of Earth actually inhabited, or those inhabited by any special peoples such as the Elves, or among Men the Numenóreans." ("Words, Phrases & Passages in *The Lord of the Rings*", *Parma Eldalamberon*, 17, 163).
5. January, 22th, 1956: "The name is the modern form (appearing in the 13th century and still in use) of *midden-erd* > *middel-erd*, an ancient name for the *oikoumenē*, the abiding place of Men, the objectively real world, in use specifically opposed to imaginary world (as Fairyland) or unseen worlds (as Heaven or Hell). ...The essentials of that abiding place are all there (at any rate for inhabitants of N.W. Europe)..." (letter to Auden, L 239).
6. October, 14th, 1958: "Middle-earth is (by the way & if such a note is necessary) not my own invention. It is a modernization or alteration (*New English Dictionary* 'a perversion') of an old word for the inhabited world of Men, the **oikoumenē**: middle because thought of vaguely as set amidst the encircling Seas (in northern imagination) between ice of the North and the fire of the South. Old English *middan-geard*, mediaeval E. *midden-erd*, *middle-erd*. (letter to Rhona Beare, L 283).
7. 1968: "The sense 'world'—applied usually to this Earth—is mainly derived from sense 'settlement': 'the great habitation' (οἰκουμένη[33]) as 'home of speaking creatures' esp. Elves and Men. (*ambar* 'world' differed from *Arda* in reference. *Arda* meant 'realm' & was this earth as the *realm* ruled by *Manwe* (the Elder King) vice-regent of Eru, for benefit of the Children of Eru.)" ("Fate and Free Will", *Tolkien Studies*, 6, 183).

---

31 We correct the edited text.
32 The reading γῆ have been approved by Christopher Gilson.
33 The reading οἰκουμένη have been approved by Carl Hostetter.

Approach and Sojourn: Structures of Arriving and Staying in *The Lord of the Rings*

Martin G.E. Sternberg (Bonn)

For a quest story like the *Lord of the Rings*, by necessity landscape is either something the characters pass through or some place where they stay, if only for a while. It is the way towards a destination or the destination itself. This paper shall deal with the question whether the way in which a destination is approached, and how this approach is described, already tells something about the destination itself. Basically, two kinds of approaching a given space or place may be discerned. The first is the sudden, leaplike crossing over a clearly defined border, the second a gradual approach where elements in the landscape the wanderer passes through already hint at the place he is going to arrive at and mediate the transition into it. As we shall see, these different modes of transition also bear a relation between landscape and time.

Sudden Crossings

The first crossing over into another landscape and country we witness in the *Lord of the Rings* is also the most extreme expression of the first kind of transition: the hobbits leaving the Shire and entering the Old Forest, or to be more precise, their entering into Tom Bombadil's land: they ride down the tunnel, and

> ...disappeared from Fredegar's sight... At the far end it was closed by a gate with thick-set iron bars. Merry got down and unlocked the gate, and when they had all passed through he pushed it to again. It shut with a clang, and the lock clicked. The sound was ominous. 'There!' said Merry, 'you have left the Shire, and are now outside, and on the edge of the Old Forest.'   (LotR I 153)

Of the Old Forest, we know very little at this point, only that it is an uncanny place where your luck will fail you. Only here at its edge Merry tells to the others that everything is more alive here than in the Shire, and relates the attack of the trees on the Hedge. Detailed knowledge about it will only be provided by Tom Bombadil later. The transition into the Old Forest is thus neither prepared by mediating elements in the landscape nor by knowledge provided before entering it, and that applies for Tom Bombadil's country as a whole. That the transition which really matters is not the entering of the Old

Forest but the passing under the Hedge is made clear by the fact that the act of entering the Old Forest is described as the hobbits looking back at the dark line of the Hedge through the trunks of the trees that are already thick about them (LotR I 154). Later on, the hobbits will leave Tom Bombadil's country in the same sudden manner: by passing a line of trees at the Road beyond which Tom will not accompany them, because 'Tom's country ends here, he will not pass the borders' (LotR I 202).

On the part of the Old Forest, an alien vegetation of densely standing, sentient trees that press in on the hobbits and give them the impression of being watched characterises this country. The trees suffer no undergrowth, which is, as there are no saplings, an indication of their agelessness. It is experienced as density and constriction: the air is sticky, Old Man Willow induces insurmountable sleepiness, rising fog obscures their ways at dusk. Fog is the element that links the Old Forest with the Barrow-downs which on the one hand are an inversion to the Forest: 'There was no tree nor visible water: it was a country of grass and short springy turf, silent except for the whisper of the air over the edges of the land, and high lonely cries of strange birds' (LotR I 187), denying the hobbits any cover. Like the Old Forest, it is a landscape of silence, and the wind grows less with every ridge the hobbits climb (LotR I 187). After the unintended nap on the mounded hilltop, the landscape will press in on them by means of that fog which 'was thick, cold and white. The air was silent, heavy and chill' (LotR I 188f).

The second characteristic experience is a loss of orientation. In the Old Forest, the paths change, and they do so at the behest of a hidden power, Old Man Willow. On the Barrow-downs, fog is taking away any sense of direction, and standing stones appear in places where they were not seen when the sun was shining.

This loss of orientation also takes the form of a changed and/or distorted experience of time. When Tom Bombadil tells the story of the Old Forest, the Barrow-downs and their inhabitants past and present, Frodo cannot tell 'whether the morning and evening of one day or many days had passed' (LotR I 180). Bombadil's tale seems to be less a tale told in words but a vision granted, which is explicitly the case when Bombadil tells the hobbits of the Men of Westernesse after their liberation from the barrow: 'as he spoke they had a vision as it were of a great expanse of years behind them, like a vast shadowy plain over which there strode shapes of Men, tall and grim with bright swords, and last came one with a star on his brow' (LotR I 199)—a prophetic vision, as this last shape obviously points to Aragorn. Stronger still is the way the past impresses itself on the hobbits fallen under the spell of the Barrow-wight. Merry re-lives (or rather re-dies) the memory of someone buried in the barrow who was killed by the Witch-king's men.

It has often been said that you cannot turn a stone in Middle-earth without finding some trace of history: 'the past is not just tributary to the present, but formative of it and immediate in it... Tolkien repeatedly underscores the imme-diacy of time past in time present and time future by introducing prophecies, old songs, and legends into his narrative' (Flieger, *Incident* 89). History is told and retold and has its ongoing effects. In Tom Bombadil's country however history does not wait to be turned upon. It has a heightened presence and an agency of its own, like the trees of the Old Forest, and the barrows act as places of lingering memories which long for new bearers after the souls of the men originally interred in them have long since passed out of this world. It is fitting that Merry has the dream of being killed by the men of the Witch-king, for he will eventually partake in his slaying, with a blade from the barrow, and act out the revenge of the man who was once laid to rest there. Merry's deed is prefigured even more closely when we think of that item of treasure that Tom Bombadil chooses to keep: a brooch set with stones of many shades of blue that once belonged to a very beautiful woman whom Tom does still remember, and it is Éowyn's beauty that stirs Merry to help her fight the Lord of the Nazgûl: 'She should not die, so fair, so desperate! At least she should not die alone, unaided' (LotR III 137). That the barrow in which the hobbits were trapped was the tomb of a king who was killed by the witch-king may be an afterthought of Tolkien's in the Appendices (LotR III 391), but it complements the picture.

The memories preserved in the Old Forest and on the Barrow-downs have in fact a common theme: revenge, aggression, and rule. The trees remember 'times when they were lords', and their hearts are 'filled with a hatred of things that go free upon the earth, gnawing, biting, breaking, hacking, burning: destroyers and usurpers' (LotR I 179). The barrows are the tombs of the ruling houses and the aristocracy of little kingdoms warring with each other and the Witch-king, and in a way, Merry carries their wrath before the gates of Minas Tirith. The Old Forest and the Barrow-downs are zones of aggressive relics, and it is a single, sharply defined, unmediated border that separates them from the surrounding world.

Embedding in Space and Time

If the Old Forest and the Barrow-downs are secluded islands of a long-gone past, then this should apply to Moria as well: a labyrinthine city stretching out for 40 miles under vast Mountains, old in itself and touching the passages dug by beings still older. The Balrog of Morgoth could be seen as the equivalent of Old Man Willow or the Barrow-wight. Yet the experience of Moria is different. Moria is of bewildering complexity, but it is the complexity of a puzzle that can be solved. It is known to have a systematic outlay of levels and halls

(LotR I 420), and Gimli knows what the Chamber of Mazarbul is. In contrast to the Old Forest, paths do not change here. The air in Moria is hot and sticky, but not foul, and is occasionally stirred by breezes of fresh air from the outside world. There is no feeling of the kind of pressing density that characterised the Old Forest: 'All about them as they lay hung the darkness, hollow and immense, and they were oppressed by the loneliness and vastness of the dolven halls and endlessly branching stairs and passsages' (LotR I 410). Moria is vast and hollow, and its experience is marked by the sudden opening-up of space: as other passages, halls, wells or chasms on the way.

Disorientation in time is absent as well: 'We had better halt here for the rest of the night,' says Gandalf. 'You know what I mean! In here it is ever dark; but outside the Moon is riding westward and the middle-night has passed' (LotR I 406 f). Despite being cut off from the sky, Gandalf is able to tell the time accurate to the hour. Neither does the experience of time in tales deviate from the quotidian norm. Gimli's song of Moria, impressive as it may be, has none of the visionary quality of Bombadil's tales. In fact, the song of the past glories of Moria does not make the past more present, but the present itself: 'I like that', said Sam, 'I should like to learn it. *In Moria, in Khazad-dûm.* But it makes the darkness seem heavier, thinking of all those lamps' (LotR I 412). The Book of Mazarbul is a record of the failed attempt to regain Moria, which gives exact dates, and is thus coherent with the flow of historical time, of which the War of the Ring is a part.

For all its strangeness and dangers, Moria forms a continuum with the outside world, and this is mirrored by the fact that Moria is not entered with a sudden leap over a defined border, but approached gradually, step by step. We are already rather well informed about it when the fellowship actually enters it: Setting its being mentioned in *The Hobbit* aside, Gloin relates the core facts already at the council of Elrond: That it is a great place from which the dwarves fled after their digging woke 'a nameless fear', and that Balin went there to reclaim it (LotR I 315).

Gimli gives the names the mountains of Moria, Caradhras, Celebdil und Fanuidhol, when the fellowship sees them from afar, and stresses their importance for the dwarves by telling the fellowship that their image is wrought in many of their works (LotR I 369). When Legolas says that the stones of Eregion still remember the elves who wrought them fair and built them high (LotR I 370), he calls attention to the elves who lived there as friends of the dwarves of Moria, whose story is already known to us. A road leads up to Moria, formerly lined with a hedge of holly-trees of which two large, immensely old holly tress still remain, standing sentinel at the gates of Moria (LotR I 394). These trees find an echo in the trees drawn out in ithildin on the gates itself. In this way, elements in the landscape hint at the place to be arrived at, and the place in turn is embedded in the landscape.

This embedding already mediates the transition into Moria, and this mediation is further intensified by the time it takes to solve the riddle how to open the gates. Finding an answer to this problem creates not only a moment of suspense, but also ample opportunity to reflect the place of Moria in history, its connections with the outside world and the ease with which this threshold was passed in former times. This means that, although the fellowship has to flee into Moria once the gates have been opened, and the Watcher in the water slams them shut, this transition is no sudden, unmediated step into a space entirely other as was the case with Tom Bombadil's country.

This kind of mediation also applies to the fellowship leaving Moria: They do so on a road, at first 'rough and broken', then 'dwindling to a mere track,' which is lined by 'ruined works of stone' and green hills which recall mounds or remnants of former buildings (LotR I 433). Only after leaving Moria do we encounter a vision with an othertimely quality: Looking down into the Mirrormere, wherein Durin's crown lies and which mirrors stars at daytime, but not the faces of those looking into it (LotR I 434). This vision however lies outside Moria, and beside the road the fellowship must take.

Approaching, entering and leaving Moria represents the second basic variety of encountering a place: however strange and hostile it may be, it belongs to the world of mortal, historical time, the time of men, when moving up to it is mediated by elements of knowledge provided beforehand, and elements of landscape that point to it and prefigure it. This is made plain by the Paths of the Dead, which have a strong structural resemblance to Moria: The way that leads up to the Gates of the Dead is lined with standing stones in the same way as the road leading up to Moria was lined with holly trees, and on the other side of the Paths of the dead stands the stone of Erech, set by Isildur, the equivalent of which is Durin's stone on the eastern side of Moria near Mirrormere. With regard to knowledge, the essentials are already explained when Aragorn declares his intent to walk the Paths of the Dead to Legolas and Gimli (LotR III 58ff). The Paths of the Dead have two arches, engraved with glyphs and pictures (LotR III 64f, 67) in the same way as gates of Moria are, but there are no gates within them, and the boundary they demarcate is blurred: dread flows out of them, and the shadows of the dead seem to be able to leave their realm. On occasion they meet at the stone of Erech, and Aragorn's command to trouble the valleys no longer (LotR III 182) implies that they have done so in the past.

Neither do we find signs of disorientation in time or space, even though the passage through the Paths of the Dead is related by Gimli who bears them worst of all the company. The embedding in the landscape reflects the embedding in mortal, historical time.

The entry into the realm of men, the men of Rohan and Gondor, is mediated in a similar way by encountering relics of a long-gone past in the landscape: the Gates of Argonath and the seat of Amon Hen. They work as mediators and announcers rather than heralds and sentinels, for they no longer demarcate a border, as the effective power of Gondor has long since retreated. They signal nonetheless that the fellowship enters a space that is governed by kings (Rohan) or their stewards (Gondor), where Aragorn will have to prove his claim, and they provide an opportunity to confer information about Gondor as a former kingdom of great power. This holds true as well for leaving the realm of men, which Frodo and Sam do at the crossroads where stands the mutilated statue of a king, 'solemn as the great stone kings of Argonath,' the decapitated head of which has grown again a crown of flowers (LotR II 390).

In this context, the Pillars of Argonath have a peculiar effect apart from their mediating function: Their own appearance is not mediated in any way, the fellowship is unstoppably carried towards them on the fast-flowing Anduin, and their recognition as gigantic statues of Elendil and Isildur overcomes the fellowship with suddenness: 'Great power and majesty they still wore, the silent wardens of a long-vanished kingdom. Awe and fear fell upon Frodo, and he cowered down, shutting his eyes as the boat drew near' (LotR I 511). In their presence, Aragorn not only stakes his claim and gives his full name and lineage, but is also transformed for a moment into a royal presence, a king returning from exile to his own land (LotR I 511), a moment that passes as soon as the river has carried the boats through the gates. Here, there are no traces of a past effective by 'supernatural' means like in the case of the barrow, but the pillars are nevertheless an example of an immediately effective and active past, solely by the landscape, the river that carries the fellowship up to the pillars.

Finally, this gradual approach applies to Mordor as well. Sam feels that the top of the Path of Cirith Ungol is a sharply drawn border, and that he will be unable to return (LotR III 207). But before this point, Mordor has already projected its presence far and wider in the landscape before the mountain ranges that are its natural walls, through devastations and the dead marches that are again relics of ancient battles and thus history.

Into the Woods of Time

Let us return now to the sudden crossing into an altogether other and alien space: the entering of Lothlórien. All we know of it when the fellowship arrives before this wood at night is what Legolas has told us of its trees that are unlike the trees in any other land. Legolas provides more detailed knowledge of the wood and its inhabitants only after the company has entered it. Unmediated by any outposts or hints in the landscape, the wood looms before them as a wide grey shadow: 'Under the night the trees stood tall before them, arched over the road and stream that ran suddenly beneath their spreading boughs' (LotR I 438). The wood poses as a wall with a gate, and thus a well-defined border.

Although Frodo has the impression of having entered a corner of the Elder Days only after crossing the Silverlode and entering the Naith, the fellowship experiences the different nature and laws of this land already after wading through the Nimrodel. Frodo feels that by its waters 'all stain of travel and all weariness was washed from his limbs' (LotR I 440). This is the first demonstration of Lothlórien's healing powers, and it shows that Lothlórien outside the Naith is already Lothlórien proper, and no space of transition, so that the first step under the Mallorn trees is already a completely valid transition. In the same sudden manner that Lothlórien is entered, it is also left again: 'Suddenly the river swept round a bend, and the banks rose upon either side, and the light of Lorien was hidden.' This sharply drawn re-entry into the grey outside world has its cognitive and emotional counterpart in a poignant feeling of loss: 'Their eyes were dazzled, for all were filled with tears' (LotR I 491). Tatjana Silec has said in her paper that there are certain words in medieval literature that signal the entry into the wild without the need for its more explicit description. With Tolkien, the word *suddenly* seems to be such a word that signals the entry into an alien space, and we will encounter it again in this role in Rivendell.

The experience of spatial disorientation is a more subtle matter. It is not confined to being led blindfolded through the Naith, and relying on Elvish guides, but goes hand in hand with a disorientation or better displacement in time: '… it seemed to him that he had stepped over a bridge of time into a corner of the Elder Days, and was now walking in a world that was no more,' 'it seemed to him that he had stepped through a high window that looked on a vanished world' (LotR 453, 455). The experience of density that we found in the Old Forest takes a more benign form here: Not only is Lothlórien, as a wood, a dense kind of landscape, but the light of this country and the ‚magic', the effects of Galadriel's ring, bears some resemblance to the power of Old Man Willow suffusing the Old Forest. What Galadriel herself calls her ‚magic', her Mirror, grants the same time-transcending visions of things past, present, and yet to come, as did Tom Bombadil in the Old Forest.

It has often been noted that time passes differently in Lothlórien, it seems to be 'a refuge from linear time' (Flieger, *Time* 93). What seems to be a few days gone by are a whole month in the outside world, and time has a different effect: as Gandalf says, its passing brings healing, not decay (LotR II 130).

Even more than the mallorn-trees of Lorien, the trees of Fangorn present themselves to the outsider in a wall-like fashion, unmediated by small groups of trees that announce the large woods in the Woody End in the Shire: 'Even as he spoke the dark edge of the forest loomed straight up before them. Night seemed to have taken refuge under its great trees, creeping away from the coming dawn' (LotR II 72). Neither is there any mediation on the level of knowledge. Fangorn's place is laid down on the maps, but all Celeborn is prepared to say that it is 'a strange land, and is now little known' (LotR I 486).

When Merry and Pippin enter this wood, its description dwells not only on the enormous age of the trees laden with lichen, but switches into another time: Merry and Pippin look out of the Forest 'like elf-children in the deeps of time peering out of the Wild Wood in wonder at their first Dawn' (LotR II 72). That Fangorn is a remnant of other times is stressed further by comparing it to the rooms of the Old Took in Great Smials, which were not changed during his lifetime and in the time since (LotR II 74f). The Entish language too has time-related aspects, for its use is very time-consuming and shows that time does not flow differently in Fangorn, but is regarded as a resource richly supplied, giving no need for 'haste' for Ents nor trees. Its words keep growing all the time, taking in and telling the history of the things they belong to (LotR II 80), in this way conserving the works of time within its words. And in a similar way to Lothlórien, the sojourn in Fangorn has healing effects: The waters of the Entwash and the drink from Treebeard's jars heal the injuries Merry and Pippin suffered from the orcs and let them grow again (LotR II 76, 87).

Fangorn complies with the rule that the alien place is left again by crossing a clearly defined border in a rather curious way: by Treebeard not leaving it at all. When he and his Ents march on Isengart and later the Hornburg, they take their wood with them by way of the moving Huorns. When they start recultivating Isengard after their victory over Saruman, they effectively extend the reach of Fangorn by adding a territory that has clearly defined borders, at the gate of which Merry and Pippin operate as gatekeepers—and from this position on the border they rejoin the other remaining members of the fellowship.

Landscape Gardening in Gondor

Judged by the criteria drawn from Tom Bombadil's land, Lothlórien and Fangorn, Frodo's and Sam's arrival at Henneth Annûn could be mistaken for a similar experience: The hobbits are blindfolded as they were while walking through the Naith, and as in Lothlórien, taking off their blindfolds is followed by an intense visual experience: The waterfall of Henneth Annûn at sunset, which is compared to a window-curtain in an elvish tower, made of gold, silver and threaded rubies, sapphires and amethysts. This image of an elvish window strongly correlates to Frodo's impression, after climbing the highest tree of Cerin Amroth, that he was looking on the Elder Days through a high window.

Indeed it is the Elder Days where we have to go to find examples for such splendid displays of gems and jewels, e.g. in the description of the seven gates of Gondolin, for the style of Elrond's household in Rivendell or of Galadriel and Celeborn is much more subdued. A window into the west is Henneth Annûn also insofar as Faramir tells Frodo and Sam about Númenor and Gondor, and

Faramir and his men turning silently towards the west before their meal make their orientation towards the west gone by and the one that will always be explicit, but there is no vision-like quality to Faramir's talk. Neither are there traces of disorientation in time.

This is no wonder, for a close examination of Henneth Annûn reveals that it does not belong into the same category as Lothlórien or Tom Bombadil's count-ry, for it is in fact tightly embedded in the landscape, and the approach to it is suitably mediated. Frodo and Sam meet Faramir near a lake in the ruins of an ancient stone basin: a piece of garden architecture. Their blindfolded walk up to Henneth Annûn is always accompanied by the sound of running water that connects this meeting place with Henneth Annûn.

As the garden of Gondor, Ithilien is a *landscaped* landscape, though we do not know the Gondorian equivalent to Capability Brown, and water features—lakes, brooks, cascades, waterfalls— are key elements of landscape design. The grotto of Henneth Annûn is no mere work of nature, but the result of a kind of hydro-engineering: the stream that cascades down before its opening did originally flow through the cave and had to be redirected (LotR II 352f). Henneth Annûn is in fact a militarised garden grotto, and grottos were a firm staple in gardening from the Renaissance onwards.

This applies not only to English landscape gardening, but also to the more formal gardens of villas of the Italian Renaissance, which would fit the Mediterranean associations of Ithilien: The large fountain in the Villa d'Este in Tivoli sports a waterfall cascading over the opening of a cave. The Ilmpark in the German city of Weimar, designed shortly before 1800, contains still the remnants of a „grotto of the Sphinx", wherein the statue of a sphinx was originally placed behind a curtain-like waterfall, which elicited in its time a description very similar to that of its Ithilian counterpart. A table in the Museum dedicated to the history of this park in the Römisches Haus gives the following contemporary description:

> The water falls down from a rocky cleft into a basin lined with tuff... Falling this way, it forms a mirror, which at some distance, and when the rays of the sun refract on it, delights the eye beyond all expression, and gains in the shadow the look of a diamond gate.

As such a garden grotto, Henneth Annûn fits in very well with the description of Ithilien as the 'garden of Gondor', and is thus embedded in time and place. To operate from a hiding place like Henneth Annûn has of course a rationale of its own, but it is tempting to see Faramir and his men, sporting masks and camouflage, as a kind of re-enactment of literary models, namely Turin and his outlaws operating from Amon Rudh, which also featured, like Henneth

Annûn, a pool (CH 130). Henneth Annûn is embedded in a landscape designed by humans, it is a place where human memory is re-enacted and shared with Frodo and Sam, and it is thus a part of human time and history. The description of the waterfall at sunset as an elvish curtain for which we find no actual elvish equivalent in the *Lord of the Rings* is thus revealed as a product of human imagination about the elves, which puts it firmly into the continuum of mortal time and history.

Befitting its role as a place of refuge, counsel and rest whose lord is half-elven, Rivendell shows characteristics both of the embedded and the separated place. Its whereabouts and its inhabitants are well known, and they are seen as accessible by both dwarves and men, otherwise Boromir, Gloin and Gimli would not have travelled there. In contrast to Lothlórien, it is not seen as dangerous to enter it, and people do not expect to be repelled at its borders. It is a fair valley, yet it is without an alien vegetation: When Bilbo, Gandalf and the dwarves ride down into it in *The Hobbit*, the successive zones of mountain vegetation are carefully described (H 55). It also has the self-embedding quality of coming out to meet the traveller if need be, as Glorfindel does, who also performs a tiny but significant act of elvish landscape gardening: The beryl he leaves in the dirt near the bridge as a sign that the passage is safe is not only a fitting symbol for Aragorn (the elf-stone, Elessar, in the mud of the road) but also recalls the Teleri who adorned the shores and waters of Valinor with the gems that the Noldor gave them (S 52).

On the other hand, the valley of Rivendell is hidden, and one comes upon it with suddenness: In *The Hobbit*, 'they came to the edge of a steep fall in the ground so suddenly that Gandalf's horse nearly slipped down the slope' (H 55). In *The Lord of the Rings*, the fellowship leaves the valley with an abrupt step onto the High moors and a last longing look backwards (LotR I 367). When the hobbits are on their way home after the fall of Sauron, it is said 'at last one evening they came over the high moors, suddenly as to travellers it always seemed, to the brink of the deep valley of Rivendell' (LotR III 320). As with Lorien, the word *suddenly* sets Rivendell apart from its surroundings.

Concerning disorientations, there is none in time. For good reason, Frodo's first questions are where he is and how late it is, and Gandalf answers both of them with accuracy. There seems however to be a slight disorientation in space within Elrond's house: 'It's a big house this, and very peculiar. Always a bit more to discover, and no knowing what you'll find around a corner,' as Sam observes (LotR I 296). Moreover, it is never described from the outside, which sets it apart from all other important buildings like the halls of Celeborn and Galadriel, Theoden, and Denethor, which are described in great detail. A feeling of displacement and a kind of vision is granted to Frodo in the Hall of Fire, when he listens to the elvish musicians and 'it seemed to him that the words took shape, and visions of far lands and bright things that he had never yet imagined opened out before him' (LotR I 306). Yet this enchantment is the effect of art, however powerful beyond human means this art may be, but not of some kind of supernatural power, befitting the intermediary position of Rivendell. So do its healing properties: 'Merely to be there was a cure for weariness, fear and sadness' (LotR I 295), but not more serious afflictions. Frodo's recovery is achieved by the actions of Elrond as a healer, not by just coming within the confines of Imladris in the way that the passing of time in Lothlórien 'brings healing, not decay.'

The Past as another Country

What do we make of it all? One concept into which to fit the places that are entered with a sudden crossing of a sharply defined border and are so different from the norm of Middle-earth reality would be to see them as heterotopias according to Michel Foucault. Heterotopias share the characteristics of the places entered with a sudden leap: clear borders, peculiar laws different from everyday normality and a time of their own. For Foucault, any society contains of lot of such segregated spaces, ranging from brothels to prisons (Foucault 11f, 16f). Society has the capacity to create and close down heterotopias at any time (Foucault 13), and this is why this concept does not fit in with our observations: The existence of Fangorn or Lothlórien does not depend on any consent of the outside world, but on their ability to defend themselves against it and to fend off the effects of the time that passes there.

Lothlórien fits much better into the concept of sacred space with a sacred time as outlined by Mircea Eliade (Hopp 145): a space of the first beginnings wherein primeaval forms are preserved and in which the time flowing is the time of creation, where 'the shapes seemed at once clear cut, as if they had been conceived and drawn at the uncovering of his eyes, and ancient as if they had endured forever'. It is a land 'that does not change or fade or fall into forgetfulness' and in which Frodo would still be walking even after having left that country (LotR I 455). This similarity to sacred spaces is to a lesser degree true for Fangorn with its healing waters, but these 'sacred spaces' do not contain a model for the world as a whole from which it could be renewed.

Nevertheless, these places influence the world outside them considerably. From Tom Bombadil's land onwards, the segregated places are pockets of a world and a time gone by elsewhere, which nevertheless have retained an agency of their own. I have already described above that this point is made, and made very strongly, when the hobbits leave the Shire and enter Tom Bombadil's land, where the past both fends off trespassers and traps and, in Merry's case, transforms them. Here, the past is more than memory, and Merry's 'dream' in the barrow does not need to rely on a concept of reincarnation or a common human memory (for this see Flieger, *Incident* 97ff), but could equally be explained by the idea of memories attaching themselves to things and places, like a kind of 'mana', and imposing themselves on sentient beings. Judith Klinger has shown how swords with Tolkien oscillate between inanimate artefact and animate being, being agents of history, fate and memory, carrying with them certain qualities of their makers or bearers (Klinger 147). There is no reason why this concept should not be applicable to lands and landscapes as well. The landscapes and the relics in them are *agents* of memory and ongoing history.

In contrast, places that are embedded in the landscape and are approached gradually are part of a continuum of world and time and are *subjects* to memory, like Henneth Annûn where a lot of history is told which holds no power beyond talk. Here, the past has no agency of its own, but is called upon, however strange and forbidding the place and the threshold to it may be. The shadow host of Dunharrow waits to be called forth by an heir of Isildur, and when Aragorn does this, he does so at the instigation of those who dwell in places of an active past, Galadriel and Elrond. Thus, the approach to a place tells us a lot of what we will find there and points to where the past will be, in a very literal sense, another country.

Bibliography

Flieger, Verlyn. *A Question of Time: J.R.R.Tolkien's road to Farie*. Kent, Ohio, and London: Kent University Press, 1997

---. "The Curious Incident of the Dream at the Barrow: Memory and Reincarnation in Middle-earth." *Green Suns and Faërie*. Kent, Ohio, and London: Kent University Press, 2012, 89-101

Foucault, Michel. *Die Heterotopien*. Translated by Michael Bischoff. Frankfurt am Main: Suhrkamp Verlag 2005

Hopp, Martin. "Das Heilige und das Andere – Weltbild und Weltbindung im *Herrn der Ringe*." *Hither Shore 2* (2005): 137-155

Klinger, Judith. "A Legacy of Swords: Animate weapons and the Ambivalence of Heroic Violence." *Hither Shore 6* (2009): 130-150

Tolkien, John Ronald Reuel. *The Children of Hurin*. London: HarperCollins, 2007

---. *The Hobbit*. London: Unwin Paperbacks, 1984

---. *The Lord of the Rings*. 4th ed. London: Unwin Hyman, 1988

---. *The Silmarillion*. Ed. Christopher Tolkien. Boston and New York: Houghton Mifflin, 2004

Die dunkle Seite des Waldes? Konkrete und ›gefühlte‹ Bedrohungen durch natürliche Räume

Patrick Peters (Mönchengladbach)

Wenn wir über den Wald bei J.R.R. Tolkien sprechen, reden wir über ein räumliches Konstrukt, das auf mehreren Ebenen eine ungemeine Bedeutungstiefe besitzt. Der literarische Entwurf des Waldes besitzt, legt man den Fokus beispielsweise auf die mit Mittelerde verbundenen Texte, Diskurse von Gut und Böse, soziale und kulturelle Aspekte und Symbolcharakter unterschiedlicher Ausprägungen und ist bisweilen vor allem auch offensichtlicher Treiber für den inhaltlichen Fortgang und die konzeptionelle Entwicklung der Texte.

Um dafür ein konkretes Beispiel zu geben: Wenn Meriadoc und Peregrin beim Angriff der Krieger Rohans unter der Führung Éomers auf die Uruk-hai am Saum Fangorns in den Wald fliehen und dort Baumbart begegnen, setzen sie damit einen nicht vorhersehbaren Handlungsteil in Gang, der mit der Schleifung Isengarts und dem Ende der Herrschaft Sarumans endet. Der Wald ist dabei unabdingbarer Raum für diese Entwicklung und setzt eine längere Episode innerhalb der Romanhandlung in Gang, die sich dann in einem Erzählmoment höchster Relevanz entlädt und sich nachhaltig auf die Gesamtkonzeption von *The Lord of the Rings* auswirkt.

Doch es soll in diesem Aufsatz nicht um den Wald an sich bei Tolkien gehen; eine Analyse des Bedeutungsspektrums würde den sinnvollen Rahmen der vorliegenden Untersuchung sprengen, aber eine Monografie zu dem Thema könnte echten Wert für die Forschung beweisen. Vielmehr steht eine raumsemantische Besonderheit im Fokus, denn J.R.R. Tolkien führt in seinem epischen Werk unterschiedliche Wahrnehmungen von Natur und Landschaft vor.

Auf der einen Seite finden sich zahlreiche positive, bisweilen ›idyllische‹ Beschreibungen von Wäldern und anderen ›natürlichen‹ Räumen, die entsprechend positiv konstruiert und funktionalisiert werden, beispielsweise Bruchtal, das Auenland, (je nach Perspektive) Lothlórien oder auch solche, die in der Tradition des topischen *locus amoenus* definiert sind.

Auf der anderen Seite werden gleichzeitig differente Darstellungen von Natur und Landschaft im Allgemeinen und von Wäldern im Speziellen positioniert, die deren dunkle Seite in den Vordergrund stellen und solche Räume als explizite und implizite Bedrohung für Physis und Psyche präsentieren. Auch dafür gibt es naheliegende Beispiele, man denke bloß an den Alten Wald und Düsterwald als die offensichtlichsten auf der Folie einer akuten Bedrohung gezeichneten Wälder beziehungsweise natürlichen Räume. Deshalb ist zu fragen, wie Bedrohung als Teil des Waldes (und damit von Natur und Landschaft) literarisch konstruiert ist: Was bedeutet Bedrohung genau und wie und in welchen Räumen äußert sie sich konkret? Mit welchen stilistischen Mitteln wird episch und lyrisch gearbeitet, um die Bedrohung zu materialisieren? Darauf haben Rimoli und Spirito hingewiesen, wenn sie die Korrelation zwischen Raumgestaltung (bezogen auf die Landschaft an sich) und Charakterentwicklung andeuten: »There are even much darker landscapes in Imlad Morgul and in the Stairs of Cirith Ungol—in Shelob's Lair—, as the darkening of Frodo's mind and soul unfolds within him while getting nearer to the Nameless Land« (Rimoli/Spirito 128).

Aber dies ist nur ein Teil der Fragestellung in diesem Kontext. Denn Bedrohung ist nicht immer konkret vorhanden, sondern ihr wird auch Bahn gebrochen durch die Dynamiken der *oral tradition*, auf die sich tragende Figuren in ihren Meinungen berufen. Damit wird ›Bedrohung‹ von außen auf die Räume appliziert, ohne geprüft zu haben, ob eine solche Meinungsapplikation im Sinne einer auf Tradition beruhenden Deutungshoheit überhaupt gerechtfertigt ist, und es entsteht dadurch eine ›gefühlte‹ Bedrohung ohne Substanz. Hier ist besonders an Lothlórien zu denken, das kultur- und traditionsbedingt als massive, magisch-mythische Bedrohung wahrgenommen und deren Herrin Galadriel als bösartige Hexe figuriert wird – ohne dass ein Beleg für diese Deutung greifbar wird.

Auf diese Weise erscheint ›Bedrohung‹ in einem doppelten Licht, und es soll Aufgabe dieses Aufsatzes sein, neben der Untersuchung der literarischen Konstruktionen dieses zweifachen Diskurses auch die Grenzen zu ziehen zwischen echter, vorhandener Bedrohung und der ›gefühlten‹ beziehungsweise der mündlichen Erzähltradition entspringenden angenommenen ›Bedrohung‹, die von den Figuren zwar als *Status quo* postuliert wird, ohne aber dabei konkrete Formungen anzunehmen.

In einem ersten Schritt werden Beispiele für positive Konstruktionen genauer analysiert und deren Bedeutung für Handlung und Figuren ermittelt. Der zweite Hauptteil befasst sich dann mit den ›bedrohlichen‹ Konstruktionen, deren Funktionalisierung ebenso untersucht werden soll wie deren formale Gestaltung sowie Bedeutung, bevor sich dem Konzept der ›gefühlten‹ Bedrohung zugewendet werden soll.

1. Das Auenland als per se ›guter Raum‹

Beginnen wir unsere Betrachtungen mit der positiven Raumkonstruktion im Auenland. Zwar kein unmittelbares Waldgebiet, steht das Auenland aber als eine Art exemplarische Idylle im System Mittelerde da; und das nicht nur aufgrund der bereits vielfach nachgewiesenen und beschriebenen Ähnlichkeit zu Tolkiens geliebter mittelenglischer Heimat. Es ist eine Interpretation der Idyllentradition, wie sie eigentlich sämtliche europäische Literaturen kennen und aus der Antike herstammt. Bei der Idylle sprechen wir, nach Gero von Wilpert, von der »Schilderung friedvoll-bescheidenen, behagl.-gemütl. Winkelglücks harmlos empfindender Menschen in e. heilen Welt harmon. Geborgenheit und Selbstgenügsamkeit und natürlich-alltägl. Land- und Volkslebens«, das insbesondere in Differenz zu städtischen Lebens- und Sozialräumen im »Land- und Hirtenleben... als glücklicherer und harmon. Zustand gepriesen« (von Wilpert 365) wurde. Diese literaturwissenschaftliche Definition lässt sich anhand Tolkiens dem *Herrn der Ringe* vorgestellter Beschreibung (»Prologue«) des Auenlandes und der darin enthaltenen Charakteristika der Hobbits nachvollziehen. Tolkien beschreibt die Hobbits als:

> an unobstrusive but very ancient people, more numerous formerly than they are today; for they love peace and quite and good tilled earth: a well-ordered and well farmed countryside was their favourite haunt. They do not and did not understand or like machines more complicated than a forge-bellow, a water-mill, or a hand-loom, though they were skilful with tools (LotR 1)

Damit bezieht er sich genau auf diese Lebensentwürfe, die der europäischen Idyllik so eigen sind, und nimmt sie als Fundament für die Konstruktion des Auenlandes auf, das »rich and kindly« (LotR 5) und damit ebenfalls einem idyllischen Landschaftsentwurf sehr nahe ist. Diese Idyllik des Auenlandes definiert somit ein Wechselspiel zwischen Natur- und Sozialraum, wenngleich diese überhaupt kaum zu trennen sind: wie das Wesen der Hobbits, so die Landschaft und wie die Landschaft, so das Wesen der Bewohner. Die beiden Raumkonstruktionen (›natürlicher‹ Raum und ›sozialer‹ Raum) sind nicht erst auf Metaebene eins, sondern bereits in der konkreten Textsituation. Beide Pole wirken befruchtend aufeinander ein, es gibt keine Fremdkörper in der ureigentlichen Konzeption und Konstruktion.

Negative Fremdkörper sind nur dingliche Einflüsse *von außen*, die keinen Ursprung im Auenland an sich haben; das Auenland bringt nichts Böses hervor, sondern ist nur Raum für Konflikte, aber niemals Ursprung. Leicht lässt sich dies anhand des vorletzten Romankapitels »The Scouring of the Shire« beweisen. Es sind Menschen, die als Handlanger des von Saruman beeinflussten Lotho für Unheil im sonst eben idyllischen – jetzt temporär nurmehr unidyllischen, da industrialisierten – Auenland sorgen:

> »Who is this Sharkey?« said Merry. »I heard one of the ruffians speak of him.« »The biggest ruffian o' the lot, seemingly,« answered Cotton. »It was about last harvest, end o' September maybe, that we first heard of him. We've never seen him, but he's up Bag End; and he's the real Chief now, I guess.« (LotR III 989)

Das Auenland ist somit ein per se ›guter Raum‹, dessen ganze Struktur auf ein idyllisches Gutsein ausgelegt ist und dessen Bewohner ebenso an diese Struktur gebunden sind; fällt eine Figur wie Lotho aus dieser Konzeption heraus, ist sie erstens von außen negativ beeinflusst und wird zweitens zu einer tragischen Gestalt, deren Schuldpotential eingeschränkt ist.

2. Negative Semantisierungen

Diese kurze Übersicht über die Struktur des Auenlandes und die dahinter liegende Bedeutung führt unmittelbar zum ersten Hauptteil des Aufsatzes über. Denn so wie im Auenland der Raum per se gut ist und damit schlechtes Personal von außen hinein transportiert beziehungsweise von außen beeinflusst wird, führt uns Tolkien in einem großen Rahmen vor, wie Räume vom Bösen übernommen werden und damit in ihrer gesamten Struktur ebenfalls böse werden und explizite Drohpotentiale entfalten.

Gemeint ist der Düsterwald, dessen Raumstruktur ganz vom Bösen durchdrungen ist. Seit 1050 DZ steht der Düsterwald – früher: Großer Grünwald – unter dem Schatten Dol Guldurs, beherrscht von Sauron in der Gestalt des Hexenmeisters von Angmar. Das hat zu einer völligen Veränderung des Naturraums geführt. Selbst der uralte Elbenpfad ist zu einem schauerlichen Weg verkommen, der die Benutzer vom ersten Schritt an in einen negativen Bann zieht und dessen Semantik ganz auf die Darstellung des Bösen fokussiert ist.

> The path itself was narrow and wound in and out among the trunks. Soon the light at the gate was like a little bright hole far behind, and the quiet was so deep that their feet seemed to thump along while all the trees leaned over them and listened... There were black squirrels in the wood... There were queer noises, too, grunts, scufflings, and hurryings in the undergrowth, and among the leaves that lay piled endlessly thick in places on the forest-floor; but what made the noises je could not see. The nastiest things they saw were the cobwebs: dark dense cobwebs with threads extraordinarily thick, often streched from tree to tree, or tangled in the lower branches on either side of them. (H 132)

Das Drohpotential dieser Beschreibung ist damit schon auf der ersten Textebene gesetzt. Tolkien macht deutlich, welche Mächte im Düsterwald wirken, der Naturraum ist durchdrungen vom Bösen, das Sauron von Dol Guldur ausgesendet hat. Dieses Böse wird vor allem in den Spinnennetzen semantisiert: Diese Netze, die sich durch den Wald ziehen, die bald den Boden erreichen, sind die Netze, die das Böse im Laufe der fast 2000 Jahre seit seiner Herrschaftsübernahme im früheren Großen Grünwald gesponnen hat. Diese Netze sind, ohne dass sie in einem ersten Schritt eine Auswirkung auf Bilbo Beutlin und die Zwerge rund um Thorin Eichenschild haben, das ultimative Symbol des bedrohlichen Naturraumes, als welcher der Düsterwald figuriert wird. Der Wald transportiert das unendlich Böse, das aus der Gestalt Saurons entspringt, auf allen Ebenen; im Düsterwald materialisiert sich das Böse an sich und beeinflusst die Struktur des Raumes derart, dass selbst der legendäre Elbenweg trotz seines ihm innewohnenden originär magischen Potentials es nur noch vermag, einen grundlegenden Schutz für sich selbst zu gewährleisten. Gegen das Umsichgreifen des Bösen, gegen das Eindringen in die originäre Struktur und deren Übernahme, hilft keine »gute«, traditionelle Magie mehr.

Der natürliche Raum des Waldes ist durch das Böse konstituiert, und diese Konstitution findet dann in der Bedrohung für Leib und Leben ihren Ausdruck. Um diese Struktur theoretisch zu verankern, lohnt sich der Verweis auf Kurt Lewin und seinen Aufsatz »Kriegslandschaft«: Darin konkretisiert der 1947 verstorbene Philosoph die Landschaft zu einem bestimmten Zeitpunkt (nämlich im Krieg). »Seine topologische Beschreibung skizziert einen Raum, der durch Gefahrenzonen, Grenzen und Stellungen bestimmt wird« (Günzel 126), diese Beobachtung bezieht sich ganz klar auf die Beeinflussung des Raumes durch die spezifischen Umstände. Dies lässt sich auch für Tolkien festhalten: Die Beschreibung und Ästhetisierung des Waldes passiert unter dem Eindruck der Spezifität des Bösen, wodurch die literarische Raumstruktur des Düsterwaldes negative Form annimmt und die Bedrohung artikuliert.

Zusammenfassend lässt sich für das Beispiel Düsterwald also Folgendes sagen: Durch das Eindringen des Bösen ist aus dem ehemals friedlichen Großen Grünwald ein expliziter Bedrohungsraum geworden, in dem nur das Waldlandreich noch in seiner Struktur widerstehen kann. Die Bedrohung kommt in diesem Kontext nicht *durch* den Wald zustande – wie etwa in Märchenliteratur –, sondern bricht *aus dem Wald heraus*, so dass das Böse, dass die Bedrohung zur Semantik des Düsterwaldes an sich gehören.

Sehr interessant in diesem Zusammenhang ist die (Teil-)Art der Bedrohung, die semantisiert wird. Die Spinnennetze sind die Merkmale und Instrumente der allbösen Spinnen, deren Urmutter Ungolianth in der Frühzeit der Welt in Beleriand hauste und im Bunde mit Melkor das Licht der Zwei Bäume in Valinor verschlang. Die zur Zeit des Ringkrieges in Mittelerde domizilierten Spinnen sind zwar nur noch Abbilder des alten Schreckens, aber sie besitzen dennoch deutliches archaisches Potential: Sie sind, strukturell, so alt wie die Welt an sich, und damit bergen sie einen Schrecken, der weit über die Erzählzeit des Textes hinausgeht. Das Böse ist zwar situativ fassbar und in der Erzählzeit beheimatet; aber der ureigentliche Schrecken entstammt einer entfernt liegenden Epoche, wodurch die Semantik des Waldes einen doppelten Impetus erhält: einmal den spezifisch-konkreten, einmal den tieferliegenden, auf die Ursprünge zurückweisenden. Dadurch erscheint Bedrohung auf gleich zwei Ebenen in der naturräumlichen Semantisierung.

Ein weiteres Beispiel für einen explizit bedrohlichen Naturraum sind der Alte Wald an der Grenze des Auenlandes und die östlich an den Alten Wald angrenzenden Hügelgräberhöhen. In *The Lord of the Rings* ist der Alte Wald die erste Kulisse, die nicht nur auf Metaebene eine Bedrohung entwirft. Nach dem Gespräch zwischen Gandalf und Frodo über die Bedeutung des Ringes in Beutelsend, die die idyllische Struktur des Auenlandes erstmals durchbricht, wenn auch nur auf einer neu eingezogenen und nicht nachhaltig verankerten Ebene, bringt der Alte Wald eine echte Bedrohung mit sich, eine Bedrohung, die dem Raum strukturell innewohnt und auch nicht davon zu lösen ist. Damit ähnelt das Bedrohungspotential des Alten Waldes dem des Düsterwaldes, dessen Bösartigkeit ebenso strukturiert ist.

Der Alte Wald besteht im Grundsatz aus zwei Naturräumen: dem Wald an sich und der magischen Globule des Tom Bombadil. Der Wald an sich ist eine explizite Bedrohung für Leib und Leben, zum einen durch das ›Naturpersonal‹, zum anderen durch den angebundenen Binnenraum der Hügelgräberhöhen. Zwar gehören diese nicht unmittelbar zum Alten Wald; jedoch ist die Poetik des Romans darauf angelegt, einen fließenden Übergang vom Alten Wald zu dem kleinen, uralten Höhenzug zu schaffen, so dass an dieser Stelle die Hügelgräberhöhen als Teil des großen Naturraumes angesehen werden sollen, um eine strukturelle Aussage treffen zu können. Beginnen wir mit dem Alten Weidenmann, dem mit bösem Willen beseelten Baum. Er greift die Hobbits an, und ohne das magisch induzierte Eingreifen Tom Bombadils wäre diese Episode unglücklich ausgegangen; das ist ein naheliegender Beleg für die These, dass Naturräume wirkliche Bedrohungen ausspielen und dadurch echten wesentlichen Einfluss auf den Inhalt nehmen können.

> They went round to the other side of the tree, and then Sam understood the click that he heard. Pippin had vanished. The crack by which he had laid himself had closed together, so that not a chink could be seen. Merry was trapped: another crack had closed about his waist; his legs lay outside, but the rest of him was inside a dark opening, the edges of which gripped like a pair of pincers. (LotR I 115)

> Setting down his lilies carefully on the grass, he ran to the tree. There he saw Merry's feet still sticking out – the rest had already been drawn further aside. Tom put his mouth to the crack and began singing into it in a low voice. They could not catch the words, but evidently Merry was aroused. His legs began to kick. Tom sprang away, and breaking off a hanging branch smote the side of the willow with it. »You let them out again, Old Man Willow!« he said. »What be you a-thinking of? You should not be waking. Eat earth! Dig deep! Drink water! Go to sleep! Bombadil is talking!« The he seized Merry's feet and drew him out of

> the suddenly widening crack. There was a tearing creak and the other crack split open, and out of it Pippin sprang, as if he had been kicked. Then with a loud snap both cracks closed fast again. A shudder ran through the tree from root to tip, and complete silcence fell. (LotR I 117f)

Die Weidenmann-Szene setzt also die Begegnung mit Tom Bombadil in Gang, und diese Begegnung ist auch entscheidend für die Abwehr der zweiten echten Bedrohung im Großraum des Alten Waldes: die Hügelgräber. Auch dort hätte die Reise der Hobbits enden können, denn der Raum ist als die Bedrohung schlechthin gestaltet. Dieser semantische Raum ist angefüllt mit den finstersten Vorstellungen und dunkelsten Einflüssen überhaupt: Düsternis, Beklemmung und außerhumane Mächte im Bündnis mit Tod und Sterben, gegen das der Einzelne keine Wirkungsmacht und Widerstandkraft hat.

Die Hügelgräberhöhen als Teil des Waldraumes werden durch den Einbruch von dunkler Magie (den Grabunholden) zu einem Bedrohungsraum existenzieller Natur, dessen Bedeutung für den Roman sowohl inhaltlich (durch den Eingriff Bombadils in Spiegelung zur Weidenmann-Szene) als auch poetisch erstaunlich ist: Tolkien gelingt hier der Kniff, innerhalb einer eigenständigen Raumstruktur (Alter Wald) einen weiteren Raum zu semantisieren (Hügelgräberhöhen als Höhenzug in Eriador), der dann wiederum um einen Subraum (Grabhöhle) erweitert wird. Um dies einmal zu strukturieren: Der Alte Wald bildet als übergeordneter Raum die Bedrohungsebene 1, darin integriert sind die Hügelgräberhöhen als implizit bedrohlicher ›Mittelraum‹ und als Hülle für die Höhlen an sich als Subraum und damit explizite Gefahr auf einer dritten Ebene. Einige wenige Zeilen des Romans können diese unglaubliche Bedrohungssituation exemplifizieren:

> When he came to himself again, for a moment he could recall nothing except a sense of dread. Then suddenly he knew that he was imprisoned, caught hopelessly; he was in a barrow. A Barrow-wight had taken him, and he was probably already under the dreadful spells of the Barrow-wights about which whispered tales spoke. He dared not move, but lay as he found himself: flat on his back upon a cold stone with his hands on his breast. (LotR I 137)

Was tut Tolkien hier? Zum einen semantisiert er die der Szene innewohnende Bedeutung für den gesamten Romanverlauf im Gedankenstrom Frodos, und zwar im Adverb »hopelessly«: Hoffnungslosigkeit hat den Hobbit ganz umfangen, er ist sich der Situation in dem existentiellen Bedrohungsraum des Hügelgrabs (»barrow«) bewusst und weiß, dass diese Gefangennahme durch den Grabunhold das Ende seiner Reise bedeuten kann, bedeuten wird, denn er hat selbst keine Möglichkeit, die Situation zu seinen Gunsten zu beenden. Zum anderen entwirft

Tolkien in der Gestalt des Subraums eine Grabessituation. Frodo liegt flach auf einem Stein, die Hände auf der Brust abgelegt; dies ist die typische Position eines Verstorbenen im Sarg, nur dass an dieser Stelle der Sarg fehlt. Frodo als metaphorische beziehungsweise durch den Grabunhold vorweggenommen gedachte Leiche steht im Hügelgrab für den Tod; den Tod, der als die ultimative Zuspitzung sämtlicher Bedrohungen des gesamten Raumes vorgestellt wird und damit die todesnahe Situation beim Alten Weidenmann spiegelt.

Der Alte Wald und in seiner Fortsetzung die Hügelgräber stehen also nicht für eine nebensächliche Bedrohung, die leicht reversible Ereignisse zu Tage fördert. Sowohl der Alte Weidenmann als auch der Grabunhold sorgen in ihren jeweiligen Räumen für wirklich lebensbedrohliche Situation, deren Abwendung nur jeweils über Tom Bombadil erfolgen kann; Frodo und die Hobbits als tragendes Romanpersonal sind nicht in der Lage, die Bedrohungssituationen der Räume selbst zu überstehen. Diese Todesnähe ist tatsächlich ein Resultat der Räume, die Tolkien entwirft und inhaltlich qualifiziert. Es sind keine zufälligen Begegnungen im Alten Wald oder dem uralten Höhenzug, die die Hobbits (und damit die ureigentliche Queste des Romans!) an den Rand des Unterganges treiben; es ist das Innenleben der Räume an sich, das Einfluss auf die gesamte Gestaltung nimmt. Wir können hier mit Shippey sprechen, der die negative Semantisierung ausgehend von Frodos Lied (LotR I 110) fasst:

> As usual we take the immediate point—Frodo and the others want to get out of the forest—while reading through a kind of universality: the ›shadowed land‹ is life, life's delusions of despair are the ›woods‹, despair will end in some vision of cosmic order which can only be hinted at in stars or ›sun‹.   (Shippey, *Road* 190)

3. Erzählte Bedrohungen

Dieser Teil bildet so etwas wie den Kern des Aufsatzes, denn er führt ein Thema vor, das bis dato in dieser Form wenig Beachtung gefunden hat. Im Mittelpunkt der Überlegungen steht folgende These: Tolkien entwirft Bedrohungen als genuinen Teil von Waldräumen, die ihren Ursprung nicht in konkreten und damit verifizierbaren Bedrohungen haben, sondern einer Erzähltradition und damit einem fehlerhaften ›kulturellen Wissen‹ entspringen. Dies wiederum ist in das kulturelle Gedächtnis der jeweiligen Völker eingegangen, um einen Begriff Jan Assmanns hier aufzugreifen. Das möchte ich anhand des Sprechens über Lothlórien verdeutlichen.

Lothlórien, auch als »Golden Wood« (LotR I 329) und von Shippey »the Earthly Paradise« (Shippey, *Author* 205) bezeichnet, ruft bei denen, die nie in unmittelbarem Kontakt dazu standen, Schrecken und Horror hervor. Boromir, ein aufrechter Gondorianer und – so lassen sich verschiedene Andeutungen und Rückblendungen verstehen – einer der größten Krieger der Zeit, ist entsetzt von der Vorstellung, durch das Land Galadriels zu reisen – und bezieht seine Kenntnis aus überliefertem Wissen aus seiner Heimat, wie das folgende Zitat zeigen wird:

> »A plain road, though it led through a hedge of swords,« said Boromir. »By strange paths has this Company been led, and so far to evil fortune. Against my will we passed under the shades of Moria, to our loss. And now must enter the Golden Wood, you say. But of that perilous land we have heard in Gondor, and it is said that few come out who once go in; and of that few none have escaped unscathed.« (LotR I 329)

Wir müssen uns diese Sprechsituation einmal im Detail vergegenwärtigen. Wer dort redet, ist nicht irgendeine periphere Gestalt, die nicht durch Mut, Kampfkraft oder ähnlichen Tugenden auffällt, sondern Boromir, Stellvertreter des Truchsess' von Gondor auf den Schlachtfeldern des Ostens, erster Gesandter des historischen Reiches in Zeiten ärgster Not. Ein Mann, der den Weg »through a hedge of swords« (LotR I 329) gehen würde, wenn denn nur dieser Weg ein gerader sei. Gerade, aufrecht, das sind die Eigenschaften, mit denen Tolkien Boromir ausgestattet hat. Und dieser Boromir bezieht sich bei seiner Ablehnung des Weges durch Lothlórien gerade nicht auf selbst gemachte Erfahrungen oder verifizierbare Aussagen seiner Soldaten etc., sondern aufs *Hörensagen*! »But of that perilous land we have heard in Gondor« (LotR I 329), übernimmt er ganz offensichtlich tradiertes Wissen seiner Heimat, um seine Gegenmeinung zum Vorschlag Aragorns damit zu untermauern.

Wir reden hier ganz eindeutig von einer Bedrohung in mündlicher Tradition, von einer Bedrohung, die keine Substanz hat; Substanz erhält diese (vermutete) Bedrohung für Boromir allein dadurch, dass sie in Gondor so berichtet wird. Der Figur also genügt der Verweis auf das kulturelle Wissen seines Volkes, das er absolut setzt und gleichzeitig als absolut gesetzt angesehen haben will.

Diese tatsächliche Substanzlosigkeit wird von Tolkien auch als solche dargestellt. Während wir bei konkreten Bedrohungssituationen entsprechende Semantisierungen vorfinden, bleibt Tolkien in seiner epischen Darstellung hier ebenso schwammig wie die Meinung von Boromir ist. Der Gondorianer hat kein Beispiel für seine Behauptung, seine Aussage bleibt dünn und dergestalt zeichnet Tolkien diese Sprechsituation: als ein reines Gerücht, das zwar im kulturellen Wissen verankert ist, aber dabei inhaltsleer bleibt. Diese Inhaltsleere findet also ihre Entsprechung in der ›dürren‹ Semantik, wodurch Form und Inhalt sehr eng an dieser Stelle korrelieren. Eine Bedrohungssemantik, wie sie in anderen Kontexten entworfen wird, findet hier keinen Raum, und der Raum (Lothlórien) an sich findet keinen strukturellen Eingang in das Denksystem Boromirs.

Der Raum ist in dieser Sprechsituation nur reine Hülle, die ausschließlich durch falsches kulturelles Wissen ausgefüllt wird. Lothlórien wird als Raum in einer *oral tradition* (wie sie Tolkien aus der germanischen und auch der keltischen Literatur bekannt war) also nur dazu verwendet, dieses Wissen zu transportieren, das Aragorn folgendermaßen kommentiert und damit seine Einschätzung dieses (offenbar gar nicht so alten) Wissens zum Ausdruck bringt: »But lore wanes in Gondor, Boromir, if in the city of those who once were wise they now speak evil of Lothlórien« (LotR I 329)[1].

Den gleichen Zungenschlag wie Boromir bringt Éomer in die Debatte über Lothlórien ein. Bei der ersten Begegnung in der Steppe von Rohan zwischen Aragorn, Gimli und Legolas auf der einen Seite und Éomer und seinen Kriegern auf der anderen Seite sagt er: »›Then there is a Lady in the Golden Wood, as old tales tell!‹ he said. ›Few escape her nets, they say‹« (LotR I 422). Obwohl wir völlig unterschiedliche soziale und intellektuelle Traditionen in den beiden Völkern vor uns haben, ist die Aussage die gleiche: Aufgrund überlieferter Geschichten wird eine gedankliche Bedrohungslandschaft entworfen, die sich wie ein Netz durch alle Schichten und alle Altersgruppen sowohl Rohans als auch Gondors zieht. Auch in Rohan fürchten sich die Menschen bis hin zum schlachtenerfahrenen und furchtlosen dritten Marschall der Riddermark vor Galadriel und Lothlórien, und genauso wie in Gondor beruht dies nicht auf Erfahrung, sondern auf der *oral tradition* des Kulturkreises. Lothlórien ist für die Menschen Rohans ein Raum voller Gefahren, beherrscht von einer hexengleichen Herrin, durchspannt von ihren Netzen – diese lassen kaum jemanden entkommen, was auf sekundärer Textebene bedeutet, dass der Raum die Bedrohung schlechthin ist.[2] Eilmann hat schon vor einigen Jahren im Zusammenhang mit der textinternen Poesie Tolkiens beobachtet, dass das »Verhältnis von ›story‹ und ›history‹ nicht immer eindeutig zu bestimmen ist« (Eilmann 110). Diese Meinung lässt sich ausgehend von den hier gelieferten Textbeispielen über den ursprünglichen Kontext hinaus stützen: *Die* Geschichte (kulturelle Tradition) ist nicht gleichbedeutend mit *der* Geschichte (konkrete Situation)![3]

---

1 Dass Aragorn darin sogar eine Kritik an den aktuellen Zuständen in Gondor verbirgt und damit impliziert, dass unter der Regentschaft der Truchsesse echte Weisheit und echtes Wissen verloren gegangen sind, sei hier nur postuliert und müsste an anderer Stelle separat ausgeführt werden.
2 Auch die formale Gestaltung ähnelt in ihrer Schlichtheit der Szene mit Boromir. Ebenso wie der Gondorianer hat ja auch Éomer nichts Substanzielles beizutragen. Das macht Tolkien durch die für ihn unübliche poetische Kargheit klar.
3 Es lässt sich auch die Frage aufwerfen, ob negative Semantisierungen im Sinne einer volkstümlichen Erzähltradition dadurch zustandegekommen sind, dass spezifische Völker kein Herrschaftsrecht über spezifische Gebiete besitzen, wie es bei Gondor und Rohan hinsichtlich Lothlórien der Fall ist. Diese Ansicht geht auf Georg Simmel zurück: »Die Herrschaftsübung über Menschen dokumentiert ihre Eigenart oft in der besonderen Beziehung zu ihrem räumlichen Gebiete. Wir erblicken die Gebietshoheit als Folge und Ausdruck der Hoheit über Personen« (Simmel 304). Ohne Einfluss auf den Raum neh-

Dass aber tatsächlich nur Erfahrung und Erleben eine Bedrohung ermessen und beurteilen können, zeigt sich am Beispiel Gimlis. Als Zwerg aufgrund von Tradition und historischer Ereignisse den Elben gegenüber kritisch eingestellt und in sorgenvollen Gedanken aufgrund der Dunkelheit in Lothlórien (»If Elves indeed still dwell here in the darkening world« (LotR I 329)), wandelt er seine Einstellung aufgrund der Begegnung mit Galadriel (LotR I 347) völlig. Und dabei geht er so weit, dass er bei der eben benannten Begegnung mit Éomer sein Leben aufs Spiel setzt, um gegen die Überlieferung, die Galadriel verunglimpft, anzukämpfen, indem er Aragorns Antwort auf Boromir inhaltlich spiegelt:

> Then Éomer son of Éomund, Third Marshal of Riddermark, let Gimli the Dwarf Glóin's son warn you against foolish words. You speak evil of that which is fair beyond the reach of your thought, and only little wit can excuse you. (LotR I 422)

4. Zusammenfassung

Der Aufsatz versucht zu zeigen, wie Tolkien zwei Ebenen von Bedrohungen im Kontext von Wald-Räumen aufbaut und auf welche Weise diese existenziellen und gefühlten/eingebildeten Bedrohungen semantisiert werden. Tatsächlich bedrohliche Räume werden von Tolkien als solche benannt und gezeichnet, deren Semantik ist düster, erschreckend und erregt Angst und Furcht; Beispiele dafür wurden geliefert. Diese Textausschnitte untermauern, im Vergleich zu den unter Punkt 3 vorgestellten, den Grundgedanken der vorliegenden Analyse. Während echte Bedrohungen von Tolkien als solche geschildert und explizit ausgeführt werden in der aus seinen Schriften bekannten ›epischen Breite‹, verlieren sich die Darstellungen der gefühlten Bedrohung an genau dieser Stelle. Formale Gestaltung und inhaltliche Bedeutung gehen eine untrennbare Verbindung ein.[4] Die Aussagen Boromirs und Éomers sind dünn und schlicht und transportieren nur mittelbares, ganz peripheres Wissen, das von Generation zu Generation mündlich übertragen wurde beziehungsweise wird. Oder,

---

men zu können, entsteht auch keine Hoheit über das darin domizilierte Personal; und aufgrund der nicht vollzogenen Herrschaftsausübung über, in unserem Falle, Galadriel, bricht sich die Negativierung des Raumes in kultureller Tradition Bahn.

4 Verlyn Flieger sagt: »The polarities of light and dark that generate the elements of Tolkien's fictive world and motivate its actions are created, reflected, and conveyed through the power of the word« (Flieger 10). Sie spricht Tolkien bei der Darstellung des Konfliktes von Gut und Böse eine enorme Macht des Wortes zu und suggeriert damit, dass die Darstellung von Gut und Böse poetisch ambitioniert abgebildet und durch die Kraft des Wortes sichtbar wird. Diese Kraft des Wortes fehlt aber Éomer und Boromir in ihren Einschätzungen, so dass die Frage nach Gut und Böse gerade nicht aufgeworfen wird, mithin die Bedrohung eine tradierte Hülse bleibt.

um mit Peter-André Alt zu sprechen: »Das Böse ist das Produkt verwickelter ... paradoxer Verhältnisse« (Alt 215). Aber diesem Wissen wohnt keine Erfahrung inne, denn Begründer und Weiterträger der mündlichen Tradition haben *Geschichten* (»old tales«; LotR I 422) entwickelt und so eine *pseudo-literarisch fundierte Bedrohung* in die kulturellen Traditionen ihrer Völker eingeführt. Diese mündlichen Überlieferungen haben schließlich dazu geführt, dass selbst die (potentiellen) Führer der wichtigsten menschlichen Völker traditionsversessen diesem Weg folgen und Wald-Räume per se als Bedrohungen disqualifizieren, dafür aber aus verschiedenen Richtungen (Mensch, Zwerg) Zurechtweisungen in Kombination mit unverhohlener Häme einstecken müssen.

Zum Abschluss soll ein Ausschnitt aus der *Poetik des Raumes* von Gaston Bachelard zitiert werden, der sich auf das Vorgehen Tolkiens beziehen lässt:

> Das Diesseits und das Jenseits wiederholen dumpf die Dialektik des Drinnen und des Draußen: alles läßt sich zeichnen, sogar das Unendliche. Man will das Sein fixieren, und indem man es fixiert, will man alle Situationen überwinden, um eine Situation aller Situationen anzugeben. Man konfrontiert dann das Sein des Menschen mit dem Sein der Welt und meint damit an eine ursprüngliche Gegebenheit zu rühren. Man erhebt die Dialektik des *Hier* und des *Dort* in den Rang eines Absolutums. Man verleiht diesen ärmlichen Adverbien der Ortsbestimmung eine kaum kontrollierbare Macht ontologischer Bestimmung.
> (Bachelard 171)

Das Absolutum des Hier und Dort wird auch bei Tolkien entwickelt. Hier sind die Tradition der Völker, das kulturelle Wissen und Gedächtnis, dort sind die Räume, die innerhalb dieser Tradition als Bedrohung semantisiert werden. Und so entsteht diese Ebene der Raumstruktur, die Tolkien als künstlerisches Element in seiner Mittelerde-Epik vorführt, und der der Autor die Ebene der echten Bedrohung entgegensetzt, um so seinen doppelten Diskurs zu entwerfen. Und in diesem doppelten Diskurs besitzen die gefühlten Bedrohungsräume die gleiche Signifikanz wie die echten Bedrohungsräume, denn sie tragen eindeutig zum poetischen Gehalt der Texte bei, sie sind Teil der Charakteristika bedeutender Protagonisten, und sie weisen auf einer sekundären Ebene auch auf die kulturellen Hintergründe in Tolkiens Weltentwurf, indem die Einflüsse einer *oral tradition* auf die nicht auf Erfahrungen basierenden Lebenswirklichkeiten von Völkern dargestellt und dabei auch von anderen Figuren kritisiert werden.

Die eigenständige Bedeutung von Wald-Räumen für die Tolkien'sche Poetik wird auch deutlich in Tolkiens Aufsatz *Sir Gawain and the Green Knight*. In dem mittelalterlichen Text findet er den Wald als reine poetische Funktionalisierung ohne eigene ›Handlungsgewalt‹ vor: »The lady was in fact his ›enemy keen‹. How then was she protected, if her lord was far away, hallooing and hunting in the forest?« (GPO 82). Während hier der Wald als Raum nur die Folie darstellt, auf der Handlung abgebildet wird, werden in *The Hobbit* und *The Lord of the Rings* Wäldern eigene Strukturen zugewiesen. Durch die unterschiedlichen Formen und Gestalten von Wäldern werden auch jeweils unterschiedliche Merkmale und Bedeutungen in die Texte eingebracht: Nicht *auf der Folie des Waldes* spielt sich etwas ab, werden Handlung und Bedeutung gezeichnet; sondern *im Wald* entscheidet sich der Inhalt, und *der Wald* besitzt Potential für kulturell bedingte Diskurse.

Der Wald ist also, das ergibt sich als Resultat über die Existenz eines Widerspruchs von ›Erfahrung‹ und ›Tradition‹ hinaus, tragende raumsemantische Säule im gesamten Weltentwurf Tolkiens.

Bibliographie

Alt, Peter-André: Ästhetik des Bösen. München: C.H. Beck, 2010

Assmann, Jan. *Das kulturelle Gedächtnis. Schrift, Erinnerung und politische Identität in den frühen Hochkulturen.* München: C.H. Beck, 1992

Bachelard, Gaston. „Poetik des Raumes". *Raumtheorie. Grundlagentexte aus Philosophie und Kulturwissenschaften.* Hg. Jörg Dünne & Stephan Günzel. Frankfurt am Main: Suhrkamp, 2012, 166-179

Eilmann, Julian Tim Morton. „Das Lied bin ich. Lieder, Poesie und Musik in J.R.R. Tolkiens Mittelerde-Mythologie". *Hither Shore* 2 (2005): 105-135

Flieger, Verlyn. *Splintered Light. Logos and Language in Tolkien's World.* Kent: Kent State University Press, 2002

Günzel, Stephan. „Einleitung". *Raumtheorie. Grundlagentexte aus Philosophie und Kulturwissenschaften.* Hg. Jörg Dünne & Stephan Günzel. Frankfurt am Main: Suhrkamp, 2012, 105-128

Rimoli, Emanuele, und Guglielmo Spirito. „Outer and Inner Landscapes in Tolkien: Between Wordworth, Coleridge, and Dostoevskij". *Hither Shore* 7 (2010): 120-136

Shippey, Tom. *The Road to Middle-earth.* Boston/New York: Houghton Mifflin Company, 2003

---. *J.R.R. Tolkien: Author of the Century.* Boston/New York: Houghton Mifflin Company, 2002

Simmel, Georg. „Über räumliche Projektionen sozialer Formen". *Raumtheorie. Grundlagentexte aus Philosophie und Kulturwissenschaften.* Hg. Jörg Dünne & Stephan Günzel. Frankfurt am Main: Suhrkamp, 2012, 304-316

Tolkien, John Ronald Reuel. *The Lord of the Rings.* London: HarperCollins, 1995

---. *The Hobbit.* London: HarperCollins, 1999

---. „Sir Gawain and the Green Knight". *The Monster and the Critics.* Hg. Christopher Tolkien. London: HarperCollins, 2006, 72-108

von Wilpert, Gero: *Sachwörterbuch der Literatur.* Stuttgart: Kröner, 2001

Zusammenfassungen der englischen Aufsätze

Tolkiens lebende Landschaften
Allan Turner

Die Landschaftsbeschreibungen in *Der Herr der Ringe* erzielen ihre Wirkung durch die Anwendung von kognitiven Metaphern, die auf einer kaum bewussten Ebene Assoziationen mit dem menschlichen Körper hervorrufen. Dieses Verfahren ist nicht mit literarischen Metaphern zu verwechseln, die durch das gewollte Zusammentreffen von sonst sinnunverwandten Begriffen eine plötzliche neue Einsicht gewähren. Vielmehr schaffen die kognitiven Metaphern in enger Zusammenwirkung mit den zugrundeliegenden Mythen von Mittelerde den unterschwelligen Eindruck von einer lebendigen, sinnlichen Landschaft.

Der Alte Wald und die Hügelgräberhöhen: ein natürliches Vorspiel zum *Herrn der Ringe*
Jonathan Nauman

Drei Kapitel in Tolkiens *Die Gefährten*, »Der Alte Wald«, »Im Tom Bombadils Haus« und »Nebel auf den Hügelgräberhöhen«, sind oft als Abweichung in Tolkiens *Herrn der Ringe* angesehen worden, die nicht ausreichend in den Plot der heroischen Romanze in ihrer Gesamtheit integriert ist. In seinen *Briefen* behauptet Tolkien allerdings, diese Episoden, über die der anomale Naturgeist Tom Bombadil waltet, bewusst behalten zu haben, um zu zeigen, dass die Macht des Ringes nicht das gesamte Bild ist.

Eine Untersuchung dieser drei Kapitel zeigt, dass sie die wichtige Rolle der natürlichen Welt in Tolkiens Romanze effektiv durch die Charaktere und Handlungen von Tom, Goldbeere und dem Alten Weidenmann einführen. Weitergehende Ereignisse nicht angeschlossener natürlicher Intervention im *Herrn der Ringe* tendieren besonders dazu, den Wert unvorhergesehener Hilfe, einem wichtigen Element in der impliziten Kritik der Ringqueste an dem Willen zur Macht, zu demonstrieren.

Melians Gürtel – Grenzen und verborgene Schwellen in Arda

Guglielmo Spirito

Die Struktur von Tolkiens Arda enthält eine Menge Grenzen, Begrenzungen, Zäune und Wegkreuzungen: Meerufer und Inseln, Wälder und Stromtäler, Berge und Täler, Sümpfe und Tunnel, Flüsse und Ströme. Manche von ihnen wurden von den Valar und Maiar am Anfang gemacht; andere wurden im Laufe der Zeit verändert oder zugefügt, um auf neue Bedürfnisse zu antworten, wie z.B. Melians Gürtel.

Was beinhalten diese mysteriösen Schwellen und verborgenen Pfade? Welche Wahrnehmung von Natur in einer gefallenen Welt wird ausgedrückt? Wieso geht man beim unbefugten Betreten verloren? Wer kann sie finden und überqueren? Diese Fragen sucht der Artikel zu beantworten.

Mitfühlender Hintergrund in Tolkiens Prosa

Annie Birks

In Anbetracht von Tolkiens poetischer Sensibilität und Liebe zur Natur überrascht es nicht, dass seine Fiktion reich ist an Naturbildern und Landschaftsbeschreibungen. In den meisten Fällen scheinen diese Bezüge zur Umwelt sich in Harmonie mit den Ereignissen oder der Erzählstruktur zu befinden. Mit anderen Worten: Tolkien scheint auf das alte universale literarische Mittel zurückzugreifen, das gewöhnlich als ›mitfühlender Hintergrund‹ bezeichnet wird, wobei die Natur auf die Taten, Emotionen oder Geisteszustände der Charaktere reagiert oder diese spiegelt oder nachahmt.

Als Beitrag zu früheren und aktuellen Studien über Natur in Mittelerde untersucht dieser Artikel Tolkiens Kunst der Naturbeschreibung – ob die unmittelbare Umgebung (Geographie, Pflanzen, Tiere) oder das Wirken der Elemente (die das Wetter konstituierenden Kräfte) – in einem Versuch, einen Subtext unter der Perspektive des ›mitfühlenden Hintergrundes‹ aufzudecken.

Landschaft als Metapher in *The Lord of the Rings*

Thomas Kullmann

Viele Leser sind von Fülle und Umfang der Landschaftsschilderungen in *The Lord of the Rings* irritiert. Tatsächlich gehören Landschaften nicht zum Motivinventar von Traditionen phantastischen Erzählens (u.a. Epen, Märchen, Kinderliteratur); sie sind jedoch zentral im ›realistischen‹ Roman des 19. und 20. Jahrhunderts.

Ausgangspunkt der Untersuchung ist die Feststellung, dass diese Landschaften fast durchweg metaphorische Funktionen haben: Sie veranschaulichen Charaktereigenschaften und psychische Befindlichkeiten der Protagonisten oder markieren Wendepunkte der Romanhandlung, so etwa bei Ann Radcliffe, Emily Brontë und Thomas Hardy.

In dieser Tradition stehen auch die Landschaftsschilderungen in *The Lord of the Rings*. Die Schilderungen, die die Bootsfahrt Frodos und seiner Mitstreiter begleiten, lassen sich als Illustrationen von deren Bewusstseinszuständen verstehen; durch Personifikationen sowie die Wahl von Adjektiven und Verben, die sich auch auf Personen beziehen lassen, werden die Parallelen zwischen Landschaft und psychischem Zustand deutlich: Die Wahrnehmung der öden und dunklen Welt am Ufer veranschaulicht die Erwartung einer langen und beschwerlichen Reise. Ähnliches gilt für die vielfältige und idyllische Waldlandschaft, deren Beschreibung der Ankunft in Lothlórien vorausgeht.

Weiterhin erhält die Landschaftsmotivik in *The Lord of the Rings* jedoch auch Funktionen, die über die der realistischen Romantradition hinausgehen. So ist der Übergang in die Welt der Elben durch Schilderungen der nächtlichen Landschaft und der Sterne markiert, die an die Darstellung erhabener Natur bei Radcliffe erinnern; in den Bergen von Moria bereiten Naturschilderungen die Reisenden und die Leser auf die Begegnung mit dem Unbekannten vor. Auch die Enthüllung der Identität Aragorns wird durch entsprechende Naturschilderungen vorbereitet.

Tolkien bedient sich der Erzählkonvention des 19. Jahrhunderts, Landschaften als Metaphern für Aspekte des Romangeschehens einzusetzen, und nutzt diese Konvention auch zur Vorbereitung der Leser auf phantastische Erzählelemente.

Der Einfluss mittelalterlicher Erzählweise, spezifischer von *Sir Degaré*, auf Tolkiens Porträtierung der Wildnis im *Herrn der Ringe*

Tatjana Silec

Tolkien schrieb bekanntermaßen, seine imaginären Welten seien seinem Wunsch entsprungen, den von ihm erfundenen Sprachen die richtige »Wohnung und Geschichte« (Brief Nr. 294) zu geben. Er war ebenso bekannt dafür, die Prozesse der Erfindung, die zu seiner Zweitschöpfung geführt haben, nicht zu sehr zu elaborieren (vgl. Brief Nr. 144). In der Forschung wurde aber herausgearbeitet, dass er zu großen Teilen von skandinavischen und finnischen Epen sowie der mittelenglischen Literatur inspiriert wurde.

Der Artikel versucht zu zeigen, dass zumindest mit Blick auf letztere Tolkiens Methode mit der eines mittelalterlichen Dichters verglichen werden kann, der Motive und Geschichten frei von existierenden Werken lieh und sie seinen Zwecken anpasste: nicht nur die besten wie *Sir Gawain and the Green Knight* oder *Sir Orfeo*, sondern auch einige weniger bekannte, wenn sie passten. Beispielsweise haben die sonderbaren Ereignisse mit dem Alten Weidenmann und den Grabunholden in ihrer Beschreibung einer quasi-bewussten Natur, deren Macht zum Teil von der Tageszeit abhängt, viel mit dem Beginn von *Sir Degaré* gemeinsam, einer Romanze, die Tolkien gekannt haben musste, da sie wie *Sir Orfeo* im *Auchinleck Manuskript* kopiert wurde.

Mensch, Natur und das Böse im *Herrn der Ringe* und in *La saga de los Confines*

Natalia González de la Llana

Es ist bekannt, dass in Tolkiens *Herrn der Ringe* die Natur eine große Rolle spielt. Denn diese ist nicht nur eine Landschaft, in der die verschiedenen Charaktere ihre Abenteuer erleben, sondern auch ein symbolischer Ort. Der Bezug der Protagonisten zu ihrer Umwelt und zu der Position in dieser, welche sie dem Menschen und anderen Kreaturen zuschreiben, ist gleichzeitig ein Zeichen für ihre moralische Haltung. Dies ist ebenso der Fall in Liliana Bodocs *La saga de los Confines*, einer Trilogie, die in den Fruchtbaren Ländern spielt, einem Ort, der stark an das präkolumbische Amerika erinnert.

In diesem Beitrag werden die beiden literarischen Werke miteinander verglichen. Zunächst sieht man, wie sich die Charaktere durch ihre Beziehung zur Natur unterscheiden: Diejenigen, die sie mehr schätzen und sich in ihr integriert fühlen, sind die moralisch höheren Wesen. Anschließend wird der Bezug zwischen dem Bösen und der Natur analysiert.

Im *Herrn der Ringe* wird durch Saruman die Technologie als Mittel zur Zerstörung der Umwelt thematisiert. Seine Suche nach einer verbotenen Erkenntnis erinnert an literarische Figuren wie Adam und Eva, Faust oder Frankenstein. Der ambivalente Wert der Erkenntnis wird hier in der Form einer Transgression gegen die Natur gezeigt.

Eine Transgression gegen die Natur ist auch schon die Geburt Misáianes, des größten Vertreters des Bösen in *La saga de los Confines*. Dieser, ebenso wie Saruman, erschafft wie eine Art grausamer Gott neue und schreckliche Kreaturen, die ihm dienen sollen. Die Suche nach Erkenntnis und die Gefahren des Hungers nach Macht werden durch Bor, den Magier, ins Spiel gesetzt. Seine Hybris zeigt dem Leser, dass man sich von den Kreaturen nicht entfernen soll, um sie zu leiten, so wie dies der Fall bei der »Laienbruderschaft des Geländes« ist, sondern eher zusammen mit ihnen leben muss, weil die ganze Natur wie ein Netz ist, in dem jeder seine Rolle spielt.

Das Böse kommt also in beiden Werken in Zusammenhang mit einem Mangel an Respekt für die Natur und der »richtigen« Position des Menschen in ihr vor.

Die Totensümpfe & οἰκουμένη: Grenzen einer Landschaft in Mittelerde

Michaël Devaux

Bekanntermaßen ist der Tod das zentrale Thema des *Herrn der Ringe* und *Der Herr der Ringe* das Hauptwerk Tolkiens. Vor diesem Hintergrund können mithilfe einer Untersuchung über das Verständnis der Landschaft bei Tolkien einige Charakteristika der Totensümpfe, eine erstaunliche Landschaft Mittelerdes, herausgefunden werden. »Die Durchquerung der Sümpfe« gehört zu den faszinierendsten Kapiteln. Aber unverzüglich stellen sich zwei Fragen, wenn man sagt, dass die Totensümpfe eine Landschaft Mittelerdes sind. Denn: Gehören die Sümpfe zu Mittelerde? Und erlauben sie die Sicht einer Landschaft?

Tolkien verwendet den Ausdruck »Mittelerde« seit 1914 im Gedicht »Éalá Éarendel« in seiner altenglischen Form. Darüber hinaus nimmt Tolkien die im *Oxford English Dictionary* genannten Bedeutungen auf. Er wählt aber *oikumene* als Äquivalent zu Mittelerde nicht früher als 1937. Hängt dies vielleicht mit einer Lektüre des großen Artikels »Oikumene« von Friedrich Gisinger in *Paulys Realencyclopädie der classischen Altertumswissenschaft* zusammen? In wessen Mitte liegt Mittelerde? Anders als in der Antike, wo primär der Charakter der Bewohnung im Zentrum stand, verbindet Tolkien Erde (mit umgebenden Gewässern) und Bewohnung mit diesem Begriff. Nimmt er erst am Ende der Inkubationszeit des Gedankens von Mittelerde als *oikumene* (1937) die Gegenüberstellung mit der Wüste, *ereme*, auf?

Unsere These ist, dass die Totensümpfe zur Mittelerde als *oikumene* gehören und eine innere Grenze konstituieren. In der Konsequenz bedeutet dies, dass wir uns jenseits der Totensümpfe außerhalb der Mittelerde als *oikumene* befinden.

Die Totensümpfe werden ausgehend von traumatisierenden Erfahrungen aus der Schlacht an der Somme während des Ersten Weltkriegs vorgestellt. Eine genaue Studie dieses Ursprungs und ihrer literarischen Präsentation erlaubt eine Antwort auf die genannten Fragen. Die Sümpfe stellen sich dem Blick nicht als Landschaft dar. Sie sind ein täuschender, unsichtbarer Ort, wobei der Nebel jede Perspektive abgesehen von der auf den Boden verbietet. Sie sind ein lügnerischer Ort: Man sieht die Toten und Illusionen auf der Wasseroberfläche. Ihre Illusion macht sie wegen der lügnerischen Repräsentation des eigenen Todes zudem zu einem tödlichen Ort. Die Sümpfe sind trotzdem bewohnt und gehören in diesem Sinne zur *oikumene*. Die Totensümpfe sind aber keine Wiederaufnahme des Niemandslandes, da Tolkien beide unterscheidet. Das Niemandsland liegt jenseits des Morannon. Die Totensümpfe gehören zur Mittelerde, das Niemandsland ist eine Wüste, das Gegenteil der *oikumene*.

Angang und Aufgang: Strukturen des Ankommens und Bleibens in *Der Herr der Ringe*

Martin Sternberg

Tolkiens *Herr der Ringe* ist die Erzählung einer Queste, und so ist Landschaft etwas, das man auf dem Weg zu einem Ziel durchquert oder die das Ziel selbst ist. Bei Tolkien zeigt bereits die Art der Annäherung an einen Ort, um was für eine Art von Ort es sich handelt.

Die erste Form der Annäherung ist die plötzliche Überschreitung einer scharf definierten Grenze. Sie führt in einen Raum mit eigenen Gesetzen und einer eigenen Zeit- und Raumerfahrung. Zu dieser Gruppe der von Normalraum und -zeit abgetrennten Orte zählen Tom Bombadils Land aus Altem Wald und Hügelgräberhöhen, die sich als einheitlich umgrenzter und auch inhaltlich verbundener Raum erweisen, Lothlorien und Fangorn.

Die zweite Form der Annäherung erfolgt dagegen schrittweise. Elemente in der Landschaft verweisen bereits auf den Zielort und vermitteln so den Übergang in den anderen Raum. Zu dieser Gruppe der in Zeit und Raum eingebetteten Orte zählen Moria, Mordor, die Pfade der Toten, die Länder der Menschen allgemein und auch Henneth Annûn, welches auf den ersten Blick zur ersten Gruppe zu gehören scheint. Bruchtal nimmt hier, wie es seiner Rolle als Rastplatz und Übergangsort, aber auch Rückzugsort entspricht, eine Mittelstellung ein und weist Merkmale beider Gruppen auf.

Es lässt sich zeigen, dass die abgetrennten Orte der ersten Gruppe Orte einer noch lebendigen Vergangenheit mit einer eigenen Handlungsmächtigkeit sind, die die Geschichte weiterhin gestalten können und religionswissenschaftlich gesehen Ähnlichkeit mit heiligen Räumen aufweisen. Die in Raum und Zeit eingebetteten Orte der zweiten Gruppe sind dagegen Orte einer passiven Vergangenheit und nur noch Objekt vor allem menschlicher Erinnerungen.

Summaries of the German Essays

Romantic Landscape in J.R.R. Tolkien's Work
Julian Tim Morton Eilmann

The interpretation of Tolkien's work in context of the Romantic literary movement is not very common among Tolkien scholars. Apart from a handful of papers and a seminar on "Tolkien and Romanticism" by the German Tolkien Society, Tolkien scholarship has not yet taken adequate notice of the Romantic spirit that underlies the middle-earth mythology. In this paper Julian Eilmann focuses on Tolkien's depiction of landscape in view of the Romantic *poetology*.

Eilmann introduces the central philosophical and poetological framework of the Romantic ideology to explain how Tolkien's approach to sub-creation and fantasy shares elements with Romantic concepts. The most important element in this discussion is imagination as in Romantic philosophy the power of human imagination gains the status of an existential force.

The Romanticists found a strong authoritative legitimization for their ambitious attempt to promote imagination in literature by referring to German philosopher Johann Gottlieb Fichte (1762-1814) and his major work, the *Wissenschaftslehre*. Adapting Fichte's highly influential theory to literature the Romanticists aimed at transcending the prosaic world by means of their artistic work and revealing another layer of reality. Thus it is the intention of Romantic art to enable the recipient to experience the poetic quality of life—the "sleeping song" in Josef v. Eichendorff's famous poem—which is nothing less than transcendence.

Eilmann subsequently elaborates on the role of nature in the Romantic poetology. In the Romantic discourse, nature is imbued with the above mentioned mystery ("the sleeping song") of creation. Therefore landscapes function as the perfect object for the Romanticist's longing and imagination. In the passionate perception of a "romantic" scenery, a sensitive individual can thus feel the poetic quality that is inherent in all things.

Also is explained how aspects of this concept of Romantic landscapes can be found in Tolkien's early manifestation of his legendarium, the *Book of Lost Tales*. In this tale, the mortal Eriol makes wonderful experiences on the Elvish Isle Tol Eressea. Tolkien describes the Elvish retreat with Romantic imagery as a wonderful and awe-inspiring landscape setting that highly contributes to the magical atmosphere of Eriol's—and the reader's—experience.

The consequence of this natural scenery is that a reader of the Eriol frame story may get the impression to be reading a Romantic novel with a mortal protagonist who strays through fairyland.

The Dark Side of the Forest? Concrete and 'felt' Intimidation through natural Spaces
Patrick Peters

This article tries to point out that in Tolkien's *Lord of the Rings* and *The Hobbit* different views on the intimidation and threat potential respectively of woods are brought up, which is a special feature in the matter of space semantics. On the one hand, there are real threats such as in Mirkwood or the Old Forest that bring danger for the life of the protagonists. On the other hand, there are threats described having their origin in an oral tradition of Rohan and Gondor. Not only does this oral tradition transport wrong images of, in our example, Lothlórien but it gives deeper understanding of the cultural background of two of the greatest warriors of the Ring War age, Éomer and Boromir.

It will be shown that according to oral traditions some threats are only 'felt' and that they do not have any concrete basis. For they are told, not experienced, and therefore they do not possess a real threat potential. Furthermore that fact evokes derisive and critical response by protagonists who have encountered those falsely accused spaces.

And beyond that, the article shows that forests in Tolkien's novels are deeply contributing to the epic structure by itself. Forests are not just natural spaces on which plot is developed; they are parts of the plot and without the forests as they are, there would be lesser plot in the novels. Forests, from the Old Forest to Lothlórien, are 'driving' different topics of the texts and are most relevant for the organisation of characters and the progress of the novels. Forests are, in short, *indispensable spaces*.

Reviews/Rezensionen

John S. Ryan: Tolkien—Cult or Culture
Armidale: Heritage Futures Research Centre
2012, 239 S.

Bei John Sprott Ryans Buch handelt es sich um eines der Bücher, deren Titel den Leser auf eine falsche Fährte locken. Denn bei einem Werk, das im Titel die von Lesern und Kritikern oftmals diskutierte Frage aufwirft, ob Tolkien zur literarischen Hochkultur gehört oder eben nicht, wird eine dezidierte Erörterung eben dieser Frage erwartet. Zwar wird dies auch am Rande angesprochen (s.u.), tatsächlich handelt es sich bei dem Buch jedoch um etwas ganz anderes: die Sammlung von Vorträgen und Aufsätzen einer Tolkien-Konferenz aus dem Jahr 1969 in Armidale (Australien) – also aus der Anfangszeit(!) der Tolkien-Forschung. Das vorliegende Buch stellt eine überarbeitete und ergänzte Neuauflage der Originalpublikation von 1969 dar. Die beiden Organisatoren und zentralen Vortragenden des Seminars waren laut Vorwort J.S. Ryan und sein Kollege Hugo Crago, damals beide Dozenten am Anglistischen Institut der Universität Armidale. Das Vorwort gewährt auch einen Einblick darin, wie es bei dieser australischen Konferenz aus der Zeit des beginnenden Tolkien-Kults zuging: »The housewife was represented, but scarecely the hippy, and so the ideas began to fly... The almost total immersion in the Tolkienian world itself caused those present to sing the songs, to draw intuited and symbolic shapes..., the older ones to relate passages to their own experience of war« (ebd. x).

Die Frage nach Sinn und Notwendigkeit, die Konferenzbeiträge über vierzig Jahre später mit einer Neuauflage zu präsentieren, hat sich der Rezensent bei der Lektüre des Öfteren gestellt. Grundsätzlich sagt das Alter der Beiträge natürlich nichts über deren Güte aus, leisten doch viele »Klassiker« der frühen Tolkien-Forschung auch im 21. Jahrhundert nach wie vor wertvolle Hilfestellung bei der Interpretation. Zwar findet sich in der vorliegenden Publikation auch ein Essay Ryans, das es in die von Zimbardo/Isaac herausgegebene Sammlung *Best of Tolkien Criticism* geschafft hat. Aber insgesamt bietet *Tolkien – Cult or Culture* dem versierten Tolkien-Leser und -Forscher des Jahres 2015 oftmals nur Altbekanntes, was heute zum Tolkien-Grundlagenwissen gehört.

Insgesamt ist das Buch wissenschaftshistorisch von Interesse, liegt sein Reiz doch darin, dass es einen Einblick in die frühe Tolkien-Forschung gewährt, die u.a. vor der Problematik stand, dass in den 1960ern nur Bruchstücke von Tolkiens Mythologie bekannt waren.

Die Aufsätze selbst erscheinen ähnlich heterogen wie das Konferenzpublikum. Grundsätzlich versuchen die Autoren, dem Leser einen Überblick über Leben und Werk der Inklings zu geben. Ihr Schwerpunkt liegt hier auf den führenden Köpfen Tolkien, Lewis und Williams, was für den heutigen Tolkien-Kenner oftmals ermüdend ist. Interessanter sind da die Ausführungen zu weniger bekannten Repräsentanten der Inklings oder Personen aus ihrem Umfeld wie R. Havard, Hugo Dyson, Christopher Dawson, Bede Griffiths und anderen. Doch an vielen Stellen würde man gerne mehr erfahren, da es sicherlich aufschlussreich wäre, manche der referierten Ansichten über Theologie, Kunst und Literatur mit Tolkiens Werk in Bezug zu setzen.

Das Kapitel über den frühen »Tolkien-Kult« im Zuge der steigenden Popularität des *Herrn der Ringe* hinterlässt einen gemischten Eindruck. Es folgen kürzere Beiträge, die sich u.a. mit den kleineren Werken Tolkiens befassen, wobei grundlegend neue Einsichten hier nicht geboten werden.

Jedoch schließt das Buch mit dem sehr lesenswerten Aufsatz »Remarks on the Nature and Developement of Fantasy«, dem aus heutiger Sicht noch am meisten abzugewinnen ist. Hugo Crago geht hier zunächst der Frage nach, wie Tolkiens Werk in der Tradition der fantastischen Literatur eingeordnet werden kann. Er schlägt den Bogen vom *Gilgamesch-Epos* über die mittelalterlichen Romanzen zu den fantastischen Autoren des 19. Jahrhunderts (William Morris, E.R. Eddison). Auch wenn Crago Epochen der Menschheitsgeschichte miteinander in Bezug setzt, die zeitlich weit auseinander liegen, gelingt es ihm doch sehr gut, zu verdeutlichen, wie die verschiedenen Autoren das Fantastische in Worte fassen. Gemeinsamkeiten und Unterschiede geraten so in den Blick. Zwar sind für die von Crago aufgeworfene Fragestellung inzwischen Standardwerke wie Weinreichs *Fantasy – Einführung* unentbehrlich, aber Crago lenkt den Blick gekonnt auf Fragen des literarischen Stils. Besonders erhellend ist sein Vergleich zwischen Beschreibungen einer dunklen Festung bei Eddisons *The Worm Ouroboros*, Tolkiens *The Two Towers* und Mervyn Peakes *Titis Groan*. Gekonnt analysiert Crago die Art und Weise, wie die Autoren das Erscheinungsbild des jeweiligen Ortes mit Worten visualisieren.

Hier lenkt er den Blick auf bestimmte Merkmale von Tolkiens Stil: u.a. die langen Sätze. Diese bergen zwar die Gefahr der Eintönigkeit beim Lesen. Andererseits weist Crago darauf hin, dass Tolkiens Sätze oftmals den eingängigen Sprachrhythmus eines Hexameters aufweisen und damit einen mündlichen Vortrag erleichtern, was Crago zu der Einschätzung führt, dass sich Tolkiens Stil in hohem Maße für die Rezitation eignet. Und dieser Aspekt von Tolkiens Werk ist wohl bis jetzt noch nicht in gebührendem Maße untersucht worden, sodass Cragos Aufsatz hier einen wertvollen Beitrag für zukünftige Studien leistet.

Das Buch schließt also mit einem sehr starken Essay, dem es zu wünschen wäre, an anderer Stelle noch einmal veröffentlicht zu werden, um ein breiteres Publikum zu erreichen.

Julian Eilmann

Helen Conrad-O'Briain & Gerard Hynes (Eds.): J.R.R. Tolkien: The Forest and the City

Dublin: Four Court Press, 2013, 197 pp.

This volume presents several papers that were given at a conference of the same name at Trinity College Dublin on 21-22 September 2013, which I attended. I remember the exciting and high academic quality of the papers that were given and reading their published versions reinforced both their interest and importance for Tolkien studies. The conference, and this volume, includes papers by the top tier of Tolkien scholars; including Verlyn Flieger, Tom Shippey, Michael D.C. Drout, Dimitra Fimi, Alison Milbank and Thomas Honegger as well as several new Tolkien scholars including Gerard Hynes (who co-edited the volume), Ian Kinane, Rebecca Merkelbach and Meg Black.

Each of the papers in this volume explores aspects of Tolkien's many landscapes. These can be physical landscapes (cities, forests, the wild, etc.) as well as linguistic and conceptual landscapes. What is most interesting, and what makes this a key volume, is that each of these explorations not only illuminates aspects of the nature of these landscapes and the people who dwell in them but also gives us more insight into Tolkien's own mythopoeic process.

The volume opens with Tom Shippey's keynote talk 'Goths and Romans in Tolkien's Imagination' which explores a rich linguistic landscape that Tolkien dwelt in from his earliest time—the Gothic language which was linked with Tolkien's coeval myth and language invention. Shippey approaches the subject from a unique perspective; namely by analysing the examination papers that Tolkien set when he was a Professor at Oxford in the late 1920s and 1930s which, as Shippey shows, included tricky questions on the Gothic language (21). Shippey explores the importance of Gothic to Tolkien and cites Henry Bradley's *The Goths* (1887), in which Bradley linked the Gothic language to the earliest English, as an important source. Shippey explores the Gothic landscape Tolkien journeyed in by suggesting that Tolkien's development of the history of Rohan and Gondor in his Middle-earth *legendarium* was a parallel, or alternative, history. It shows what might have occurred if the Goths had not turned Arian and moved away from Roman Catholicism (a point Tolkien great lamented—see Scull and Hammond, *Companion and Guide*, vol. II, p. 467). As always with Tom Shippey's academic scholarship this gives the Tolkien scholar much to study and think about.

Bookended with Shippey's exploration is Michael D.C. Drout's incredibly revealing analysis of two key markers of many of Tolkien's landscapes—the tower and the ruin. This is a theme that Drout has continued to explore and refine—with the hope of a new book on this subject on the publishing horizon. Drout masterfully argues how the structure of the tower in Tolkien is intrinsically neither good nor evil but represents aspects of power. The fate of almost all the towers in Tolkien is their fall (mirroring what Tolkien said about 'fighting the long defeat'), which turns them into the second element that populates Tolkien's landscapes—the ruin. Drout makes the key point that the 'tower is the achievement but the ruin is the permanent memory, or at least a trigger for memory; so that what falls to entropy can still endure *æ mun uppi* as long as people live' (177). A ruin lives in the past, present and future while at the same time showing that the past can never be recaptured. This leads to the sadness that permeates all of Tolkien's works which Drout links to concepts of nostalgia, *heimweh* and what Shippey, in *The Road to Middle-earth*, identifies as *langoth*, a longing for the straight road to Valinor coupled with a recognition that such a road is no longer accessible. Drout's exploration is rooted in elements of Tolkien's landscape and offers an incredibly insightful framework for understanding how Tolkien creates in his works a sense of 'sadness that was blessed and without bitterness' (186).

Exploration of the nature of objective and subjective perception of sentient landscapes and how Tolkien honed his skill as a mythopoeist is a hallmark of Verlyn Flieger's 'The Forest and the Trees: Sal and Ian in Faërie'. Flieger launches into her discussion by focusing on the sentient nature of Tolkien's trees and juxtaposes her analysis by using two characters from Alan Garner's 2003 fantasy novel, *Thursbitch*: Ian, a highly rational priest and Sal, a deeply imaginative geologist who in the novel debate the possibility of sentient landscape. Flieger suggests that it was the mark of Tolkien's skill that he could create the dichotomy of subjective and objective realities in his invented world. Flieger shows how Tolkien's forests are closely connected to this idea and she cites several examples in the texts, especially the scene in The Old Forest, where Tolkien plays with the idea of the perception of sentient nature. One key element is the number of times Tolkien uses the word 'seems' to create this dichotomy—'There is no echo or answer, but the wood seems to be more crowded and more watchful' (112). Flieger also masterfully contrasts two examples of Tolkien attempting to make sentient nature fit into his mythology (evoking the 'green suns' idea from Tolkien's talk *On Fairy-stories*). First, there is the scene in *The Hobbit* when Tolkien explains the storm on the mountain Thorin and company are crossing as due to the wrath of the Stone Giants (*Hobbit*, pp. 56-57). Flieger characterises this as 'lack[ing] inner consistency; their ball game smacks more of a nursery game of 'let's pretend' than serious sub-creation and elvish skill' (109). Compared with, and showing the growth of Tolkien's skill, is his description of the storm on Caradhras the Cruel in *The Fellowship of the Ring* where the mountain itself is sentient and the nature of the storm does not need to be explained, thus making it fit more into the reality of the secondary world and also reflecting the 'luxuriant animism' Tolkien finds so attractive in the *Kalevala*. Flieger also explores the nature of 'intent' to shed light on one of the most enigmatic concepts of Tolkien studies which Flieger's pioneering work is illuminating—Faërian Drama. In this case she ties together the idea of sentient nature, as represented by Old Man Willow in The Old Forest and Caradhras, as being the weavers of the dream that others are dreaming. Flieger ends by treating another landscape that she has done much work on, namely Faërie in Tolkien's last work *Smith of Wootton Major* and the role of the birch tree as a sentient object in this landscape.

Dimitra Fimi's 'Wildman of the Woods: Inscribing Tragedy on the Landscape' explores the opposition of civilised city and rough wilderness in Tolkien's *The Children of Húrin* (one version of Tolkien's key story cycle of Túrin Turambar) and convincingly shows that this opposition in the story can be best illuminated by contextualizing it with the third often overlooked source Tolkien indicated in his letter to Milton Waldman for the Túrin character, Oedipus (*Letters*, p. 150). Indeed Fimi's suggestion here is intriguing given that one of the earliest descriptions Tolkien would have read of the *Kullervo* cycle was in the introduction in Eliot's *Finnish Grammar* which said that Kullervo's tragedy rivalled Oedipus (Eliot 1890, p. 237). Fimi convincingly and thoroughly explores the parallels between the fated and doomed stories of Túrin and Oedipus as portrayed in Sophocles's *Oedipus the King* and how both their tragic tales interact with the different landscapes they inhabit.

In a similar fashion, Alison Milbank explores the role of the city and wilderness through the work of Dante's *The Divine Comedy* and specifically the landscape of 'The Earthly Paradise' in Dante's *The Purgatorio* which Milbank contrasts with several of Tolkien's landscapes, especially Lothlórien and Minas Tirith.

Jane Suzanne Carroll's 'Civil Pleasures in Unexpected Places: An Introduction to the Etiquette of Middle-earth' explores concepts around Tolkien's depiction of manners and hospitality in different landscapes. Carroll uses textual analysis to convincingly show that there is definitely no direct and expected correlation between civilised spaces offering good manners and hospitality and the wilderness offering the opposite. Indeed, quite the opposite is true with more instances of rough manners being met in the cities of Middle-earth (Gondor, Rohan) and good manners, hospitality and 'rustic politeness' being met in the wild and forests (such as Tom Bombadil's House).

Rebecca Merkelbach's 'Deeper and Deeper into the Wood' focuses on the role of the forest as a place of transformation and suggests that Tolkien drew upon similar roles of forests in folk- and fairy-tales. As with Carroll, Merkelbach shows that while Tolkien's use of the forest certainly has parallels with English folk- and fairy-tales, the key difference is that in these types of stories the danger comes from the forest (e.g. Snow White, Hansel and Gretel) while in Tolkien's depictions it is the forest itself that is dangerous, which provides a nice counterpart to Flieger's thoughts on sentient nature in her paper.

Erin Sebo's 'Sacred and Immense Antiquity' analyses Tolkien's use of riddles in *The Hobbit* by suggesting influence from classical, medieval and English folklore and fairy-tales. Sebo's attempt to link this to the themes of forest and the city by suggesting that the two riddle contests in *The Hobbit* (Gollum and Smaug) take place 'in cities' (enclosed spaces—under mountains) does seem a bit of a stretch.

Dominika Nycz's 'The Forest and The City: the Dichotomy of the Istari' again contextualises the city and the wilderness with the role of the five wizards in Tolkien's work; especially the wizards Radagast and Saruman as well as the mysterious Blue Wizards. Nycz suggests that these wizards become too tied to their environment and lose their way as Istari. Interesting, although I thought Nycz's characterization of Saruman as a 'hermit in Isengard' was a bit stretched and some of Nycz's ideas need more development.

In a similar way there are some intriguing germs of an idea in Ian Kinane's 'Less Noise, More Green' which explores Bilbo as a 'proto-cultural materialist' moving from the landscape of a comfortable material-filled Shire into the wild where Tolkien 'frees his protagonist from the burdens of materialism' (147).

In 'Fractures, Corruption and Decay' Jennifer Harwood-Smith explores the more nuanced nature of some of Tolkien's key cities (Minas Tirith and Minas Morgul) with the divided nature of the city in Fritz Lang's *Metropolis* which offers a more straightforward structure of the 'good' above and the 'bad or oppressed' below (again Tolkien not following the normal binary rules!).

Thomas Honegger's 'Raw forest' versus 'Cooked City' brilliantly juxtaposes the way food is prepared and consumed in Middle-earth, and by whom, with anthropologist Claude Lévi-Strauss's culinary triangle of the raw and the cooked and draws some intriguing conclusions which again (as with Harwood-Smith) shows that Tolkien did not work on strictly binary lines in regard to how food was prepared and consumed in the wild and the city. Another great example of using a different type of contextual framework to better understand Tolkien's mythic process.

Gerard Hynes's 'The Cedar is Fallen—Deforestation and the Fall of Númenor' is a brilliant eco-critical examination on how the growing imperialism of the corrupted Númenórians led to environmental destruction and the deforestation of the Middle-earth and explores what messages Tolkien was looking to communicate through this story. Meg Black's 'The Party Tree and Its Roots in the Spanish Civil War' focuses on one tree in Tolkien's *legendarium*—the Party Tree in Bag End (where Bilbo delivers his farewell speech) and suggests a connection between Tolkien's adding of the Party Tree in the early drafts of *The Lord of the Rings* and the oak of Guernica, the symbol of Basque national pride which was featured in London papers as surviving the bombing of 1937.

One of the most unique treatments of landscapes in the volume is Karl Kinsella's 'A Preference for Round Windows—Hobbits and the Arts and Crafts Movement'. Kinsella puts the architecture of the Arts and Crafts movement in connection with the description of architecture in Tolkien's landscapes. He focuses the greatest part of this analysis on the work of Edward Schroder Prior (1852-1932) whose designs for such buildings as St Andrew's in Roker, Sutherland, brought nature into the edifice of the building by creating 'convivial caves' that bear striking resemblances to the hobbit holes of the Shire. Kinsella states: 'Both Prior and Tolkien have quite literally subsumed all activity to nature, where the landscape has become an integral part of the architecture, being essentially indistinguishable from the surrounding environment' and opens up a really interesting area for further exploration.

Each of these papers in this important volume for Tolkien studies will take the reader through the many different landscapes that Tolkien thought about, engaged with and constructed in his own mythopoeia. Helen Conrad-O'Briain and Gerard Hynes should be applauded for putting together a brilliant conference and important follow-up volume of papers.

I recommend this book not only for the landscapes it illuminates but for the better understanding it offers of the creative and mythic mind which dwells in all of them. Andrew Higgins

Stefan Ekman
Here Be Dragons. Exploring Fantasy Maps and Settings

Middletown, CT: Wesleyan University, 2013, 284 pp.

Stefan Ekman's study endeavours to tackle an important but as yet neglected subject in fantasy: maps and settings. He approaches the topic from different angles, focussing in each of the four main chapters on one central aspect, which are: maps (chapter 2), border and boundaries (chapter 3), nature and culture (chapter 4) and realms and rulers (chapter 5). First in each chapter comes a discussion of the central terminology used. Ekman makes thus a laudable effort to establish discursive clarity while retaining at the same time a firm pragmatic grasp on the practical purpose of the terminology—namely to illuminate the phenomena discussed in the following paragraphs. The works selected to illustrate his theoretical points are, as he argues, central to the fuzzy set of texts that constitute the genre of fantasy. While he strives to exemplify his points with a fairly wide selection of texts, he always includes *The Lord of the Rings* as *the* prototypical work of fantasy so that the interpretation of Tolkien's epic runs like a golden thread through all chapters—and makes Ekman's study worth reading for Tolkien aficionados. In the following I will discuss each chapter in turn, focussing on the more general quality of Ekman's approach to the theme under consideration.

The first, introductory chapter provides a discussion of central terms such as 'fantasy' or 'secondary worlds' and a sketch of Ekman's 'genre theory'. He favours the prototypical genre-model with some 'prototypical' or central works at the centre of a fuzzy set, which may overlap with other genres. His corpus consists of two hundred randomly chosen works of fantasy, of which he treats in greater detail only those which he believes to be, on the one hand, well known and which, on the other, have a (close) affinity to Tolkien's *The Lord of the Rings* as the work at the centre of the fuzzy set. This approach works quite well and all those not interested in discussing theoretical terminology may simply skip this section.

In the following chapter, Ekman analyzes the use and function of maps first by presenting statistics based on his corpus and, second, by discussing in depth two of Tolkien's maps to *The Lord of the Rings*. As to the first point: it may come as a surprise for many readers that maps are not as widespread in works of fantasy as popularly believed. According to Ekman, only 27% to max.

40% of the works analyzed feature maps. These maps, then, function either as paratexts (to use Genette's terminology—assuming an author external to the 'text world') or as docemes (assuming a text-internal author). The larger map 'The West of Middle-earth' found in *The Lord of the Rings* would be an example of a paratextual map since the text makes no references to it and it is unlikely that the implied narrator(s) (i.e. Bilbo, Frodo and Sam) are to be credited with the drawing of it. The situation is different with the map 'A Part of the Shire', which Ekman identifies as a doceme since we have textual references to maps of the Shire and its compiler is likely to be identified with Bilbo or Frodo (in spite of the small-scale initials of Christopher Tolkien in the left-hand corner of the box identifying the map as 'A Part of the Shire').

The graphic conventions used in fantasy maps are another interesting aspect explored by Ekman. He shows that fantasy maps mix elements from different epochs but in general prefer to give a 'pre-Enlightenment' (or pre-technological revolution) feel which coincides with the preferred setting for the great majority of fantasy texts. The important point here is the rather pragmatic approach by most authors, who refrain from taking recourse to authentic medieval ways of representing landscape features, such as serrated lines for hills, but prefer the more familiar triangles or even the application of shading or contours. Ekman's argument is clearly put forth and sufficiently bolstered by secondary literature, but the Tolkien scholar may have wished to see in this context the inclusion of Karen Fonstad's *The Atlas of Middle-earth* (1991) or Rainer Nagel's *Hobbit Place-names: A Linguistic Excursion through the Shire* (2012).

The third chapter investigates thresholds, borders and boundaries, with the latter defined as areas demarcated by borderlines, whereas thresholds allow crosshatching. The main function of all these 'areas' is that when you cross a border or boundary you may enter a place (e.g. Faerie) with another order of reality where the rules are different. Also important for the discussion of the different 'realms of Faerie' is Ekman's definition of 'domain' (p. 71) as "a part of a world where the laws of nature and causality differ from the rest of the world." Furthermore, he coins the term 'mundanity' (p. 71) to refer to that which is not Faerie and thus introduces and expands a terminology by means of which he and later researchers will be able to describe the related (yet not identical) phenomena encountered in a variety of texts. In his case the works chosen for analysis are Steven Brust's *Dragaeran* books, Neil Gaiman and Charles Vess's illustrated novel *Stardust* and Garth Nix's *Abhorsen* series.

Of interest for Tolkien scholars is Ekman's discussion of polders in Tolkien, Holdstock and Pratchett. In the context of fantasy, a polder is an active microcosmos with its own set of rules. Furthermore, it is "not so much a protected area as a protected era... [since] [t]hrough polders, past eras are given spatial locations, past and present are juxtaposed, and the journey across the land turns into time travel" (p. 125f). Lothlórien is a typical example of a polder since it preserves a piece of the Elder Days.

The following chapter widens the scope even more by investigating the function of nature and culture in fantasy. Again, Ekman opens with a discussion of the central terms, though this time (maybe due to the vastness of the concepts involved) it struck me as not very useful for the average reader of fantasy. What is of use, however, is the differentiation he makes between 'nature' in the sense of primordial wild nature, and 'second nature' as a category between original 'wild' nature and culture.

The case studies comprise cities found in the works of Tolkien (Minas Tirith), Charles de Lint (Newford), China Miéville (New Corbuzon and Armada) and Patricia McKillip (Ombria), all of which differ in their relationships between 'nature' and 'culture'. Minas Tirith (at least before the accession of Aragorn to the throne) shows a clear separation between nature and culture, while we have blurred boundaries in China Miéville's cities and also in Charles de Lint's Newford, which is more of a 'socialscape', i.e. constituted by how people perceive the town. McKillip's Ombria, finally, contains instances of representations of nature, but nature itself hardly plays a role and the conflicts are all situated in the domain of culture.

Realms and Rulers and the link between the two are the theme of chapter five. The concept linking the person of the king or ruler with his realm goes, of course, back to time immemorial—as shown most prominently by Frazer's monolithic study *The Golden Bough*, which is listed in the book's bibliography but which does not feature very prominently in Ekman's argument. He starts with giving an overview of works that see marriage, just governance and healing as the happy ending of the plot. They typically end with the rightful king ascending to the throne and ensuring the aforesaid things. Ekman rightly stresses the important distinction we have to make between political rule and 'rule of the land', as implied by the direct link ruler-realm.

As examples he discusses Tim Powers's Fisher-King Trilogy—a work that draws inspiration from the symbolism of the Tarot, from the works of Frazer, Weston and Eliot and in which the domains of the mythical and the mundane are basically separated by knowledge (or the lack of it). The 'other side of the coin' of the link between ruler and realm is shown graphically by means of the landscapes of Mordor (J.R.R. Tolkien), the Spoiled Plains (Stephen Donaldson), and the Blight (Robert Jordan). Whereas Sauron's landscape of evil is a 'secondary product' of his industrialization, those of Lord Foul's counterpart in the Spoiled Plains are due to his primary aim of destroying nature per se. In the Blight, then, the landscape and its fauna and flora are not sterile but show a perverted and twisted fecundity reminding the reader of the effects of nuclear radiation. The discussion of the three examples illustrates convincingly the different functions of the same topos.

Ekman concludes his study with a chapter that once more recapitulates and summarises his findings.

All in all I enjoyed reading *Here Be Dragons*, not least since Ekman's book seems to be the first scholarly study to focus exclusively on space and its representation in works of fantasy. His great achievement is to have established a framework that can be expanded and developed—and used for exploring other 'fantastic worlds' and their relationship with mundanity, such as found in the *Harry Potter* books or in the works of H.P. Lovecraft, to name but two out of a dozen possible candidates.

Thomas Honegger

Peter Hunt (Ed.): J.R.R. Tolkien. New Casebooks Series
Basingstoke: Palgrave Macmillan, 2013, xi + 185 pp.

This book, which forms part of a series devoted to critical essays on children's literature, should offer both a provocation and a challenge to Tolkien specialists, who have to recognise that Tolkien wrote a number of stories specifically for (his own) children, but usually feel a sense of resentment when the whole of the Middle-earth canon is popularly perceived as adventure stories for boys. That tension is heightened by the editorial choice not to consider stories explicitly for children, such as *Roverandom* or *Mr Bliss*, but to concentrate solely on *The Hobbit* and *The Lord of the Rings*. The best of these essays do in fact address questions of genre, what features of language and content suggest that a book is addressed to children, and what features of *The Lord of the Rings* make it a crossover text, that is one which appeals to both adults and children, regardless of which group it may originally have been written for.

The topics covered are sources and successors, the pastoral aspect, the relationship to traditional dragon tales, language, gender, world-building, landscape, trees, and adaptations in other media. However, the volume is uneven in quality and in its appeal to the Tolkien expert, largely because of the different interpretations of the editorial policy. The intention is to present a range of new critical approaches to the texts in a form intended for "university and other students". The greatest problem that students complain of when presented with a specialised critical text is that, even if they understand all the words, the argument means nothing to them because they are not familiar with a discourse which may have been ongoing in that field for a number of years, so the writer of the article has taken a knowledge of it for granted. A work of this kind should therefore ensure that the theoretical position adopted is explained in some detail, with some indication of how it arose in the first place, to provide the necessary background information for B.A. students (and also in this case for Tolkien specialists who may not be familiar with recent research in the field of children's literature). However, in a world where academics are increasingly called upon to justify their existence, it is not surprising that some of the authors feel compelled to take an approach that can count as "original research" rather than a pedagogical presentation of "known" material. It is the tension between these two perceived needs that perhaps accounts for an overall lack of focus in this collection.

The other problem is that the application of a theory usually involves a degree of significant generalisation, and it has been amply demonstrated that Tolkien's concentration on concrete detail can make it difficult to do this meaningfully. Critics more used to dealing with other authors sometimes get themselves into difficulties through being unaware of this characteristic, as has occasionally happened in this volume. The most successful articles are those which keep their argument on a clear and concrete level, such as the interesting introduction by Peter Hunt which attempts to resolve the critical confusion over Tolkien and children's literature, a line which is then further developed by Keith O'Sullivan in his investigation of the implied child reader.

The articles by Kate Harvey on adaptations, Shelley Saguaro and Deborah Cogan Thacker on Tolkien and trees, and Maria Sachiko Cecire on sources and successors all provide sufficient background information for students without simply reproducing well-known material, although Cecire suddenly veers off into explaining how the influences on Tolkien fed into the syllabus of the Oxford English School and the children's authors who studied there, rather than establishing a direct connection through Tolkien's own fiction.

Rather less successful are the articles by Jane Suzanne Carroll and Zoë Jacques. Carroll contends that Tolkien's landscapes are to be seen not as individual visualisations but as a version of medieval topoi or stylised settings. To demonstrate this, she argues that most of the stages on the journey take place in settings that can be categorised as "sanctuaries", which separate the inside area from the outside world and imply some kind of spiritual protection. Therefore Meduseld and Bag End both evoke the idea of the Anglo-Saxon hall and suggest Beowulf's defence of Heorot. No doubt the first part of this is true in as far as all enclosures separate the inside from the outside, but to conflate all of them with *Beowulf* is a generalisation too far. Interestingly, Carroll's counter-example is based on a misreading. She claims that Frodo is vulnerable to the Ringwraiths on Weathertop because that is not a proper sanctuary as the circle of stones is not continuous and the site is not "sacralised". However, she has overlooked the fact (or maybe she was influenced by the film version) that the attack takes place not in the ruins of Amon Sûl but in a dell some distance away. In fact Weathertop could be taken as a sanctuary in Carroll's sense because Gandalf is able to hold out amongst the ruins, and the presence of *athelas* not far away shows that it has been sacralised by the presence of the Númenoreans. However, the point is not whether a defence was possible or not, but of the usefulness of ignoring concrete details in order to demonstrate an underlying pattern that may or may not be there. Carroll's conclusion: Tolkien distinguishes each instantiation of the topos by giving it an individual description. *Quod erat demonstrandum*!

Jacques deals with the thorny topic of gender. She deliberately ignores the question of Tolkien's (lack of) female characters, arguing that since gender is "a mode of behaviour, separate from sex, in which cultural norms associated with sex are enacted, resisted, and reshaped", it is impossible to have a text in which gender does not play a part, so female characters are not needed for its discussion. Unfortunately her definition of gender is so broad that she is able to use "gendering" as synonymous with any kind of gaining experience. At the beginning of his story, Bilbo is a prime subject for an adventure because as a young child masquerading as a 50-year-old bachelor he's "a bit of an old woman"—although of course Jacques does not use this particular colloquialism. An interesting enough argument, but it does not introduce or refer students to any of the secondary literature already available on this topic.

The remaining articles which have not been treated here individually at least manage to avoid the worst of these pitfalls of over-generalisation. The collection is worth reading by anyone with an interest in children's literature, but they must be prepared to apply their own large pinch of salt.   Allan Turner

J.S. Ryan:
In the Nameless Wood: Explorations in the Philological Hinterland of Tolkien's Literary Creations
Zurich/Jena: Walking Tree Publishers, 2013, xv + 365 pp.

This collection of articles by J.S. Ryan is a follow-up to the previous volume, *Tolkien's View*, published by Walking Tree in 2009 and reviewed in *Hither Shore* 6 by Jason Fisher, many of whose remarks are equally relevant to this new selection. Most of them have been assembled from a variety of Tolkien journals and fanzines, some no longer in existence, and varying in length from just three pages to 22. In addition, there are two original pieces, labelled "Prequel" and "Appendix" respectively. The first of these, "'The Nameless Wood' and 'The Narrow Path'", traces the medieval origins and associations of these two well-known Tolkienian topoi, while the second, "J.R.R. Tolkien and the *Ancrene Riwle*, or Two Fine and Courteous Mentors to Women's Spirit", not only draws attention to an important area of Tolkien's research which has seldom been mentioned in the context of his literary works, but also draws a parallel between the author of the Middle English text and the modern Professor, emphasising Tolkien's generous contribution to the supervision of female Catholic students at a largely male university.

The re-printed essays are grouped into four main sections, the first of which deals with the ancient Middle East and its associations in Tolkien's fiction. Tolkien maintained a keen interest in Middle Eastern archaeology as a possible source for tracing cultural and linguistic influences on western Europe, so it is not surprising that Ryan sees significance in his use of the names Uruk (as in Uruk-hai) and Erech, both of them variant forms of the name of a powerful Sumerian city and a source of fear to its neighbours. It should be mentioned that although it is closely argued, this section contains a lot of speculation; like Mark T. Hooker, Ryan believes that Tolkien liked to fill his fiction with philological references and double meanings, so all names and invented words are open to scrutiny for possible associations.[1]

The second part deals with the importance of Tolkien's experience at the Romano-British site of Lydney for the development of his *legendarium*. Ryan remarks that it was a hint from the medievalist and Celtic scholar Nora Chadwick which first led him to investigate that field. In particular Lydney had once been an ancient centre for mining, and the remains from that period were known locally as Dwarf's Hill, so according to Ryan, not only did this provide the association of dwarves with mining, but it also suggested the secret passage to Smaug's lair in *The Hobbit*. It is also suggested that the temple of Nodens, which appears to have been visited by people seeking a cure from illnesses, could have been a source for the Houses of Healing. However, there is a curious error about this temple; Ryan quotes from an archaeological report that it overlooked the Severn Valley, and adds a footnote to specify that therefore it faced west (130). However, since Lydney lies west of the Severn, it must have faced towards the east. Similarly, he places Caerleon in south-west Wales (121), whereas of course it is in the south-east.

The third part deals with North and West Germanic traditions and Christianity, which is an area that has been well explored, although Ryan has some new sidelights to shed. However, the last part, devoted to 20th century Oxford and England, is of great importance because two of the three articles are based on Ryan's personal knowledge of Tolkien and his circle of acquaintance. Here the topic is his interactions specifically with Roy Campbell and W.H. Auden.

---

1 Tolkien was not always impressed by Ryan's guesses about the origin of his names; see *Letters*, 380 (footnote).

However, in a number of the articles there are passing references, such as the one to Nora Chadwick mentioned above, which suggest that Tolkien had an easy relationship with a good many other Oxford academics familiar with his personal interest in creating a mythology. This is a very different picture from the one presented by Humphrey Carpenter, of someone who was certainly sociable but nevertheless really opened up only in a close circle of friends. Possibly Ryan's impressions are those of a much younger man who saw at the time only the affable social exterior. Certainly he claims that Tolkien and Auden had "a close friendship for many years" (243), and had kept in touch ever since Auden's student days, although the conventional version is that they started to correspond only after the publication of *The Lord of the Rings*. Indeed, they led such different lifestyles that it would be difficult to see many points of contact, but the speculation is an interesting one.

All in all, this is a fascinating volume to dip into. Since the articles were written at different times and for different readerships, there is a certain amount of repetition between articles, so browsing is probably more rewarding than reading from cover to cover. What comes across most strongly in every article is the personality of the author and his enthusiasm for what he is writing about.

Allan Turner

Roberto Arduini & Claudio A. Testi (Eds.): Tolkien and Philosophy
Zürich/Jena: Walking Tree Publishers, 2014, 159 S.

Mit dem vorliegenden Band – der englischen Version eines schon 2011 in italienischer Sprache erschienenen Tagungsbandes – verfolgen die Herausgeber das Ziel, die Beziehung zwischen Philosophie und Philologie bei Tolkien genauer in den Blick zu nehmen. Näherhin solle das Buch »in both method and content, an essential point of reference for anyone interested in better understanding the significant connections that sometimes link, sometimes divide, ›philologist‹ Tolkien and the proper philosophical speculation« (11) werden. In Anbetracht von lediglich vier inhaltlichen Beiträgen, die durch die Einführung und zwei Dokumente der King Edward's School ergänzt werden, dürfte dies Ziel vielleicht etwas hochgegriffen sein. Die Beiträge (z.T. aus der Feder so renommierter Tolkienforscher/innen wie Tom Shippey oder Verlyn Flieger) können indes durchaus mit Gewinn gelesen werden. Wirklich neue philosophische Einsichten sollten allerdings nicht erwartet werden, da zu vielen der diskutierten Fragen wie Vorsehung, Macht, Tod etc. schon Forschungen vorliegen.

In der Einführung diskutieren die Herausgeber den Forschungsstand und bemängeln eine geringe Anzahl an Büchern und Aufsätzen, die sich mit philosophischen Fragen bei Tolkien auseinandersetzen. Während der allgemeine Befund durchaus zutreffend sein dürfte, weist die von ihnen angeführte und mithilfe gängiger bibliographischer Werke zu Tolkien erstellte Bibliographie doch (vermutlich aufgrund ihrer Suchmethode) in einigen Bereichen erhebliche Lücken auf: Beispielsweise fehlen die einschlägigen Beiträge aus der *Tolkien Encyclopedia* sowie einige Beiträge zur Willensfreiheitsdebatte (u.a. von Frank Weinreich in *Hither Shore 1*, Jason Fisher in *Tolkien and Modernity 1*, Verlyn Flieger in *Tolkien Studies 6* und Thomas Fornet-Ponse in *Tolkien Studies 7*). Dies schränkt den Nutzen ihrer Bibliographie leider deutlich ein.

Der erste Beitrag ist ein Dialog zwischen Franco Manni und Tom Shippey, in dem Manni zunächst den Befund bezüglich der Nennungen von »Philosophie« und einzelnen Philosophen in Tolkiens Werk erläutert, was von Shippey mit Verweis auf die unterschiedlichen Denkweisen von Philologen und Philosophen begründet wird. In einem zweiten Schritt nennt Manni einige philosophische Überlegungen, die sich in Tolkiens Werk zeigen, was von Shippey mit Bezug auf Plato, Boethius und Robin Collingwood vertieft wird. Drittens nimmt Manni das Verhältnis von Philologie und Philosophie in den Blick und weist auf zahlreiche Zusammenarbeiten hin, worauf Shippey mit Rekurs auf die Spezialisierung in den Wissenschaftsdisziplinen sowie auf die Problematik von Quellenstudien antwortet. Viertens werden biographische Überlegungen zu Tolkiens Persönlichkeit angestellt, um schließlich ausführlich das Thema der Vorsehung in Tolkiens Werk in den Blick zu nehmen. Dieses trägt nach Ansicht Shippeys deutlich boethianische Züge, sei aber durch den narrativen Kontext für viele Menschen besser nachvollziehbar bzw. klarer ausgedrückt als die abstrakte philosophische Spekulation.

Im zweiten Beitrag widmet sich Verlyn Flieger Tolkiens Sprachphilosophie bzw. genauer dem Verhältnis von Sprache und Mythologie. Im Ausgang von *On Fairy-stories* diskutiert sie vor allem die Frage der Namengebung bzw. den Zusammenhang von Namen und Wesen, insbesondere am Beispiel Tom Bombadils, der Elben und ihrer Sprache bzw. ihren Benennungen sowie der Inschrift an den Toren Morias, und betont, wie Tolkien Sprache als Prozess verstehe und seine Praxis Vehikel für seine Philosophie sei.

Anschließend findet sich der zweite Dialogbeitrag in diesem Band – von Andrea Monda und Wu Ming 4 – zur Frage, ob Tolkien ein katholischer Philosoph gewesen sei. Hierzu plädiert Monda zunächst dafür, der Begriff »katholischer Philosoph« treffe weniger auf Tolkien zu und möglicherweise auch nicht der des »katholischen Autoren«, während Wu Ming 4 Tolkien als Geschichtenerzähler charakterisiert. Vor diesem Hintergrund diskutiert Monda die Hobbits und die Rolle »kleiner Leute« für die »große Geschichte« als Tolkien-Erfindung, wobei sich eine gemeinsame Präsenz von Paganismus wie Katholizismus finde. Wu

Ming 4 nimmt die meta-narrativen Kommentare in den Blick und sieht darin »a virtuous cycle between past, present, and future which has narration at its centre« (107). Schließlich betont Monda die Bedeutung des Themas der Freude für die Geschichte und insbesondere ihr Ende, während Wu Ming 4 eher das Thema des Mutes und der Macht hervorhebt. Wenngleich ihre Erläuterungen interessante Aspekte hervorheben bzw. deutlich machen, verbleiben ihre jeweiligen Ausführungen recht monologisch, da nur sehr begrenzt argumentativ aufeinander eingegangen wird.

Der letzte Aufsatz stammt von Christopher Garbowski und widmet sich der Frage nach Tolkiens Philosophie und Theologie des Todes mit einem klaren Schwerpunkt auf theologischen Erwägungen. Er nimmt dabei eine sehr breite Perspektive ein, nämlich die von Tolkiens Verständnis des Lebens als auf ein Ziel hin geordnet und in einer Theologie der Narrative verortet.

Den Abschluss machen zwei von Giampaolo Canzonieri zusammengestellte und eingeleitete Dokumente aus der King Edward's School: das Curriculum zu Beginn des 20. Jh. und ein kurzer Bericht über die Prüfungsergebnisse in Alter Geschichte mit namentlicher Nennung u.a. von Gilson und Tolkien.

Angesichts dieser thematischen Akzentsetzungen der Beiträge erscheint der Anspruch, ein wesentliches Referenzwerk für die Frage von Tolkien und Philosophie sein zu wollen, doch einiges zu hoch gegriffen, bleiben doch viele wesentliche philosophische Fragen unerwähnt. Dies schmälert indes nicht die grundsätzliche Qualität der einzelnen Beiträge. Allerdings hätte das eine oder andere Argument noch stärker in Auseinandersetzung mit bereits bestehenden Überlegungen profiliert werden können.

Thomas Fornet-Ponse

Thomas Honegger & Dirk Vanderbeke (Eds.): From Peterborough to Faëry. The Poetics and Mechanics of Secondary Worlds. Essays in Honour of Dr. Allan G. Turner's 65th Birthday

Zürich/Jena: Walking Tree Publishers, 2014, 165 S.

In dieser Festschrift für Allan Turner anlässlich seines 65. Geburtstages haben sich die Herausgeber entschieden, keinen Band zu Fragen der Übersetzung oder des Stiles bei Tolkien herauszugeben – was angesichts der Forschungsschwerpunkte des Geehrten nahegelegen hätte –, sondern sich mit vielen unterschiedlichen Autoren und ihren Sekundärwelten auseinanderzusetzen. Dementsprechend folgen nach einer kurzen Einführung mit biographischer Skizze Turners sowie seiner Bibliographie acht Aufsätze, die sich Sekundärwelten von Chaucer bis hin zu Neil Gaiman widmen, wobei ein deutlicher Schwerpunkt bei Autoren des 20. Jahrhunderts liegt.

Zu Beginn erläutert Wolfram Keller anhand von *The House of Fame* und dem Prolog von *Legend of Good Women* und dem dort geschilderten Weg des Dichters durch die drei Gehirnventrikel, welche Bedeutung dissonante Bilder bei Chaucer als Ausdruck der Imagination einnehmen, nicht mehr von Logik und Gedächtnis aufgelöst werden, sondern unvermeidbarer Ausdruck historiographischer und literarischer Narrative sind.

Andrew Listen wendet sich Robert Burns' Gedicht *Tam o' Shanter* zu und legt den Akzent auf den Einsatz des Übernatürlichen, der nicht nur als Spezialeffekt dient, sondern auch eine positive Anerkennung dessen impliziert, was das Übernatürliche repräsentiert, insbesondere Aspekte der menschlichen Psyche wie Genuss.

Im dritten Beitrag nimmt Julian Eilmann die Tolkien'sche Sekundärwelt unter der Perspektive des Kontextes der Romantik in den Blick und stellt dabei die Parallelen zwischen Tolkiens Verständnis eines Märchens als Vehikel seiner poetologischen Ideen mit zentralen Ideen romantischer Dichter heraus.

Einem eher unbekannten Autor, Jack Vance, widmet sich Tom Shippey, der anhand dreier Serien (*Dying Earth, Planet of Adventure, Lyonesse*) die besonderen Fähigkeiten Vances bei der Schöpfung von Sekundärwelten herausarbeitet und damit einen Beitrag zu dessen Rehabilitierung als höchst lesenswerten Autor leistet.

Die Bedeutung von Geschichten und ihrer Auswirkung auf konkrete Leben (mit einer ökokritischen Dimension) illustriert Doreen Triebel anhand Terry Pratchetts *The Amazing Maurice and His Educated Rodents*, insofern verschiedene Charaktere in diesem Buch Geschichten zur Problemlösung heranziehen und auch die Frage gestellt wird, wie wörtlich sie genommen werden können (oder sollen).

James Fanning untersucht mithilfe der Narratologie Genettes die verschiedenen fiktonalen Ebenen in Jasper Ffordes Serie *Thursday Next* und stellt dabei heraus, wie die zunehmende diegetische Komplexität den komischen Effekt der Serie herstellt bzw. verstärkt.

In einer detaillierten Auseinandersetzung mit einschlägigen Forschungspositionen plädiert Thomas Honegger mit Blick auf Howard Phillips Lovecrafts »Mythos« dafür, deren Dynamik anzuerkennen und nicht vorschnell auf der Basis seiner ideologischen Überzeugungen zu interpretieren. Dabei betont er auch, wie Lovecraft im Unterschied zu Tolkien die Entfremdung des Menschen von der metaphysischen Welt verstärkt.

Abschließend diskutiert Dirk Vanderbeke mit Neil Gaiman und China Miéville zwei urbane Sekundärwelten (bzw. Sekundär-Londons), bei denen Elemente unterschiedlicher Genres wie Fantasy, magischer Realismus, Satire und Steampunk verbunden werden, und betont dabei den politischen Aspekt als Inversion oder satirische Überzeichnung.

Die durchweg sehr lesenswerten Beiträge fügen sich zu einem hochinteressanten und breiten Spektrum literarischer Sekundärwelten zusammen und illustrieren somit die herausragenden Möglichkeiten der (im wahrsten Sinne des Wortes poetischen) Sprache bei der Schöpfung von Sekundärwelten. Solche Sekundärwelten dienen nicht als Orte einer eskapistischen Flucht ohne Relevanz für die reale Welt, sondern als Zufluchtsorte bzw. Refugien, die bei der Kontingenzbewältigung helfen oder Kritik an der Primärwelt formulieren können.

Thomas Fornet-Ponse

Raymond Edwards: Tolkien

London: Robert Hale, 2014, 336 pp.

Oh no, not yet another Tolkien-biography-rehash! This was my first thought when a helpful cookie made Raymond Edwards's publication pop up on the list of books that may be of interest to me. Yet after scanning the information about the book and the author and after reading the blurb, I re-considered my initial judgment. First, 300-plus pages would be a bit too much trouble for a simple re-hash of Carpenter's study. Second, the author is said to have worked some years for the OED and done doctoral research into medieval manuscripts. This was motivation enough for me to give the book a chance—and I have no reason to regret it.

Edwards makes it clear right from the beginning that he cannot go beyond Carpenter if it comes to access to Tolkien's private documents (unpublished letters, private diaries etc.). However, since Carpenter's authorised biography in 1977 we have seen the publication of many of Tolkien's unpublished writings (e.g. *The History of Middle-earth* series, *The Fall of Arthur* etc.) and of several important studies (e.g. by John Garth or Wayne G. Hammond & Christina Scull) into his (and his contemporaries') life and work, not to mention an impressive number of studies of Tolkien's work in form of academic papers, journals and monographs. What Edwards does, then: to 're-write' and update Carpenter's original biography—in the positive meaning of these words. He retains the basic chronological structure and skilfully weaves a plethora of (post-Carpenter) information into a dense but readable 'biographical narrative'. That he places greater emphasis on Tolkien's Catholicism—in contrast to Carpenter who, as the son of the Anglican bishop of Oxford, had a somewhat distanced view of Tolkien's Catholic convictions—may be understandable. It is also a sign for the Catholic 'reconquista' that has been under way over the last two decades or so (cf. the publications by Joseph Pearce or Stratford Caldecott).

All in all, Edwards's study may not be as easily readable as Carpenter's original—Edwards tends towards complex sentences—but due to its comprehensiveness, it is likely to become the new 'standard biography' for the next decade. Deservedly so, I would say. Thomas Honegger

Fastitocalon. Studies in Fantasticism Ancient to Modern Vol 4-1&2: Crime and the Fantastic
Trier: WVT, 2014, 104 S.

Nachdem die Herausgeber Fanfan Chen und Thomas Honegger für die ersten drei Jahrgänge von *Fastitocalon* verantwortlich zeichneten, haben sie sich angesichts der sich schnell entwickelnden Forschungslandschaft entschlossen, bisweilen Gastherausgeber einzuladen. Die erste Frucht dieser Entscheidung liegt mit dem vierten, dem Thema *Kriminalität und das Fantastische* gewidmeten Band von Marek Oziewicz und Daniel Hade vor.

Nach einer kurzen Einführung der Gastherausgeber, in der sie vor allem die Beiträge vorstellen, folgen sechs Aufsätze (von primär in den USA tätigen Wissenschaftler/innen), die sich sehr unterschiedlichen Werken widmen –

angefangen mit der Zeichentrickserie *Adventure Time* bis hin zu Eoin Colfers *Artemis Fowl*.

Katarzyna Wasylak beginnt mit einer Skizze der unterschiedlichen Ansätze zur Ungerechtigkeit in der genannten Zeichentrickserie aufgrund der divergierenden Zugänge von Jake, dem Hund, und Finn, dem Menschen, zur Frage von Gesetzesbruch und den damit verbundenen moralischen, emotionalen und rechtlichen Urteilen. Sie attestiert der Serie ein kontextsensitives und pluralistisches Gerechtigkeitsverständnis.

Eine werkübergreifende Themenstellung wählte Emily Midkiff mit der Frage, wie verschiedene literarische Drachen die Gerechtigkeitsvorstellungen von Menschen infrage stellen bzw. herausfordern – beginnend mit theoretischen Überlegungen zum Verhältnis von literarischen Drachen und Menschen über Fáfnir und dem Drachen des *Beowulf* sowie Grahames und Tolkiens Drachen bis hin zu Le Guin und McGaffrey.

Der Frage der sozialen Gerechtigkeit anhand multikultureller Sekundärwelten widmet sich Nicholas A. Emmanuele in seinem Beitrag, in dem er vor allem die Unterrepräsentanz farbiger Personen moniert und dies anhand der unterschiedlichen Charakteristika von »touchstone fantasy«, inklusiver Fantasy und rassenkritischer Fantasy illustriert.

Marek Oziewicz diskutiert die Ansätze zu Fragen der Umweltgerechtigkeit in Susan Fletchers *Ancient, Strange and Lovely*, Isabel Allendes *City of the Beasts* und Terry Pratchetts *The Amazing Maurice and His Educated Rodents* und arbeitet heraus, wie sie ihre Leserschaft mit solchen moralischen, für die Zukunft der Menschheit zentralen Fragen konfrontieren.

Auch der Beitrag Patricia R. Cardozos kann im sozialethischen Rahmen verortet werden, da sie sich mit der patriarchalen Ordnung und sexueller Gewalt in der *Twilight* Saga auseinandersetzt, insofern sie nicht nur die Heldin Bella Swan, sondern auch die Vergewaltigung Rosalie Hales untersucht und dort deutlich macht, wie einerseits traditionelle Narrative weiblicher Vampire verlassen werden, dies sich aber andererseits in den Bereich des sexuellen Anderen einfügt.

Im letzten Beitrag des Bandes zeigt Rose Miller anhand der Charakterentwicklung der Titelfigur in der *Artemis-Fowl*-Serie, wie traditionelle männliche Machtstrukturen und Genderstereotype dort durchbrochen werden, insofern der Protagonist Selbstlosigkeit und Akzeptanz sowie die Notwendigkeit der emotionalen Entwicklung lernt.

Wie die bisherigen Bände, zeichnet sich auch dieser durch kenntnisreiche Beiträge aus, die interessante Schlaglichter auf das Oberthema Kriminalität und Fantastisches werfen. Erfreulich ist auch zu bemerken, dass nicht nur etablierte Forscher/innen hier publizieren, sondern auch Nachwuchskräfte.

Thomas Fornet-Ponse

Deborah A. Higgens:
Anglo-Saxon Community in J.R.R. Tolkien's
The Lord of the Rings

Oloris Publishing, 2014, 180 pp.

In order to do justice to this book, I have to write two reviews—one from the point of view of the general non-academic reader, the other from the point of view of the Tolkien scholar and professional academic. Let me begin by putting on my 'lay reader's hat'.

The first thing that may strike you as a European lay reader is that the author has used her academic title on the front cover. This is not so unusual in the US for academics writing for a more general audience, yet (outside the medical profession) not really common in Europe and if I were to use my titles on my publications, my colleagues would (rightly) think that I'm getting somewhat megalomaniac. Academic credentials thus established, the author proceeds in reader-friendly and easily understandable language, which is assisted by the appealing layout of the text on the page. The text is also carefully proofread and—disregarding the use of 'Wealtheow' instead of 'Wealhtheow' (an *h* does make a difference in pronunciation in Old English!)—without typos (no matter of course these days). The four chapters that constitute the study all follow the same pattern. First the author introduces the main theme (e.g. the role of the mead hall, the role of the *comitatus*-fellowship, the motif of the cup-bearing lady etc.), discusses the most relevant texts from Anglo-Saxon literature (most notably the Old English epic poem *Beowulf*) and then points out the parallels and analogues of these motives in Tolkien's *The Lord of the Rings*. The arguments are set forth clearly and are easy to follow, so that the lay reader will get a good grasp of the general relationship between Tolkien's Anglo-Saxon sources of inspiration and their transformations in his own epic.

So far, so good. Now let me don my 'academic hat'. Colin Duriez, in his 'Foreword' to Higgens's book, writes: "She wears her learning lightly, as she enthusiastically and lucidly explains and shares her discoveries" (p. iii). True, but sometimes the learning is worn a bit too lightly and the 'discoveries' are now and then only discoveries because the research into the secondary literature on the topic(s) is patchy. Thus the discussion of the Rohirrim as a 'calque' (or 'loan translation') of the Anglo-Saxon heroic ideal as presented in Old English poetry should acknowledge Tom Shippey's masterly discussion of this phenomenon as well as my more recent paper on the Rohirrim.[1] The same is true for Higgens's analysis of the woman as the cupbearer and the 'presenting of the cup' ritual. Higgens misses an important aspect by not having read (sorry for blowing my own trumpet) my paper[2] on the 'wassailing ritual' and the connection between Éowyn's presentation of the cup to Aragorn and the 'wassailing' episode in medieval chronicles featuring Vortigern, Rowena and her father Hengest. In these two cases it is not simply a matter of not having reviewed all the publications on the topic in question (an MLA bibliography search would have done the trick), which is not always necessary since many studies tend to repeat the findings of others in slight variation, but of having missed two important discoveries about the way Tolkien uses his 'sources' in his own epic. This has, in one case, led Higgens to misinterpret (in my view) the cup-bearing scene between Éowyn and Aragorn (p. 139).

It is, of course, easy to pick bones with a PhD in hindsight, but the fact that some standard monographs on the topics discussed are missing (e.g. John Garth's *Tolkien and the Great War* or Dimitra Fimi's *Tolkien, Race, and Cultural History*) or that the representation of Danish culture in *Beowulf* is often uncritically taken to represent Anglo-Saxon culture (p. 61) or that information found in Tacitus' *Germania* (98 AD) is transferred onto the much later Anglo-Saxons (e.g. p. 113) made me wrinkle my academic brow. I would also have liked to see a widening of the rather limited scope of texts consulted. The use of some Welsh sources is the laudable exception and could have been complemented by an inclusion of Old Norse texts. The same is true for the selection of texts from the Tolkienian canon, which is more or less limited to *The Lord of the Rings* and his *Letters*. A discussion of the Christian element in Tolkien's *legendarium* (cf. p. 31) must at least mention his 'Athrabeth Finrod ah Andreth' and not only the information found in his letters.

As you may have guessed by now, I am in two minds about this book. On the one hand it provides the layperson with an introduction to some of Tolkien's sources of inspiration from Old English poetry in a clear and structured way. On the other it does not fully live up to academic expectations and often fails to develop the full potential of its ideas—which is a pity since there is room for a specialised study on these aspects.   Thomas Honegger

---

[1] See Thomas Honegger, 'The Rohirrim: "Anglo-Saxons on Horseback"? An Inquiry into Tolkien's Use of Sources' in Jason Fisher (ed.), 2011, *Tolkien and the Study of His Sources: Critical Essays*. Jefferson NC and London: McFarland, 116-132.
[2] See Thomas Honegger, 'Éowyn, Aragorn and the Hidden Dangers of Drink' in *Inklings* 17. Jahrbuch für Literatur und Ästhetik. Moers: Brendow, 217-225.

Reviews / Rezensionen　　　　　　　*Hither Shore* 11 (2014)　　189

Stuart D. Lee (Ed.): A Companion to J.R.R. Tolkien
Chichester: Wiley Blackwell, 2014, xxxiv + 568 pp.

There can be no doubt that this is a major new reference work on Tolkien, appearing as part of a well-established series by a respected academic publisher. It would hardly do the work justice to say only that it contains 36 essays arranged in five sections: Life, The Academic, The Legendarium, Context, and Critical Approaches. On the other hand, it would clearly be impossible to discuss each of the contributions here. Therefore my approach will be to give the potential reader an idea of what kind of book to expect, and what to compare it with, before going on to comment on a few individual articles.

The term "companion" perhaps needs some comment, since we already have the two publications containing this word by Christina Scull and Wayne Hammond. It has been a familiar concept in British publishing since the 1930s, when the *Oxford Companion to Music* presented a reference work written by a well-known scholar but aimed at a readership of non-specialists, who were meant to feel that they were exploring the field in the company of someone older and more experienced: a companion in the literal sense. Nowadays the format is usually that of a collection of essays specially commissioned from experts on a particular topic or period, or, as in this case, author, while the readership is also expected to include university undergraduates. The essays present a cohesive introduction to their topic, but are intended to be dipped into at will rather than read from beginning to end. They are not meant to be original research articles, nor are they a critical review of previous research, but rather they give a picture of the current state of knowledge and critical assessment. In short, the companion as a genre belongs to the middle ground on which Anglo-Saxon publishers have been notably more successful than their German counterparts with their more rigorous distinction between "academic" and "popular".

This should help to place the present volume in relation to critical works that are already on the market. It is not designed for looking up the wealth of specific information to be found in the *Tolkien Companion and Guide* by Scull/Hammond, while the greater length of the articles means that it can offer more interpretation than the relatively short entries in Michael Drout's *Tolkien Encyclopedia*. In its format it is comparable to the Palgrave Macmillan Casebook edited by Peter Hunt (also reviewed here), but it offers a much broader spectrum of topics.

Rather more than a third of the volume is taken up with introducing Tolkien and his works, both fictional and academic, and it is here, where the remit for each chapter is particularly wide, that the greatest variation in conception of the task and potential readership is to be found. For example, Gergely Nagy and John Holmes take widely differing approaches to an almost impossible task: to say something significant about a major work in only about twelve pages. Nagy's contribution is densely written and presupposes a certain theoretical background, arguing that the publication of both the edited *Silmarillion* and whole "Silmarillion" corpus as a complex text or set of documents corresponded to Tolkien's own later concept. Holmes, writing in a deliberately simplifying manner, aims at readers who come to *The Lord of the Rings* via the films and attempts to point out what additional depth they might find in the book. There is a useful synopsis of the plot to differentiate it from the film version, although there is one example of interference where it is stated that the kings of Gondor are "in exile until the sword of their ancestor can be reforged" (135). There are also two small slips that were not caught during proof-reading: the name *Eorl* once appears in place of the obviously intended *Elendil* (142), while in the bibliography Julian Eilmann is transformed into Julie (145). Perhaps the most factual approach is taken by Arden Smith in his discussion of invented languages, since he bases himself largely on linguistic details, although he is not always rigorous in making clear whether he is taking a story-internal or story-external viewpoint.

The topics of the individual chapters are chosen to cover a wide range of approaches to Tolkien, including art, music, film adaptations and games. There is some overlapping and repetition of information, for example between Thomas Honegger ("Academic Writings") and Tom Shippey ("Tolkien as Editor"), or between Mark Atherton ("Old English") and Elizabeth Solopova ("Middle English"), but this is not really a fault since, as mentioned above, the book is meant for dipping; only reviewers have to read it from cover to cover! There are some minor inaccuracies, probably caused by over-familiarity with the material rather than the opposite. Verlyn Flieger refers to "Humphrey Havard" without noting that this was a nickname used only by the Inklings and he was actually named Robert (165). Mark Atherton suggests that "the name Buckland perhaps recalls a golden age when there was a King in the South, who granted land and protection" (223), but the whole point of Tolkien's little joke is that the Buckland is *not* early medieval English ("book-land"); it is named after the faintly comic Brandybuck dynasty. Leena Kahlas-Tarkka ("Finnish") and J.S. Lyman-Thomas ("Celtic") both repeat the old half-truth that Quenya is based on Finnish, but fortunately Arden R. Smith gives the more accurate information straight from Tolkien that it is "composed on a Latin basis with two other (main) ingredients...: Finnish and Greek" (203).

However, overall the scholarship in this volume is exemplary. As already mentioned, this is not intended to be original research, but there are frequent little flashes of insight which offer a new understanding even to those who have been reading Tolkien and Tolkien criticism for years. So for instance Corey Olsen points out that in the intermediate version of the Eärendil poem published in *The Treason of Isengard* we have another poem that is valid in its own right and offers a further "cautionary tale of the Perilous Realm" (186), although unfortunately for the first-time reader, he does not explain what that means or point out explicitly the similarity to "Looney". John Garth manages to produce a refreshingly different potted biography of Tolkien after all the re-hashes of Carpenter that have appeared in recent years, achieved by basing it around the texts that Tolkien was working on at any given time.

Finally, there are plenty of opportunities for newcomers to Tolkien criticism to follow up what they have learnt here. In addition to the usual bibliography of references at the end of each article, some authors offer a list of suggestions of related articles, while the General Bibliography at the end contains four and a half pages of "Further Reading".[3] This is definitely a book to recommend both to the student and to the general reader. However, it would be advisable to wait until a cheaper paperback edition comes out; the vastly inflated price of the hardback edition (120 £) is clearly intended to milk libraries which recognise it as essential reading. Allan Turner

Friedhelm Schneidewind & Heidi Steimel (Hg.): Musik in Mittelerde
Saarbrücken: Verlag der Villa Fledermaus, 2014, 224 S.

Dieses Buch ist die deutsche Übersetzung des vor vier Jahren erschienenen *Music in Middle-earth*. Nun bietet sich also die Möglichkeit, die Artikel von Julian Eilmann, Fabian Geier, Norbert Maier, Friedhelm Schneidewind und Mira Sommer auch in der Originalsprache zu lesen.

Da die englische Ausgabe in *Hither Shore* 7 (246-251) von Margaret Hiley ausführlich besprochen wurde, ist es wohl überflüssig, im Detail auf den Band einzugehen. Trotzdem sei kurz daran erinnert, dass die Beiträge vier verschiedene Gebiete behandeln: Schöpfung und Musik; Musik in Tolkiens Welt; Einflüsse unserer Welt; Interpretationen in unserer Welt. Die drei Aufsätze in der ersten

---

3 Just as an aside, it is noteworthy that Pat Pinsent's chapter ("Religion: An Implicit Catholicism") cites only one critical article less than 40 years old, and the "Further Reading" section is also very scanty on this topic. This is a striking omission in view of the interest shown in recent years by theologians in Tolkien and the other Inklings.

Abteilung behandeln Tolkiens Schöpfungsmythos von der Musik der Ainur. Das ist ein sehr relevanter Ausgangspunkt, denn der ganze Tolkien'sche Kosmos beginnt mit den drei Themen Ilúvatars und soll mit der Vervollkommnung der großen Musik enden. Es folgen drei fantasiereiche Artikel, die darüber spekulieren, wie die Musik in Mittelerde geklungen haben könnte. Die vier nächsten befassen sich mit den musikalischen Traditionen in unserer Welt, die Tolkiens Darstellungen vom Musizieren in der Sekundärwelt vermutlich geprägt haben.

Zum Schluss bieten weitere vier Beiträge einen Überblick über Realisationen von Musikstücken in verschiedenen Stilrichtungen, die durch Tolkiens Welt inspiriert wurden.

Da dieses Buch eine der insgesamt nur zwei Publikationen ist, die sich mit dem musikalischen Aspekt von Tolkiens Schaffen befassen (neben *Middle-earth Minstrel*, herausgegeben von Bradford Lee Eden), ist es allen musikalisch interessierten Lesern zu empfehlen, die die englische Version noch nicht gekauft haben.

Allan Turner

Our Authors

Annie Birks teaches English language, literature and translation at the Université Catholique de l'Ouest, Angers, France. Her long-lasting interest in J.R.R. Tolkien and C.S. Lewis, together with her doctorate on "Retribution in the Works of J.R.R. Tolkien" (Université Paris-Sorbonne), have led to articles and lectures on these two authors. annie.birks@neuf.fr

Michaël Devaux holds a Ph.D. from the Sorbonne in Paris, has worked extensively on Leibniz, Descartes and is currently teaching philosophy of education at the University of Caen - Lower Normandy in Alençon. He has published numerous articles on the theological dimension of Tolkien's works and is president of the French Tolkien Society *La Compagnie de la Comté* and is editor-in-chief of *La Feuille de la Compagnie* (last volume entitled *J.R.R. Tolkien, l'effigie des Elfes*, Paris, Bragelonne, 2014, 500 p., including 30 pages of unpublished texts by Tolkien about elvish reincarnation). michael.devaux@gmail.com

Julian Tim Morton Eilmann studied History, German Philology, and History of Arts at Aachen and Nottingham and is currently working as teacher. Furthermore, since three years he is working as a journalist and author of films and TV productions, and as a developer of historical TV documentation. His works on Tolkien focus an Tolkien's songs and poems and the adaptation by Peter Jackson. julianeilmann@web.de

Natalia González de la Llana has studied Literary Theory and Comparative Literature at the Complutense University in Madrid. After winning research scholarships for stays at La Sapienza University in Rome and Humboldt University in Berlin, she received her PhD at the Complutense with her thesis *Adam and Eve, Faust and Dorian Gray: Three Myths of Transgression*. She has taught at the Romance Language Departments of the University of Münster and Aachen University where she is now preparing her habilitation with the title *Multimedia narrative forms in 'high fantasy': a model of analysis*.
natalia.llana@romanistik.rwth-aachen.de

Andrew Higgins is a Post Graduate Research Student at Cardiff Metropolitan University, currently working on his thesis *The Genesis of Tolkien's Mythology* which examines Tolkien's early mythology and invented languages. Andrew is also Director of Development at Glyndebourne Opera in East Sussex, England. He has given several Tolkien related papers at The Return of the Ring, the UK Tolkien Society, the 2013 Mythopoeic Conference, and 49th International Congress on Medieval Studies at Kalamazoo in May 2014. ashiggins@me.com

Authors/Autoren

Thomas Kullmann is Professor of English Literature at the University of Osnabrück. Currently, his main research interests are Shakespeare and Renaissance Culture; English Children's Fiction and Images of India in 19th-century Britain. His publications include two books on Shakespeare, one on landscape and weather in the nineteenth-century English novel and one on English children's and young adults' fiction as well as numerous articles on English Renaissance Literature, Victorian and twentieth-century literature and culture, and children's literature. He also edited two volumes of essays on aspects of English children's fiction. He recently published three articles on Tolkien: "Intertextual Patterns in *The Hobbit* and *The Lord of the Rings*" (online), "Songs and Poems in *The Lord of the Rings*"(*Connotations*, 23.2) and "Metaphor and Metonymy in *The Lord of the Rings*" (*Transitions and Dissolving Boundaries in the Fantastic*, ed. Christine Löscher et al.). tkullman@uos.de

Jonathan Nauman has authored *The Franklin Trees*, a children's book. As Secretary of the Vaughan Association (USA), he often speaks on seventeenth-century poetry in England, Wales, and America. jonnauman@hotmail.com

Patrick Peters, Dr. phil. studied German, English, and American Literature at Universities of Duisburg and Essen and gained his doctorate with the study *Männer aus dem Hain. Studien zur Männlichkeitskonstruktion in der Lyrik der Göttinger Hainbündler* (Essen: Oldib Verlag, 2014) at University of Wuppertal. He runs his own company as an economic journalist, PR consultant, and writer. Next to his dissertation and several articles he has published *Edda. Einführung* (Essen: Oldib Verlag, 2007) und *Von Jerusalem nach Paris. Der Heilige Gral zwischen Mythos und Literatur* (Essen: Oldib Verlag, 2009).

info@pp-text.de

Tatjana Silec-Plessis has been working at Paris-Sorbonne University (Paris IV) as a Lecturer in English Medieval Studies since 2009, after defending her PhD dissertation on the relationship between the court jester and his king in English medieval and Renaissance literature at the same university. She has penned papers on the topics of madness and folly in medieval literature as well as on Tolkien, her other area of interest. Her most recent work in that field is to be found in Vincent Ferré's recent Dictionnaire Tolkien published by CNRS Éditions (2012), for which she wrote six entries. tatjana.silec@gmail.com

Martin Sternberg studied Ancient History, Mediaeval History, History of Arts, and Law at Münster, 1990-1996. He is currently working in a federal authority. During his studies, he specialised in Late Antiquity and Early Christianity.

lasgalen@web.de

Guglielmo Spirito is a conventual franciscan friar (Minorit) and works and lives in Assisi. In Rome, he got his Doctorate in Theology with specialitation in Spirituality at the ANTONIANUM. Since 1994 he is professor at the Theological Institute of Assisi (ITA) and at the Pontifical Faculty of Saint Bonaventure (SERAPHICUM) in Rome. He gave courses of Theology in Canada, Croazia, Romania, Russia, Mexico, Lebanon and Kenya, and lectures on Tolkien in England, Germany, France and Canada. On J.R.R. Tolkien he had published essays, articles and books, as *Fra San Francesco e Tolkien* and *Lo specchio di Galadriel with Il Cerchio* (in italian) and several papers with Walking Tree Publishers and *Hither Shore*. fraguspi@gmail.com

Allan Turner has recently retired from a career spent as Lecturer in English, most recently at the Friedrich-Schiller-Universität Jena. He looks forward to being able to spend more time on research into translation studies and stylistics, particularly in relation to Tolkien. allangturner@gmail.com

Unsere Autorinnen & Autoren

Annie Birks unterrichtet Englische Sprache, Literatur und Übersetzung an der Université Catholique de l'Ouest, Angers (Frankreich). Ihr lang anhaltendes Interesse an J.R.R. Tolkien und C.S. Lewis führte mit ihrer Dissertation *Vergeltung in den Werken J.R.R. Tolkiens* (an der Universität Paris-Sorbonne) zu Vorträgen und Aufsätzen über beide Autoren. annie.birks@neuf.fr

Michaël Devaux promovierte an der Sorbonne in Paris, arbeitete ausführlich über Leibniz, Descartes und unterrichtet gegenwärtig Philosophie der Erziehung an der Universität Caen – Niedernormandie in Alençon. Er veröffentlichte viele Artikel über die theologische Dimension der Werke Tolkiens und ist Präsident der französischen Tolkien Gesellschaft *La Compagnie de la Comté* und Hauptherausgebet von *La Feuille de la Compagnie* (jüngst *J.R.R. Tolkien, l'effigie des Elfes*, Paris 2014). michael.devaux@gmail.com

Julian Tim Morton Eilmann studierte in Aachen und Nottingham Geschichte, Germanistik und Kunstgeschichte und ist gegenwärtig Gymnasiallehrer. Neben seinen akademischen Arbeiten ist er bei einer Film- und TV-Produktion als Autor von Reportagen und historischen Dokumentation tätig. Schwerpunkte seiner Tolkien-Forschungen sind Tolkiens Lieder und Gedichte sowie die Filmadaption durch Peter Jackson. julianeilmann@web.de

Natalia González de la Llana, Dr. phil., studierte Literaturtheorie und Komparatistik an der Universität Complutense in Madrid und promovierte dort nach Aufenthalten an der Universität La Sapienza in Rom und der Humboldt-Universität in Berlin mit einer Arbeit namens *Adam and Eve, Faust and Dorian Gray: Three Myths of Transgression*. Gegenwärtig ist sie Wissenschaftliche Mitarbeiterin an der RWTH Aachen und arbeitet an einer Habilitation zum Thema multimedialer narrativer Formen in „High Fantasy". natalia.llana@romanistik.rwth-aachen.de

Thomas Kullmann, Prof. Dr. phil., ist Professor für Englische Literatur in Osnabrück. Gegenwärtig sind seine primären Forschungsinteressen Shakespeare und Renaissance-Kultur, englische Kinderliteratur und Bilder Indiens im Britannien des 19. Jahrhunderts. Er publizierte u.a. zwei Bücher über Shakespeare, eines über Landschaft und Wetter im englischen Roman des 19. Jahrhunderts und

eines über englische Kinder- und Jugendliteratur sowie zahlreiche Artikel über englische Renaissanceliteratur, Literatur und Kultur des Viktorianismus und 20. Jahrhunderts sowie Kinderliteratur. Jüngst publizierte er drei Beiträge über Tolkien: "Intertextual Patterns in *The Hobbit* and *The Lord of the Rings*" (online), "Songs and Poems in *The Lord of the Rings*"(*Connotations*, 23.2) und "Metaphor and Metonymy in *The Lord of the Rings*" (*Transitions and Dissolving Boundaries in the Fantastic*, ed. Christine Löscher et al.).
tkullman@uos.de

Jonathan Nauman schrieb das Kinderbuch *The Franklin Trees* und hält als Sekretär der Vaughan Association (USA) Vorträge über Dichtung des 17. Jahrhunderts in England, Wales und den USA. jonnauman@hotmail.com

Patrick Peters, Dr. phil., studierte Germanistik, Anglistik und Amerikanistik in Duisburg und Essen und wurde mit der Arbeit *Männer aus dem Hain. Studien zur Männlichkeitskonstruktion in der Lyrik der Göttinger Hainbündler* (Essen: Oldib Verlag, 2014) an der Bergischen Universität Wuppertal promoviert. Er ist als Wirtschaftsjournalist, PR-Berater und Autor tätig. Neben seiner Dissertation sind bereits erschienen: *Edda. Einführung* (Essen: Oldib Verlag, 2007) und *Von Jerusalem nach Paris. Der Heilige Gral zwischen Mythos und Literatur* (Essen: Oldib Verlag, 2009). info@pp-text.de

Tatjana Silec-Plessis arbeitet nach der Verteidigung ihrer Dissertation über die Beziehung zwischen dem Hofnarr und seinem König in englischer Literatur des Mittelalters und der Renaissance seit 2009 an der Universität Paris-Sorbonne als Dozentin in Englischer Mediävistik. Sie veröffentlichte verschiedene Aufsätze über Fragen des Wahnsinns und der Torheit in mittelalterlicher Literatur sowie Tolkien. Ihre jüngsten Beiträge über Tolkien finden sich im *Dictionnaire Tolkien* (ed. Vincent Ferré). tatjana.silec@gmail.com

Guglielmo Spirito, Prof. Dr. theol., ist ein Franziskaner-Konventuale (Minorit) und lebt und arbeitet in Assisi. Er promovierte in Rom am *Antonianum* in Theologie mit dem Spezialgebiet Spiritualität und ist Professor am Theologischen Institut Assisi und an der päpstlichen Fakultät Sankt Bonaventura (Seraphicum) in Rom. Über Tolkien hat er in Italien, England, Deutschland, Frankreich und Kanada Vorträge gehalten und mehrere Essays, Bücher (*Tra San Francesco e Tolkien* und *Lo specchio di Galadriel*) und Aufsätze (bei *Walking Tree Publishers* und *Hither Shore*) veröffentlicht. fraguspi@gmail.com

Martin Sternberg hat in Münster 1990-1996 Alte Geschichte, Mittlere Geschichte, Kunstgeschichte sowie Rechtswissenschaft studiert und arbeitet als Referent bei einer Bundesbehörde. Bei seinem Geschichts- und Philosophiestudium bestand ein Schwerpunkt in der Beschäftigung mit Spätantike und frühem Christentum. lasgalen@web.de

Allan Turner, Dr. phil., ist kürzlich von seinem Berufsleben als Dozent in englischer Sprache, zuletzt an der Universität Jena, in den Ruhestand gegangen und freut sich darauf, mehr Zeit auf die Forschung über Übersetzungsstudien und Stilfragen, insbesondere in Beziehung zu Tolkien, aufwenden zu können.
allangturner@gmail.com

Siglenverzeichnis

Die Schriften von J.R.R. Tolkien werden im Text jeweils ohne Angabe des Verfassernamens mit den folgenden Siglen zitiert. Die jeweils benutzte Ausgabe findet sich im Literaturverzeichnis.

AI:	The Lay of Aotrou and Itroun
ATB:	The Adventures of Tom Bombadil and other Verses from the Red Book / Die Abenteuer des Tom Bombadil und andere Gedichte aus dem Roten Buch
AW:	Ancrene Wisse and Hali Meiðhad
B:	Die Briefe von J.R.R. Tolkien
BA:	Bilbos Abschiedslied
BB:	Baum und Blatt
BGH:	Bauer Giles von Ham
BLS:	Bilbo's Last Song
BMC:	Beowulf: The Monster and the Critics
BT:	Blatt von Tüftler
BUK:	Beowulf: Die Ungeheuer und ihre Kritiker
BW:	Die Briefe vom Weihnachtsmann
CH:	The Children of Húrin
CP:	Chaucer as a Philologist
EA:	The End of the Third Age (History of Middle-earth 9). Auszug
EW:	English and Welsh / Englisch und Walisisch
FA:	The Fall of Arthur
FC:	Letters from Father Christmas
FGH:	Farmer Giles of Ham
FH:	Finn and Hengest
FS:	On Fairy-Stories
GD:	Gute Drachen sind rar
GN:	Guide to the Names in the Lord of the Rings
GPO:	Sir Gawain and the Green Knight, Pearl, and Sir Orfeo
H:	The Hobbit / Der Hobbit / Der kleine Hobbit
HB:	The Homecoming of Beorhtnoth Beorhthelm's Son
HdR:	Der Herr der Ringe
HdR I:	Der Herr der Ringe. Bd. 1. Die Gefährten
HdR II:	Der Herr der Ringe. Bd. 2. Die Zwei Türme
HdR III:	Der Herr der Ringe. Bd. 3. Die Rückkehr des Königs / Die Wiederkehr des Königs
HdR A:	Der Herr der Ringe. Anhänge
HG:	Herr Glück
HH I/II:	The History of the Hobbit
HL:	Ein heimliches Laster
KH:	Die Kinder Húrins
L:	The Letters of J.R.R. Tolkien
LB:	The Lays of Beleriand (History of Middle-earth 3)
LN:	Leaf by Niggle

Siglenverzeichnis

LotR:	The Lord of the Rings
LotR I:	The Fellowship of the Ring. Being the first part of The Lord of the Rings
LotR II:	The Two Towers. Being the second part of The Lord of the Rings
LotR III:	The Return of the King. Being the third part of The Lord of the Rings
LotR A:	The Lord of the Rings. Appendices
LR:	The Lost Road and other Writings (History of Middle-earth 5)
LSG:	The Legend of Sigurd and Gudrún
LT 1:	The Book of Lost Tales 1 (History of Middle-earth 1)
LT 2:	The Book of Lost Tales 2 (History of Middle-earth 2)
MB:	Mr. Bliss
MC:	The Monsters and the Critics and Other Essays
ME:	A Middle English Vocabulary
MR:	Morgoth's Ring (History of Middle-earth 10)
My:	Mythopoeia
NM:	Nachrichten aus Mittelerde
OE:	The Old English Exodus
OK:	Ósanwe-Kenta
P:	Pictures by J.R.R. Tolkien
PM:	The Peoples of Middle-earth (History of Middle-earth 12)
R:	Roverandom
RBG:	The Rivers and Beacon-hills of Gondor
RGEO:	The Road Goes Ever On (with Donald Swann)
RS:	The Return of the Shadow (History of Middle-earth 6)
S:	Silmarillion
SD:	The Sauron Defeated (History of Middle-earth 9)
SG:	Der Schmied von Großholzingen
SGG:	Sir Gawain and the Green Knight / Sir Gawain und der Grüne Ritter (Essay)
SM:	The Shaping of Middle-earth (History of Middle-earth 4)
SP:	Songs for the Philologists
SV:	A Secret Vice
SWM:	Smith of Wootton Major
SWME:	Smith of Wootton Major Essay
TB:	On Translating Beowulf
TI:	The Treason of Isengard (History of Middle-earth 7)
TL:	Tree and Leaf
ÜB:	Zur Übersetzung des Beowulf
ÜM:	Über Märchen
UK:	Die Ungeheuer und ihre Kritiker. Gesammelte Aufsätze
UT:	Unfinished Tales
VA:	Valedictory Address
VG 1:	Das Buch der Verschollenen Geschichten 1
VG 2:	Das Buch der Verschollenen Geschichten 2
WJ:	The War of the Jewels (History of Middle-earth 11)
WR:	The War of the Ring (History of Middle-earth 8)

Index

Ælfwine	69
Ainur	34, 57
Alter Wald	72, 142, 147ff
Alter Weidenmann	147ff
Arda	32, 34, 46, 54, 116f, 128
Auenland	142-147
Barrow-downs	9, 18, 21ff, 26f, 35, 44, 92, 99, 131f, 148
Bombadil, Tom	17f, 20-27, 35, 49, 55, 96, 100, 130-134, 136ff, 140, 147ff
The Book of Lost Tales	13, 117
Buckland	19, 35, 53
Caradhras	13, 27, 44, 87, 132f
Cirith Ungol	16, 38, 135, 143
Dead Marshes	44, 116f, 122-126
Dickens, Charles	62, 80
Elbereth	44, 53f
Eldar	53, 71
Emerson, Ralph	55f, 62
Eriol	69ff, 75-78
Fangorn	14f, 27, 136, 140, 142
Flieger, Verlyn	97, 101
Galadriel	36, 42ff, 47, 49, 58, 83, 96, 136f, 139, 141, 143, 150ff
Gandalf	12, 18, 23, 27ff, 36, 86, 105, 110f, 133, 136, 139, 147
Gildor	35, 39, 54
Goldberry/Goldbeere	18, 20-28, 36, 55
Gollum	11f, 38, 97, 122ff
Gondolin	40, 61, 137
Gondor	27, 105, 108, 134f, 137f, 150f
Hammond, Wayne	56, 123, 168
Henneth Annûn	28, 37, 137ff, 141
Herr der Ringe, Lord of the Rings	9, 11-14, 18, 26f, 69, 72, 75, 78, 80, 83, 89, 92, 95, 97f, 104-111, 114, 116, 126, 128, 130, 137, 139, 142, 144, 147, 154
Ilúvatar	19, 42, 46, 57, 60f
Isengart/Isengard	27, 56, 108, 137, 142
Jackson, Peter	32, 92
Keats, John	58f
Lothlórien	14, 41, 57f, 71, 78, 85, 96, 105, 135-143, 149-152
Macbeth	52f
Melian	32, 42-47
Melkor/Morgoth	26, 34, 43, 54, 57, 61, 132, 146
Metaphor/Metapher	8-16, 71, 80, 82, 89, 98
Minas Tirith	11, 29, 61, 132
Mordor	13, 15f, 27, 29, 37, 39, 85, 108, 110, 120, 122, 124ff, 135
Moria	28, 38, 41, 58, 85f, 132ff, 150

Index

Novalis	65, 67
Old Man Willow	18-27, 92, 97, 131f, 136, 147
Petty, Anne	56, 58
Rivendell	13, 34, 37, 39, 136f, 139f
Rohan	15, 27f, 37, 85, 134f, 142, 151
Romantik	64-78
Ryan, John S.	96, 98
Saruman	15, 27f, 54, 61, 105-114, 137, 142, 144
Sauron	16, 18, 23f, 28f, 34, 45, 61, 87, 89, 105f, 108-111, 124, 139, 145f
Scull, Christina	56, 123, 168
Shire	18, 34f, 53, 58f, 97f, 105, 136, 140, 144
Silmarillion	13, 26
Shippey, Thomas A.	20, 85, 92, 149
Sir Gawain and the Green Knight	92f, 95, 97f, 153
Smaug	32, 58
Tolkien, John R.R.	8, 11-16, 18-21, 24, 26, 28, 33, 42, 52-62, 64, 66, 68-71, 74, 77f, 85f, 89, 92ff, 97f, 100f, 104f, 108ff, 112, 114, 116-128, 132, 136, 141-154
Treebeard	11, 15, 109, 137
Valar	29, 42, 46f, 54

www.ingramcontent.com/pod-product-compliance
Lightning Source LLC
Chambersburg PA
CBHW070329230426
43663CB00011B/2264